This Jewi

Stories of Discovery, Connection and Joy

Debra B. Darvick

Read The Spirit Books
an imprint of
David Crumm Media, LLC
Canton, Michigan

For more information and further discussion, visit
http://www.ThisJewishLife.com

ISBN: 978-1-934879-36-8
version 2.0 2012/12/01

Cover art and design by
Rick Nease
www.RickNeaseArt.com

Published By
Read The Spirit Books
an imprint of
David Crumm Media, LLC
42015 Ford Rd., Suite 234
Canton, Michigan, USA

For information about customized editions, bulk purchases or permissions, contact David Crumm Media, LLC at info@DavidCrummMedia.com

Contents

Dedication

In memory of my grandparents—
Estelle and Abe Berkowitz

Foreword

JUDAISM IS A culture that has been sustained by books. That is the common view, and it contains a great deal of truth. But of course, books are carried along the current of people's lives, and in the pages of a vital book we hear a living voice. The Torah enshrines the living voice of God. Rabbinic commentaries celebrate the living voices of those who seek to live a life of faith, of commitment and of community. But throughout our history many people have not been heard. Scholars speak through texts. But what of the salesman, the housewife, the baker? Who records the laughter evoked by the storyteller, whose tales do not make it into the sacred halls of study, into the pages of learned tomes?

Debra Darvick's book is an act of reclamation and joyous discovery. She searches for the immediacy of living voices. Here are people seeking community and spirit from all walks of life, in every situation of life. Here are stories of holidays and life-cycle events, of marriage and divorce, told by those learned in the tradition and those who are taking their first tentative steps toward involvement and understanding. Here is the story of a woman entering the mikvah for the first time; a man who guarded Paul Robeson; a teen's trip to Israel and the meditations of a recovering alcoholic.

In other words, this is a profoundly Jewish book. It retells the tales of our people as they are, in all their glorious diversity, their raucous integrity, their wonderful, infuriating, stiff-necked exuberance. Debra Darvick has given us the voices. We give her our thanks.

—*Rabbi David Wolpe*

Introduction

A person reaches in three directions: Inward, to oneself; up, to God; out, to others. The miracle of life is that in truly reaching in any one direction, one embraces all three.

Rabbi Nachman of Breslov

YOU MIGHT SAY that Jewish life is one story after another. Each spring, we mentally shed our business suits and wingtips, donning sandals and desert robes as we retell the story of our exodus from Egypt. Fall brings the unsettling story of a father who, at God's command, places his son upon a sacrificial altar and holds a knife to the cherished boy's throat. In between we have tales of great battles and miraculous oil lamps. We have the story of a reluctant queen who saves her people and a young Moabite woman whose loyalty to her mother-in-law is still remembered. Our Torah is a storybook on the grandest of scales

We don't forget our stories but pull them along with us. I once read an account of California's fires and mudslides. A displaced resident commented to a reporter, "It was just like in the Exodus. We were fleeing for our lives." A tale thousands of years old was so real to this woman it had the immediacy of the recent past. That is the power of our literature. We are our stories.

Thus, in addition to being Israelites and Maccabees, we are also the Inquisition's martyrs. We are exiles from Babylonia and the victims of Babi Yar.

In the shadow of the Holocaust we have come to see ourselves, exclusively I sometimes think, as Holocaust survivors. Enormous funds and energies are expended to ensure the telling and retelling of this calamity.

While there is merit in remembering and retelling, the idea for this book grew out of my desire to provide a counterweight to the shelves of Holocaust literature. This book grew out of my need to hear from fellow Jews who felt a different connection to Judaism about Jewish experiences that enlightened and invigorated.

This Jewish Life is the story of EveryJew, a composite Jew whose experience, told in a mosaic of voices, portrays the many facets of Jewish life at the end of the twentieth century and the beginning of the twenty-first. You will read stories of joyous engagement and poignant loss. You will read about men and women who turn to Judaism in their struggles with drug addiction and spousal abuse. You will read of a bar mitzvah service in rural Illinois and a commitment ceremony in a California metropolis. And you will also read stories about the Holocaust. It wasn't long before I realized I could not avoid this horrific period in our recent history and so set for myself the task of finding stories of triumph in the face of near obliteration.

Those who share their experiences come from a wide range of backgrounds. Not everyone belongs to a synagogue, celebrates Jewish holidays on a regular basis or even believes in God. Nevertheless, they have all experienced something wonderful by virtue of being connected to the Jewish community. Their Judaism matters.

Perhaps, if the future is anything like the past, you will take these stories to your heart. Some will become a part of you and you will carry them in your own spiritual rucksack, retelling them when the moment is right.

* * *

I wrote the above words nearly a decade ago; they still stand as an accurate reflection of the genesis of this book. With this new edition, an update is in order. Some of my interviewees became dear friends. Others have gone on with their lives, content to have had a pivotal Jewish experience recorded for posterity. Two beloved participants—Jules Doneson and Arthur Ost— have since died. Every time I read their stories, they come to life once again.

This edition of *This Jewish Life* includes the story of a devoted wife and mother who, while retaining the religion of her birth, has lovingly committed herself to Jewish life and practice. A chance encounter with a friend at Rosh Hashanah services led to the inclusion of a story rooted in practices of ancient Israel's priesthood. Those of you intending to read a story a week will have to double up somewhere along the way.

I am grateful to David Crumm, colleague, friend and now publisher, for his enduring support and enthusiasm for my work. My children and husband remain eternal sources of discovery, connection and joy, Jewish and otherwise, for which I am daily blessed. Above all, I give thanks to God, source of all that is, was and will ever be.

—Debra B. Darvick, Birmingham, MI

PART 1

Birth

Each child carries his own blessing into the world.

—*Yiddish proverb*

ON THE EIGHTH day of his life, a Jewish boy is circumcised in a ritual ceremony called a *b'rit milah*. Commonly known as a *b'ris*, the Hebrew word for covenant, the circumcision or *milah*, is performed by a *mohel*, who has been thoroughly trained not only in the surgical procedure but also in the study of all the laws concerning the rite. Since the time of Abraham, it has been the father's responsibility to circumcise his son. Thus, all *mohelim* have traditionally been men. In the more liberal movements, a few women have recently undertaken the training as well.

Since the 10th century, a close relative or friend has customarily been invited to be the *sandak* (derived from the Greek word for godfather) to act as a *ba'al* b'rit, or master of the circumcision ceremony. It is the sandak's responsibility and honor to hold the infant during the actual circumcision. Many families place beside the sandak an empty chair called the Chair of Elijah. According to tradition, the prophet Elijah attends every b'ris in order to protect the infant from danger.

B'rit milah is a holy moment, and the emotions surrounding it are manifold. There is joy, and naturally there is anxiety. Some Jewish parents, unwilling to subject their son to the procedure, forgo the rite, but they are very much in the minority. A b'ris is the first of many religious opportunities for Jews to create a new link in the long chain of Jewish history. It is the first of many joyous milestones in the life of a Jewish family.

When parents adopt a baby not born of a Jewish mother, Jewish law (though not the Reform movement) requires conversion of the child by immersion in the *mikvah*, ritual bath. When the infant to be converted is a male, a ritual circumcision must then be performed by a mohel. If the infant has already been circumcised, the mohel performs a symbolic circumcision called a *hatafat dam b'rit*. This procedure consists of a pinprick that results in the letting of a speck of blood. A *beit din*, rabbinic court comprised of three qualified rabbis, must oversee and approve of the conversion.

There used to be little fanfare celebrating the birth of a daughter. It was custom for the infant girl's father to name her, in absentia, in the synagogue. Since the '70s, however, parents, inspired by feminism, have welcomed their infant girls into the covenant with a ceremony called a *simchat bat*, or celebration of a daughter. Since there is no set ritual or liturgy, families have been free to structure their own, combining both traditional and contemporary blessings, psalms and readings from secular literature. In some cases, rituals such as foot-washing or candle-lighting are incorporated into a ceremony that celebrates the arrival of a daughter with as much festivity as that traditionally summoned for her brother.

CHAPTER 1

And on the Eighth Day You Shall …

The Story of Debra B. Darvick

"AND WHO'S GOING to be there to celebrate if we have a boy?" I was eight months pregnant and about to be transferred from New York to the wilds of the Midwest.

I had just realized that if our first child was a boy, we would have only the barest handful of family at his *b'ris*. Our immediate family would make the spur-of-the-moment trip no matter when the eighth day fell, but my aunts, uncles and cousins wouldn't travel from Manhattan to Michigan for a b'ris—nor would my husband's 30 or so relatives who had watched my pregnancy with loving and not-too-overbearing interest. All of our friends would be left behind. How many caring friendships could be cultivated in 21 days—the time between our arrival in Michigan and my due date? I began hoping for a girl, even though I'd been getting "boy" vibes ever since the little blue circle had appeared in the glass tube seven months before.

But when the plane touched down in Detroit, a b'ris was the last thing on my mind. We had three weeks to settle in, unpack, scope out the grocery and drug stores, interview pediatricians and learn the shortest route to the hospital.

As it turned out, I did have one acquaintance: a woman I'd known briefly from B'nai B'rith Girls during my high school years in Atlanta, who now lived 10 minutes away. Our first weekend in Michigan, she and her husband threw us a party to introduce us to their circle of friends. Her friends were in various stages of diaperhood and warmly invited me to join their playgroups when I felt ready. There were few Jews in our neighborhood, but in a procedure reminiscent of the old Farmer in the Dell game, one introduced us to another until we had met them all. The couple from whom we'd bought our house kept in touch, even offering to take me to the hospital if my husband couldn't make it home from work in time.

One morning I called a baby nurse recommended to me by our future pediatrician. "Lord, you called way too late," she said when I asked if she could come 12 days hence. "But I will give you this: If you have a boy, don't let anyone near him but Cantor Greenbaum. I've taken care of plenty of boys in my time, and Cantor Greenbaum does it better than anyone else." Her well-meaning advice only reminded me that we knew barely enough people to make a *minyan*. I called the cantor and then, feeling lonelier than ever, hoped against hope I wouldn't need his services.

I went into labor on my due date. Eight days later, Cantor Greenbaum showed up at the appointed hour. My friend's friends and the neighbors we had met during the past few weeks arrived with cookies and cakes, bunting blankets and knitted sweaters. My grandfather was in classic form: Every few minutes, I heard the punch line to a Yiddish joke, followed by ripples of laughter. My stepmother had set up a wonderful brunch. Maybe living in Michigan wouldn't be so bad, after all.

And then, all of a sudden, it was time. My grandfather held his great-grandson in our new maple rocker while the *mohel* chanted blessings over my son. Well into his 70s and feeling frail, my grandfather had been reluctant to participate so directly in the ceremony. I had insisted, as there was no greater honor I could give him than to make him *sandak*, the overseer, as our son was entered into God's covenant with Abraham. I knew his strength wouldn't falter.

I looked around the tiny room that was our son's nursery and was overcome at the tableau before me: People who barely knew us had skipped work to be with us, to welcome our child into the Jewish community with fanfare and affection. The woman who'd sold us our house held my hand as the mohel made his dreaded cut. When my son wailed, my knees buckled. "Did you ever think you could love something so much?" she whispered to me, squeezing my hand. She had seen straight into my heart. Then, with shouts of "**mazel tov!**" drowning out our son's cries, it was over. God's pledge of loyalty to Abraham's offspring now included our son.

Thinking back on that day, I am reminded of the passage in Exodus when the Children of Israel proclaim to God, "We will do and we will listen." In the desert, they promised action and had faith that understanding would follow. In my own Michigan desert, the day of my son's b'ris taught me the power of Jewish ceremony. It taught me the value of following ritual for no other reason than "just because." It taught me that our tradition cherishes community, and that by embracing the former, we are richly rewarded with the latter.

CHAPTER 2

Oh, but She's Perfect!

The Story of Anita Landy

WHEN WE CALLED my parents to tell them we were going to pick up our soon-to-be-adopted infant, my mom asked, "Anita, what does she look like?" What she meant was, "How bad are her disabilities?"

"I have no idea, Mom. She's a baby."

"So you're taking her sight unseen?"

"Mom," I said, "I didn't see Jaime, Noah or Adam before I gave birth to them. You took *me* sight unseen. So it's sight unseen with this one, too. She needs us. She needs a home. And we have a home."

My husband, Doug, and I love children. At the time we had three biological children and wanted more; however, I had ruptured a disc with each child, and I knew my back couldn't take another pregnancy. Noah, our second, was a preemie and has problems related to his premature birth; Adam, child no. 3, had a stroke when he was an infant due to an inherited condition that left him with a hearing impairment and minor learning disabilities.

Adoption seemed the best course of action for more children, not only because of all the medical histories but because, on the plus side, Doug is a doctor and I am a special education teacher. Plus, given the fact that our boys' births had given us lots of experience navigating medical and insurance issues, it all just made sense.

We were specifically looking for Jewish kids. Once we started researching adoption, we learned that not only was there a real need to place Jewish kids with disabilities, but on the flip side, few Jewish couples were lining up to adopt kids with special needs. I don't know why more Jewish couples are not willing to adopt less-than-perfect children, but the result is that a lot of Jewish kids grow up not knowing what it is to light *Shabbos* candles or celebrate Passover.

A comment we heard among some of our Jewish acquaintances was: "Why would you do this? It's not necessary. What difference will it make if these kids are raised Jewish or not?" Doug and I felt it was necessary. A Jewish soul is a Jewish soul. Looking back now, adopting our last three kids has certainly made a difference to them! There are lots of kids with special needs who are cognitively intact. Just because kids have medical problems doesn't mean they can't go on and have kids of their own, thereby keeping the Jewish line going. You know that saying about "saving one life means saving the world"? Well, who knows what kind of world can be saved by adopting kids with special needs?

Doug and I settled on seeking out children with medical problems like cerebral palsy or spina bifida, because we had experience with these things both professionally and personally. Since our son is hearing impaired, and we knew how to sign, taking a deaf child was another option.

We wrote to every Jewish Family Service agency in the country. Some wrote back; some didn't. Without exception, however, those who wrote back told us to contact the Jewish Children Adoption Network in Denver. It's not an agency, but more of a clearing-house for Jewish kids with special needs.

We set in motion our home-study process and within two weeks got calls from two agencies. One call was from Adopt a Special Kid, and one was from the place in Denver. Two little girls had been born within a day of each other, one who was deaf and one who had spina bifida. Four or five families were already in line to adopt the deaf baby; no one had stepped forward to take the infant with spina bifida. Doug and I decided that she was the child for us.

On the plane to New York City, I fretted to Doug about my capacity to love this little baby as much as I loved my birth kids. He reminded me that he hadn't carried our kids, but the minute he held them, he loved them. He also reminded me that I had worried about loving my second child as much as my first. Love is love. It's independent of birth order. Adopting Rachel, and later Becky and Stephanie, taught me that loving children has nothing to do with how they find their way into your arms.

When we got to the hospital, I took one look at our daughter-to-be and I said, "Oh, my God. She's perfect!"

"No one's ever called this baby 'perfect,'" the NICU nurse told me. And I suppose to an outsider she wasn't. She had a large lesion on her back where her spinal cord had been protruding in a sac. Normally the first thing they do is remove the sac and close the opening, but the surgeons couldn't do it yet in this case. She had club feet and had already needed a brain shunt, so her hair was shaved and she had stitches across her scalp.

But she had the biggest, brownest eyes in the world, and she looked perfect to us. We knew in an instant that she was a fit, that she was our child. What was unbelievable to me was that somehow God had worked it so that someone else had given birth to our child. It was clear that she was ours. All my fears of bonding were left behind somewhere in the skies over New York.

The baby's parents were Russian immigrants who had only been in the U.S. a couple of years and didn't feel equipped to care for her. In Russia, it's a real taboo to have such a kid. There, these children are literally left to die in the streets; and because the couple lived in a tight Russian community, word of her condition would have made the mother's two younger sisters ineligible for marriage. But they were adamant that she go to a Jewish family if at all possible. We named our new daughter in synagogue soon after we got home. Her name is Rachel, after my grandmother, Rochel.

Half a year later we got another call. A couple had given birth to a child with spina bifida. They had heard about us from one of their NICU nurses who knew about Rachel. Would we adopt their baby? We were not even home when the call came. We were 250 miles away visiting our parents. Our friend had gone into our house to get something, and for some reason she couldn't even explain herself, she answered the phone when it rang. The timing of our friend's presence in our house was nothing short of miraculous.

We called the couple right away and told them that we had just adopted Rachel and weren't sure we were ready to take on another infant so soon. They had no family support, and they were scared; we offered to be that support and help them through the rough spots. But they insisted. They wanted someone to adopt their child and, without even meeting us, the someone they wanted was us.

Parents who have given birth to a handicapped child have a tremendously hard time giving up their children. Society applauds teenage girls who give their babies up for adoption into a better situation. We say, "How wonderful. How courageous you are for making such a sacrifice." Well, the same is true for parents of disabled children. These babies are not unwanted. They are loved, and their parents are in agony because, for a variety of reasons, they don't feel they can care for their own child. They decide, just as the teen moms do, that it would be in the best interest of their child that she be raised by someone else. But no one applauds these parents. People either shrug and say, "Yeah, I would too if I had such a kid," or they silently criticize them for not being "courageous enough" to stand by their child. Let me tell you, it takes an enormous amount of courage to give up a disabled child. To trust that your child, whose needs are so great and whose future is so uncertain, is going to be raised with love and care.

What were the chances of this happening? Of the NICU nurse knowing about us? Of our friend being at our home just at the moment the couple called? Of the couple learning about us and not taking no for an answer? Once again, I was certain there was some sort of divine intervention going on.

Rebecca was truly a beautiful baby. I'm not heavily into looks, but she was strikingly beautiful. Her spinal lesion was closed, and our expectation was that since she could move her legs she'd be running rings around her sister Rachel. We also thought that it would be easier for both girls to have each other.

Becky was coming with another issue we had to deal with. Her birth parents were Irish Catholic, and we were very up-front about the fact that their child would be raised in a Jewish home—no Mass, no Christmas trees. We would convert Becky to Judaism as soon as we could. Were they prepared to accept this?

Jim and Sally told us that they had already discussed it with their priest and they were OK with it. No, not only OK, but that it was good. Their daughter would be raised within a religious framework by parents concerned for her spiritual life. Again I felt that a gentle nudging from God had led Becky's parents to us.

When the girls were three years old, we moved to Rochester, New York. We'd been living in Traverse City, Michigan, but the girls' conditions required access to hospitals better equipped to deal with their ongoing needs. While we thought Becky's disabilities would not be as harsh as Rachel's, she has had a difficult time of it. She has a complication of spina bifida called a Chiari malformation. Her cerebellum is misshapen, and the malformation sits on her brain stem, exerting persistent pressure. The malformation cannot be changed, but doctors can surgically make room for it within the cranial cavity—if you live near enough to doctors who can operate. Becky has a tracheal tube now and is dependent on a ventilator to breathe.

For a while, we held off Becky's conversion, but each time we had a crisis I realized that I couldn't deal with another Chiari surgery if she weren't converted. What if something happened? Where would Becky be buried? Complicating the situation was the fact that there were no Orthodox rabbis in our area to oversee the conversion. An Orthodox rabbi in Rochester had agreed to perform the conversion when we moved to the community, but only if we agreed to commit to leading an observant life—totally keep kosher, keep Shabbos, no eating out in non-kosher restaurants. Our lives had been moving in that direction, but with no firm commitment. Was the family prepared for such a change?

Our kids had been so enthusiastic up to this point. They loved their new little sisters and had rolled with all the adjustments of living with not one, but two disabled kids. They were willing to go for it, and even Jaime, who was well past *bat mitzvah* age and not entirely sold on the idea, promised not to do anything inappropriate in our home or flout any discrepancies with our observance. We took the plunge.

Every Shabbos is so special now. I love it each week as Doug and I take turns blessing our six kids. We are together—playing games, reading with one another. The girls all light their own candles. Doug and I married when Jaime was three and we fell into having her light candles with me. So when the little girls came along, we started the tradition of giving them their own set of candlesticks for their third birthday. When Becky is home, she lights her own candles, and when she is in the hospital, she gets frustrated and feels it's not a true Shabbos. Stephanie, our third adopted daughter, just turned three and is proud to share the privilege of lighting candles the way her big sisters do.

Growing up, I loved being Jewish but always wondered, "Is there really a God?" I struggled to believe that there was, but without much success. It took Rachel and Becky and then Stephanie to bring God into my life with absolute trust and belief. True, I had given birth three times and recognized the miracle in each and every birth. It certainly was miraculous that our preemie son lived and that our son who had a stroke could walk and talk. But somehow those were miracles derived from human endeavors—the efforts of wonderful doctors and teachers. I wanted to feel that God had guided them but still could not accept with complete surety God's hand in those miracles.

Then I held each of our adopted daughters. They felt so right in my arms, and I knew for the first time in my life, "Yes, there is a God. These children, my children, could not have been brought to me—physically, emotionally, spiritually—in any other way. This could not have happened without God."

Doug and I set out to give Jewish children a home. Along the way we even brought another Jewish soul into being. We've never regretted our decision for a moment, for our daughters have brought our family joy, triumphs and a deeper understanding of God and Judaism. More miraculous than what we have done—negotiating wheelchairs, breathing tubes, countless surgeries, and heart-stopping races to the hospital—is what other parents have done. They gave us, sight unseen, their children.

CHAPTER 3

Cutting the Cord

The Story of Marcia Ferstenfeld

AS MY DAUGHTER grew close to delivering our first grandchild, it became important to have her and her husband stay with us over *Shabbos*. If you're not part of the observant community, this isn't an issue. But if you are, as she is and as my husband and I have become by extension, you understand that this one-chance-in-seven occurrence means no phone calls can be made to expectant family members. Having them stay with us meant that if Bethie went into labor on Shabbos, we would know right away.

As it so happened, during the wee hours of a Saturday morning in June, Bethie did go into labor. My husband and I stayed behind while our son-in-law took our daughter to the hospital (another Shabbos restriction—only one person is allowed to accompany the laboring mother to the hospital). We were consumed with frustrated glee awaiting the phone call telling us of the birth of our first grandchild.

My daughters' choosing observant life altered so many of the anticipations I'd had of being a Jewish mother and grandmother:

kids and grandkids around my table Friday night; Passover Seders in our home; taking everyone out to restaurants to celebrate birthdays, good report cards and graduations. I gladly *kashered* my kitchen so that everyone was comfortable eating with us during the week, but, practically speaking, Shabbos was out. My husband and I were only occasionally willing to observe in the way that my daughter and son-in-law did: by entering into a 25-hour period from sunset to sunset during which turning on a reading light, adjusting the oven temperature for dinner, or raising the thermostat for comfort were forbidden. As Beth's due date drew near, we were more than willing to make the accommodations.

Long before becoming a grandmother, or even a mother-in-law, I had developed my own sense of spirituality and religiosity. Then, as they became young adults, my daughter Lisa moved toward living a *frum* life and Bethie followed later in her wake. Amy, our middle daughter, remains committed to the Reform values she was raised with. Lisa and Bethie's choices threw a monkey wrench into my devotion to ritual and observance. If the path that two of my daughters and their husbands were following was purported to be the right way, where did that leave me? It left me challenged to allow them the space to live their own lives. It left me feeling like a woman in a Botero painting—huge and overblown, expanding beyond all normal parameters. And just as I thought I had made every possible accommodation to their lifestyle, my expectations of being close at hand while my daughter was in the labor room, of holding my grandchild moments after birth, now went out the window, too.

But soon enough, Arianna—in Hebrew, Emunah—was born. Beth and Riffy had agreed to have a non-Jewish nurse call and leave the good news on our answering machine if we promised not to pick up the receiver—another Shabbos prohibition. We listened to the joyous news on the machine, barely able to contain ourselves. Come sundown, we tore to the hospital and finally held our granddaughter. All frustration melted the minute

I held that tiny being; my heart swelled as I breathed in her new-baby smell.

A few months after Emunah's birth, Beth's husband, Riffy, was stricken with leukemia. Six years before their wedding he had been diagnosed with and survived a bout with aplastic anemia. Bethie was sure he would make it once again. But it wasn't to be. Despite our prayers, despite all the doctors' care, despite even the bone marrow transplant from 9-month-old Emunah, Riffy suffered a cerebral hemorrhage and died.

We had gone to Boston that spring for the transplant. *Pesach* fell while Riffy was in the hospital for the procedure and, during the *Seder*, Bethie stunned us with the news that she was newly pregnant with their second child. Their enormous love for each other and immutable faith that Riffy would recover must have tipped the scales for them to try and conceive while there was still a chance. I still see my daughter standing by her husband's bedside, fragile, slender, beautiful, struggling to accept the most horrible truth imaginable. Just twenty-two, she returned home from Boston to bury her husband and live nearby while she completed her pregnancy.

I don't know if the pregnancy helped or forestalled Beth's healing, but I know she couldn't allow herself to dissolve into grief. She needed to persevere for the baby she was carrying and for the child she was raising. It was good that she had her mothering to do, because it gave her a purpose in life. At a time when she might have doubted the purpose of living, there she was living life in every intensity: feeling the baby kick inside of her; chasing an active toddler all over the house, in the back yard and through the park near our home.

And while Bethie could throw herself into mothering to hold her pain and grief at bay, my mothering instincts were completely sidelined. If I moved to hug my daughter, she would go stiff on me. If I tried to reach out, she would shut down. I desperately wanted to scoop up my little girl and comfort her, but she would turn her face, hold her arms to her sides, and resist me.

Struggling to understand, I came to realize that if she had allowed herself to take in my comfort, she would have fallen apart. And she didn't dare. Her own vulnerability was too terrifying; she couldn't be a daughter, because she had to be a mother. She had to stay spiritually connected and hold on to the belief that this was God's will. It took her two years to get good and angry with God. Over the years, I had gotten ticked off in waves at the impediments their observance had placed in my path. In the wake of Riffy's death, a tsunami of rage overtook me. I've always been the family's emotional barometer. *Where is the justice*, I silently shouted, *in a 31-year-old man dying and leaving behind a wife and budding family?*

From my front-row seat I have learned that, for my children, observance isn't about getting their own way. They do it because they are commanded to. Life is filled with loss and pain, and that doesn't stop because they are observing the commandments. I see that, for them, living a frum life is a path toward attaining spiritual elevation. And for the promise of that spiritual potential, I had to give my daughter space.

As Bethie's delivery date drew near, I was faced with another "Botero" growth moment. She was determined to honor mother and mother-in-law equally by having us both be with her in the delivery room as her birth coaches. Inwardly, I heaved a sigh of resignation. This was the child of Beth's *machataynister's* dead son. Who was I to complain or stake out territorial rights in my daughter's delivery room? And then, surprise! That which had taken away so much from me loosened its grip and gave a little back. Shabbos. One-in-seven chance. Again, a quiet knock at my door in the wee hours of the morning. At first I thought Beth wanted me to take over with Emunah so that she could get some sleep. But no. She whispered to me that her water had broken and she needed to go to the hospital. Now. And in a flash I realized what had just been carved out for me—the chance to be with my daughter, just the two of us, at this extraordinary time in her life. It was a gift beyond anything I'd envisioned.

All the things I couldn't do for her for months and months, I finally could. All the love and caring that had been penned up, seemingly forever, flowed out. During her pregnancy, Bethie had been returning to me in increments, and while the hours of her labor were a very sweet connecting experience, there was still this little rivulet of caution on my part. My reserve in the face of her pain was a gentle way of honoring her. I was wary of her fragility even as I was completely taken up with massaging her back and legs while the contractions did the work of readying her body for birth.

Finally, after hours of waiting, miles of walking the hospital halls, onto the bed for a nap, off the bed for one last trip to the bathroom, back onto the bed for the final phase, Bethie let out that cry: "***I have to PUSH!***" The doctor assigned me to her left side to act as a stirrup while the nurse took up the mirror position at Beth's right side, and again she shouted, "***I have to PUSH!***" All of a sudden I saw this black, mushy, furry top of the head through an opening of what? Four inches? And then my daughter pushed again and the head was out, looking like that of a beautifully-fashioned doll—so beautiful, so beautiful. And then the next push and a tiny bit of upper chest appeared. Then another contraction and push and, contrary to any engineering principle, a shoulder, altogether too wide to ever emerge from so little an opening, squeezed forth and popped into shape like a blow-up doll. In another split second I saw those wide, if tiny, shoulders narrow into a slender waist. Then, like the genie spilling forth from Aladdin's lamp with a mighty whoosh, the baby was out.

I searched around the cord to see a baby girl and felt an instantaneous awareness of the losses of that—no boy from Riffy's seed; and all the joys—a sister for Emunah! She! She!

"Who's going to cut the cord?" the doctor asked. I shot a look at Beth and she shot one back to me. I took the scissors from the doctor and with my right hand cut the translucent lifeline linking my granddaughter to her mother. Natanya Rafaela was free in one sense, only to be bound through nursing and Bethie's mothering for the next 18 years.

The cleanup began. Beth's bloody right sock was sacrificed to the cause. The baby was wrapped up and placed upon her mommy's belly. The delivery room was alive with energy and excitement. In the wake of so much sadness and grief, the birthing room throbbed with the triumph of life.

Bethie's observance, and her sister Lisa's before her, had stolen so much from me. Their choices had forced me to grow past my own limitations of acceptance. I later realized that I, too, was forced through an opening so small—hemmed in as I was by dashed hopes, confusion, resentment. I had a birthing of my own to endure—cutting the cord of my expectations again and again and again.

Moments after Riffy's death, Beth had painfully accepted God's judgment. Barely nine months after the most excruciating experience of our lives, my daughter and I were again in a hospital room. God had taken, and now God had given. Blessed be the name of God.

PART 2

Rosh HaShanah and Yom Kippur

On Rosh HaShanah it is written; on Yom Kippur it is sealed.

—From the Un'taneh Tokef, High Holiday Liturgy

ROSH HASHANAH, THE Jewish New Year, and Yom Kippur, the Day of Atonement, are often referred to as *Yamim Noraim*, the Days of Awe. Indeed, the 10 days that begin with Rosh HaShanah and conclude with Yom Kippur are filled not only with prayer but with soul searching, pleas for forgiveness and a commitment to spiritual and moral renewal. A special *siddur*, or prayer book, is used at this time. Called a *machzor*, this book contains not only the daily and Sabbath prayers said during this time, but also special readings and prayers pertinent to the High Holidays.

Tradition holds that during the days between Rosh HaShanah and Yom Kippur, God reviews the deeds of each and every Jew during the past year and judges whether the individual merits inclusion in the Book of Life for the coming year. Through proper atonement and asking forgiveness (not only from God but from those whom we may have wronged), every Jew hopes to be sealed in the Book of Life for the year to come.

One of the most stirring elements of the High Holidays is the blowing of the *shofar*, ram's horn. Remember that in the last moment before Abraham sacrificed his son Isaac, God called out to him and instructed him to sacrifice a ram, caught in a nearby thicket, in place of Isaac. The use of the shofar (plural, *shofarot*) commemorates this event and reminds God to take note of His Jewish people and their prayers for life.

The shofar is blown according to specific musical patterns named *t'kiah, t'ruah, sh'varim*. At the very end of the shofar service, these patterns are followed by a *t'kiah g'dolah*, one long blast of sound that, depending on an individual's lung capacity, can last up to, or even longer than, a minute.

On the afternoon of the first day of Rosh HaShanah, many Jews walk to a nearby body of water to perform *Tashlich*, or casting off. Emptying their pockets of breadcrumbs (which symbolize their sins), they throw the crumbs into the water and then recite prayers of penitence.

The Days of Awe culminate with Yom Kippur. Next to the Sabbath, it is considered to be the most sacred day of the Jewish calendar. Yom Kippur is given over to prayer and self-reflection. Jews who have reached the age of religious maturity (13 for boys, 12 for girls), and whose health would not be compromised, are expected to fast from sunset to sunset.

The hymn "*Avinu Malkeinu*," "Our Father Our King," sung on Rosh HaShanah and Yom Kippur, is a stirring component of each High Holiday service. The words of the hymn offer admission of transgressions as well as pleas for compassion, blessings and an end of suffering. On Yom Kippur the cantor chants the haunting melody of the *Kol Nidrei* prayer. Kol Nidrei means "all vows," and it is the prayer by which Jews nullify any vow made by force or frivolity during the previous year. Yom Kippur services the next day include *Yizkor*, a service that memorializes deceased relatives. The mourner's *Kaddish* is recited once again at this time, and services end at sunset.

Apples and honey are eaten during this season, in hopes of a sweet year. *Challah*, the rich and braided bread that is part of every festive meal, is also eaten, but during these holidays the loaf is shaped into a circle to symbolize the unending cycle of Jewish life.

The day concludes with a *Havdalah* service. Derived from the Hebrew word for "separation," the weekly Havdalah ceremony separates the holy from the mundane, the Sabbath day from the rest of the week. Once three stars appear in the sky, the ceremony can be performed. Blessings are said over wine, a special braided candle and fragrant spices, and wishes for a *shavuah tov*, a good week, are sung.

CHAPTER 4

Beginning the New Year at Sea

The Story of Deanna Silver Jacobson

ONE OF THE biggest reservations I'd had after learning I'd been accepted into the University of Pittsburgh's Semester at Sea program was the realization that I would be spending Rosh HaShanah and Yom Kippur away from my family for the first time in my life. I wouldn't hear the cantor's familiar High Holiday melodies or be with my loved ones for our family's legendary holiday meals. I didn't even know if I would be with other Jews at all; it was quite possible that I would mark the Jewish New Year in private, by myself.

All my friends and family said holiday homesickness wasn't reason enough to miss the opportunity of a lifetime. "Go," my mother said. "You'll find a way to make it meaningful." I didn't know how that could possibly be, but I sent in my deposit anyway, got all my shots and started packing.

There were 400 of us altogether, college students from all across the country. During our three months at sea we would tour Japan, Korea, Taiwan, China, Hong Kong, and Malaysia. Bombay, India; Odessa, USSR (now Russia); and Cadiz, Spain, were also to be ports of call, as were stops in Istanbul, Turkey, and Dubrovnik, Yugoslavia (now Croatia). Leading professors from universities in each country gave onboard lectures. A major goal of the trip was to show us that, beyond the differences in geography and appearance, we would have a lot in common with the people we were to meet. I didn't realize at the time how much I would also learn about the commonality between Jews.

Rosh HaShanah would fall between Taiwan and Korea, and as it drew closer, my homesickness only grew. Each time we docked, I would seek out a telephone, only to turn away from dialing. The thought of calling home tightened my throat with such longing that I couldn't speak. I didn't know how I would make it through. Then, somehow, via that radar we all seem to have, word got passed among the Jewish students that a group was getting together to hold Rosh HaShanah services. This was something I knew I could do. And, for the first time ever, I got involved in High Holiday services not as a passive congregant but as a leader.

At our first planning meeting, Steffie, a student who had her sights set on rabbinic school, took stock of our various skills and aptitudes. She had brought a prayer book from home and had gone on a scavenger hunt that netted us a battered but usable Torah scroll. We decided who had skill enough to read Torah and who would lead prayers. Since the *siddur* was not a High Holiday prayer book, others were assigned the task of writing prayers appropriate to Rosh HaShanah that would be inserted into the service. I was given the challenge of writing a sermonette and the honor of reading the Torah.

We knew that it was up to us and us alone to make the services meaningful for everyone. We also planned to invite non-Jewish students—we wanted it to be a learning experience for them, as well. Many of our shipmates had never even met a Jew before and it made sense to invite them. The raison d'être of this trip was to learn about other cultures. What better way than this?

Over the course of the week, as we created our service, individual memories of our holidays at home began to surface. Some of us had grown up observing Rosh HaShanah for two days; others for one; still others came from families who observed the holiday only intermittently. We talked of *mandelbread* and *mechitzahs*. There was such a free exchange of experiences, I think in part because so many of us were incredibly homesick. Hearing stories about one another's temples and *shuls*, trading tales about eccentric uncles and exploded *kishkes* at holiday dinners helped us through our longings for home.

Magically, that Rosh HaShanah service, marking the Jewish year 5747, was the most meaningful one I have ever attended. We students had barely known each other two weeks, but repeating the *Sh'ma* joined us; singing the *V'ahavta* united us. From the first reading to the final *Adon Olam*, we became a community. Just like that. Not only were we linked to one another, but we felt the presence of all of our families, knowing that on the other side of the dateline they would soon be awakening, dressing hurriedly, and walking to shul or finagling a parking spot in the synagogue's crowded lot, praying and singing as we had. I had new friends simply because I was a Jew and they were Jews; we had an unspoken agreement that we could turn to one another if we needed to. I was halfway across the world from home, but I realized somewhere between my sermon and the Torah reading that Judaism is my home. Much in the way a turtle carries her house on her back, I realized that I carried my Judaism with me wherever I went. No matter where I am, I thought, all I have to do is link up with fellow Jews and I can be home once again.

That evening, after a festive holiday meal prepared by the Asian chefs on board (yellow tablecloths and lots of rice, but apples, honey, and a *challah*, too), about 40 of us, some Jewish, some not, went up to perform *Tashlich* and *Havdalah* on the sun deck. Water is a big image in Judaism and I thought about Noah, surrounded by floodwaters on all sides, on a journey whose outcome he couldn't fathom. The Israelites passed through the amniotic waters of the Sea of Reeds to be reborn into freedom. Rebecca and Isaac fell in love at her father's well. Though 21 years old and 10 time zones from home, I threw my breadcrumb sins into the inky darkness of the East China Sea and felt an entirely new dimension of my Jewish identity come into being.

Havdalah was as electrifying as our morning services. Standing in a circle, we watched the sun slip beneath the waves, leaving behind a horizon of brilliant blue. The ship's whistle bellowed low and loud, a good enough substitute for the *shofar* we did not hear this year. We passed around the spice box, then the braided candle whose flame flickered in the wind. We blessed wine, sang songs, and wished one another *shavuah tov*, a good week, and began to scatter.

Just then Alisa, the student from Mexico, approached Steffie and asked if she could help her find the *Kaddish* in the prayer book. Several of us within earshot stopped in our tracks and began counting. Just like that. We called others back to be sure we had enough for a *minyan*. We didn't yet know that Alisa had just received a wire from home that her grandfather had died, and we didn't have to know it. She didn't ask us to stay or ask for a minyan, but we understood and were there for her. Plain and simple, that's what it means to be Jewish. As we stood around, giving our silent support while Alisa said the words to the Kaddish, I felt an indescribable solidarity with the Jewish people. It occurred to me then why you need ten for a minyan. So that you are not alone. You might feel desolate and grief-stricken, but Jewish tradition has structured itself so that you will not be alone in your grief. Your community will come forward for you.

The semester passed quicker than a black-market deal in Moscow, and before I knew it I was home, attending my brother's *bar mitzvah*, celebrating Passover with my family, looking forward to graduation and my first move into the adult world. That was 26 years ago. I'm married now, raising kids of my own. When they dip their apples into honey each year, they leave sticky golden trails on my white tablecloth. Each year when the cantor blows the shofar in synagogue, I hear an echo of the ship's horn, loud and mighty as Moses. I've forgotten Korea's GNP and how to say "excuse me" in Turkish, but I will remember this forever: *am Yisrael chai*, the people of Israel will live.

CHAPTER 5

"Quick! Beneath the Tallis!"

The Story of Paul Darmon

"*VAS-Y EN DESSOUS du tallit de ton grand-père; il va te protéger*," my father whispered every Rosh HaShanah before the *duchaning* began. "Get under your grandfather's *tallis*; he will protect you." Protect me from what? I wanted to ask. But I never did. Over the years, huddling beneath my grandfather's large, white prayer shawl with my father, my uncle and my cousin Jacques became an unquestioned tradition. I sensed something holy and ominous was taking place during this part of the service. Else, why would my father urge me under grand-père's tallis for "protection"?

Duchaning is a strange and mysterious ritual. During Rosh HaShanah morning services, the *Kohanim*, those males in the congregation who are descendants of the priests of ancient Israel, recite over the entire congregation the same blessing uttered by the priests in Temple times. The ancient Kohanim would ascend daily to a platform (a *duchan*) to bless the Jewish people with the threefold benediction known today as the Priestly Blessing:

Yevarechecha, adonai veyishmerecha. Yaer adonaiy panav elecha vichuneka. Yisah adoniay panav elecha veyasem lecha shalom. May God bless you and protect you. May God cause His face to shine upon you and enlighten you. May God raise up His countenance toward you and grant you peace.

As the Kohanim do today, the Priests would hold out their hands toward the congregation, palms forward, thumbs touching at the tips, the fingers parted between the middle and ring finger. If you're having trouble picturing this, imagine the Vulcan salute: Leonard Nimoy borrowed it from Jewish tradition.

So why did we have to huddle beneath my grandfather's tallis? In ancient times there was the belief that God's emanation rested upon the hands of the Kohanim while they recited the blessing. Based on the warning in Torah that anyone gazing upon God's presence will be struck down, the superstition developed that looking at the Kohanim's hands during duchaning will blind you—hence the protection beneath my grandfather's tallis. I knew nothing of divine emanations or going blind back then. When my father urged me to stand close, I did, period. My cousin always tried to make me laugh but somehow, even as a young child, I knew something important was going on. I stayed as still as I could, inhaling the scent of my father's Old Spice cologne, keeping my eyes averted from my cousin's mischief and from anything going on outside the safety of my grandfather's prayer shawl.

My parents are Sephardic Jews—Mom is from French Algeria and my dad is from French Tunisia. The male-dominated culture in which they both grew up naturally extended to synagogue life. That's why it was males only beneath the tallis. Girls and women had their own section of the synagogue. What they did during the duchaning I never thought about. But that doesn't mean females didn't also have ritual power of protection. In Sephardic tradition, there is a part of the Passover Seder when the family's matriarch takes the Seder plate and passes it over everyone's head, symbolizing God's literal passing over the children of Israel during that deathly night of the Tenth Plague, the Death of the Firstborn. As my mother walked over each of us we would sing, together, *"Etmol haynu avadim, hayom beney chorin kan- beshana haba'a beney chorin be'ara d'Israel,"* which means "Yesterday we were slaves, today (tonight) we are free people here—next year free people in the land of Israel."

During my father's recitation of the Ten Plagues, Mom had another role, every bit as ominous and powerful as the duchaning. After naming each plague, my father would spill a bit of wine from his *Kiddush* cup into a bowl. As he poured, my mother would recite in Hebrew: "*Simsilenu*," "God will save us (from the plagues)." We were dead quiet as my parents performed this ritual.

When my father reached the Tenth Plague, he would pour the remainder of his wine into the bowl and my mother, again repeating "Simsilenu," emptied the rest of the water from her pitcher. Then, she would take the bowl of powerless plagues to the bathroom and we would all wait for the comic relief of the ceremonial flush before she returned to the table and continued serving the meal with my aunts and my sister and my grandmother. Twice a year, on *Pesach* and Rosh HaShanah, these rituals of protection played out.

Even after my grandfather died, the four of us still gathered beneath the tallis during that mystical part of the Rosh HaShanah service. Until my cousin and I went to college, we stood shoulder to shoulder each year, quietly remembering with our bodies the years when three generations sought protection during the duchaning.

It's been a long time now since I've been under my father's tallis. I don't go to the Sephardic *shul* in our community. My wife and I joined an Ashkenazi congregation—at the time, the cantor had a very Sephardic way of chanting that felt like home. Unlike Sephardic tradition, my wife and our daughters have equal opportunities to participate. The first Rosh HaShanah our family attended, when the rabbi announced duchaning it sparked something in me. I realized I was the head of the household; it was up to me to protect my family. So I gathered everyone around and spread my tallis over us. Like my father before me and his father before him, it is now our family's tradition. The kids giggled at first but my wife loved it from the start. She stands beside me and I feel such gratitude for her and for the life we are making together. In the five minutes the ceremony takes, my head goes somewhere else. It's peaceful. I remember Old Spice and my cousin's antics and the feel of my grandfather's wool suit against my cheek. The Kohanim recite blessings that go back thousands of years. Under the protection of my tallis, all our family becomes one soul.

CHAPTER 6

Never Too Late

The Story of Hannah Dietz

"I'VE BEEN GIVEN a good deal of money to hire a High Holiday cantor, and I have no idea where to begin the search," Steven Richman told me. Steven, my friend and first rabbi, was back for a visit. Several years earlier he had been the student rabbi for our small congregation in northern Michigan. He's warm and lovable, has a great talent for fun and I've always enjoyed time spent in his company. Since his ordination a few years earlier, he has been the spiritual leader of a thriving congregation in New Hampshire.

"I'll do it," I said as a joke. "Hire me."

Two months later he called. "The High Holiday material is on its way to you—sheet music, our prayer book and some CDs that might get you started." My heart raced twice its normal pace. Steven had taken my offhand joke about being his cantorial soloist seriously! I realized with dread that there was no getting off the hook at this stage of the game; he was counting on me. I had to make good on my commitment and I had only the summer to prepare.

Becoming a High Holiday soloist was a challenge on two fronts. I had been a professional musician in Denmark, but I had always sung with others—in the royal opera choir, in Copenhagen's symphony choir. I put myself through college by singing in church choirs all over the city. But paralyzing stage fright made solos out of the question for me. I had tried early in my career, and as soon as things started flowing well on stage, I would sabotage myself with doubt: "What if your knees buckle? What if you forget a line?" I would completely self-destruct. It was 20 years before my husband even heard me sing, that's how under wraps I kept my voice.

The other challenge was the not-so-minor fact that I had never attended High Holiday services. Not once. I didn't know *Kol Nidrei* from *Avinu Malkeinu*. In Denmark, our parents raised us to be proud and knowledgeable Jews; our home was filled with books about Jewish art and history. My family was strongly Zionist. But there was no Jewish ritual in my upbringing—none. Any references to *shul* came from my aunts and uncles, who occasionally mentioned during their visits whom they had seen at services. My grandmother, whose Danish was heavily accented with Yiddish, came each fall and cooked these wonderful meals for us. It wasn't until I began going to services many, many years later that I realized what she cooked for us all those years were the traditional Jewish holiday meals. We knew we were Jews, and Hitler certainly did, but the religion of Judaism had nothing to do with us.

I think my father became an atheist after the war. His involvement in the Resistance didn't sit well with the leaders of the Jewish community, and they let him know it. They thought it inappropriate for a married man to leave home and put himself and his family in danger. Also, they feared that his actions would expose Copenhagen's Jews to retaliation from the Nazis. Somehow, though, I don't think my father's activities were the reason my mother, my sisters, and I and nearly our entire community had to escape over the sea to Sweden to wait out the war.

Earlier that fall, my father and other members of his group had been captured by the Gestapo in a raid at the printing plant where they produced and distributed underground literature and helped communicate between different resistance groups. He was sent to a camp in Germany and miraculously survived to return to us after the capitulation.

All I understood of Judaism in those years was danger and fear; after the war and our return from Sweden, Judaism became who I was but had no bearing on anything I did. I married an American man, not a Jewish man, but a man who lives by a strong sense of honor. When we came to America, Judaism was the farthest thing from my mind. We owned a ranch in Texas right in the middle of the Bible Belt. In all those years I never felt the need to seek out other Jews or any kind of worship. I wasn't hostile; Judaism just didn't play any role in my life.

So there I was, nearly 50, happy with my life, yet indifferent to the fact that two aspects of my identity were completely submerged. Music was tugged into the light after my husband saw an announcement that an amateur group was holding auditions for *Annie Get Your Gun*. He bugged me so much that I started to work on "*Habañera*" from *Carmen* as my audition piece. I practiced before him every evening, figuring if I could sing in front of him, I could sing in front of anybody. Audition night, no one could believe that the shrinking violet they had known for years had a voice! Eventually I had parts in several musicals and stayed with the group in Texas until our move to Michigan.

Soon after our arrival in Traverse City, another bulletin notice caught my attention: The student rabbi of the local synagogue was sponsoring a summer of ethnic cooking at members' homes. I thought, *What the heck? I'll go*. We cooked a lot of foods I had eaten on visits to Israel, and before too long I wanted a little more connection. I started attending Rabbi Richman's Intro to Judaism class. I had always been so embarrassed at my ignorance of Jewish ritual and Torah. I began attending services, mostly out of courtesy to the young rabbi. I had taken a real liking to him, and I went more out of friendship for him than any need for spiritual connection.

A funny thing happened on the way to services. I kept hearing Hebrew phrases that sounded familiar. Maybe I had picked them up long ago when my uncles sang prayers in our home. I would look at the faces in the synagogue and find them familiar. I had this rudimentary feeling that I belonged. There was a connection, and over the weeks and months it grew and grew.

Those initial echoes of connection, however, were not going to help me sing High Holiday services three months down the road. I had to get to work. I listened to the CDs and began some research of my own. I looked through all the sheet music Steven had sent me and picked things that seemed appropriate. Never having been to a High Holiday service before, I had no idea what melodies people expected to hear, what was traditional and what wasn't. Steven had also sent me a list of prayers sung in the service, so I sought out that music to learn, too. Rewriting the materials for solo voice, my old self-destructive doubts began to bubble up. I wrote faster, transcribed more quickly and practiced harder to silence them. I consulted with Steven throughout the summer, then booked my ticket and went out to New Hampshire, shaking like a leaf.

Five minutes before Rosh HaShanah evening services began, I looked out into the congregation. The sanctuary was filled to overflowing; there was a light of expectation in everyone's eyes. Steven was a new rabbi there, and I wanted to do well for him and for his congregants. I didn't want to let them—or myself—down. I was overwhelmed at the role I was playing. I was acting as their clergy, responsible for their experience. I prayed I would be worthy.

When it was time, I stood up and opened my mouth, and the music just flowed out in waves of inspiration. My voice rode on unknown sources. From then on, I couldn't get enough. I saw in everyone's eyes that I was reaching them. It was the most powerful experience of my life. I was carrying them and they were carrying me. I had finally broken through a wall that I should have broken through 30 years before.

Another fear I brought with me was my choice of music. These were people who had been attending services all their lives. I had no clue which melodies they were accustomed to hearing. Luckily, some unknown hand had guided me in the void, because most of the melodies I picked were the traditional High Holiday ones with which the congregation was familiar.

In their faces I saw the faces of people I had grown up with in Denmark—all repeated in Steven's temple in New Hampshire. It was something in the corner of a mouth, in the rise of a cheek or slant of an eye. It hit me that we were all of the same stock.

At the close of *Havdalah* after Yom Kippur, 10 days later, Steven came to my side of the *bimah*, took my hand and drew me to the front of the congregation. He told them that I wasn't trained as a cantor and that not only was this the first time that I had ever sung High Holiday music, but it was the first time I had ever attended High Holiday services. Everyone seemed to gasp at the same moment. Steven spoke of new beginnings and of rebirth.

Earlier, during Rosh HaShanah, he had shared with them in an emotional sermon the fact that he was gay. The outpouring of warmth, love, and acceptance with which the congregation had embraced him after his courageous announcement had been a powerful emotional experience. He and I had never discussed his sexual orientation years before in Michigan. I had figured it out, and it made no difference to the way I felt about him. The qualities that I love and admire in him have nothing to do with his sexuality.

When he spoke of breakthroughs and confronting one's "what ifs", he was speaking for us both. We had both stepped out over a cliff. What really mattered was not that he was gay or that I had never sung Jewish liturgical music before, but that we had made new beginnings in our 10 days together and had grown spiritually because of it. They had truly been "Days of Awe."

Since that first High Holiday encounter, I have been on a voyage of discovery. I never knew there was all this wonderful music written for the synagogue. I still love church music; I just never thought there was Jewish music that could match up with the great hymns of the Lutheran church, but there is. Judaism opened up an aspect of music for me that I never knew existed, and music opened up Judaism to me as never before.

We now have a permanent rabbi in Traverse City, and I am our congregation's regular soloist. *Avinu Malkeinu* has become my own conversation with God each year. Music is how I connect with the Divine. The *Avot* prayer begins with the plea, "Adonai, open my lips that my mouth may declare Thy glory." That's what it is for me. I begin to sing, and music takes the place of prayer.

The biggest surprise for me in all this is that music has returned my father to me. When he died, he had a Jewish funeral, and I remember being so angry. There was a rabbi, a cantor, Hebrew music and prayers. I was furious because my father's funeral service had absolutely nothing to do with who he was or how he lived. But somehow, everything I do that is religious is a tribute to him. I always have the feeling when I sing that he knows and is proud of it. I feel him hovering all around me. The Resistance fighter who was rebuked for his courage, the father who divorced himself from religion but bequeathed his Jewish pride, now has a daughter who brings 55 Jewish families in a small Michigan town closer to their God.

My whole life I wondered why I had survived the war, why our boat made it safely out from under the guns and searchlights of the Nazis. I used to think: *So many died for their faith. I am barely a Jew. I didn't marry a Jewish man and don't live a Jewish life—why me?*

Now I realize that I still have something to give the Jewish people this far along the road. Maybe someone will hear me and have a spiritual experience that connects them to God. Maybe my singing will reinforce another's commitment to Judaism. Some people bake for *Kiddush*; others raise money. Singing is something I can do that no one else can. My having been saved was for a reason after all.

CHAPTER 7

So, Who Is a Jew?

The Story of Ahuva Newman

SO HERE IS this question: What kind of Jew am I? I am Israeli born, but am I Conservative, Orthodox, Reform? I don't know what I am.

You do a *Pesach* Seder. Do you do it because it is custom, or because you are commanded to? Where do you draw the line between traditions, behaviors, and ethnic food? Maybe because my parents didn't have a label around religion, I had freedom to choose, but I don't even know what to call what it is I have chosen. It doesn't have a name.

What I do know is this Yom Kippur I felt I wanted to go to evening services for *Kol Nidrei*. I usually go in the morning each year, since I lead junior congregation in my synagogue. Since I was 12 I have fasted on Yom Kippur. But this year I needed to feel more of a connection again. My son is in college; my daughter is in her teen years and off doing her own thing. What can I say? I felt very disconnected from the things I had been connected to before. And when I look at it now, I know that the bond I needed to feel started in Israel, even though my parents weren't the religious type at all.

Growing up in Israel in the 50s and 60s, you could be only one of two things—*chilonit*, secular, or *datiyit*, observant. There wasn't anything in between. I don't know if my parents ever even went to a synagogue—they weren't the religious type at all. The extent of it was that my mother lit *Shabbat* candles, and come Passover and *Shavuot*, my father took the responsibility of cooking everything himself. But when I was a young girl, every Friday night I would go to my girlfriend's apartment on the floor below us and do *Kiddush* with her family. My parents never said, "Don't go." They weren't anti-religion, but it wasn't anything that involved them.

On Yom Kippur I would go with these same girlfriends to the Beit HaKnesset HaGadol, the Great Synagogue in Mercaz HaCarmel, and afterward we would walk and walk through the streets of Haifa. In the Great Synagogue, the men were downstairs and the women upstairs behind an elevated *mechitzah*. We would always look over and try to see the boys we knew, try and see what was going on down there. It left its mark on me. Did I pray? I don't particularly remember. I went because my girlfriends were going and I liked being with them.

Once we experimented and went to a Reform service in an old movie house. It was crazy to me, boys and girls, men and women all sitting together. It was so different from what we were used to. When I came to the United States I realized that that was one way of Judaism. You could go that way if you wanted to. It took me many years to adjust to the fact that men and women were sitting together. Yet, I don't consider myself an observant Jew; I'm a religious person, but I'm not *Shomer Shabbat*. The sitting together didn't bother me from a religious point of view; it was just very, very strange to me

But still, when I need my religion, I go back to the strictest form that I can. When my son was born, I made sure that an Orthodox rabbi performed the *b'ris*. Why him and not the cantor at the Conservative synagogue? I don't know. When my father had a heart attack, I had a flight booked for Pesach to go and see him. I remember praying, "Wait for us, Daddy, wait for us." He died a week before I was to go. I didn't go to his funeral. I sat *shivah*, following the rule to the best of my ability and knowledge. I wore black, sat on a low chair, prayed and followed the *minhagim*, the customs, as best I could. I probably did my own picking and choosing, but I leaned toward the more strict ways, and that comforted me.

The Shabbat of the week I sat shivah, I went to *shul*. How can I describe it? I felt like I was in the middle of those funny mirrors at the county fairs. I felt isolated from everyone around me. Totally separate. It was the hardest, most painful time of my mourning. Then *Kaddish* was recited, and I felt the community praying next to me. That Kaddish healed me, made me feel that I belonged once more.

This past Yom Kippur I felt isolated again. I needed some kind of connection, not necessarily to Israel or to my parents. I don't know how else to say it except that I needed connection. I had only one thought—to go to an Orthodox shul.

I have a friend who goes to this shul. We've been friends for 20 years, and though she is older than I am, we are each other's support system. But attending her shul created a lot of conflict. I didn't want to drive. I hadn't paid for a ticket, and I didn't want to be a *shnorrer*. I didn't feel right. Do I go? Don't I go? I was debating until the last minute, and then I said, "I'm going. We'll see what happens."

I drove to my friend's house, and then we walked to her shul. A neighbor joined us; we were our own community walking to Kol Nidrei together. My friend and I entered through the *ezrat nashim*, the women's section, and I was immediately struck by the emptiness of it all. I was expecting to see barely an empty seat, and instead it was like, "Well, you can sit here or there or over there." There were so many places it was as if someone was saying, "Here, it's open for you to choose your place."

I assumed I wouldn't know many people, but soon after I arrived, a woman came in whom I had tutored for her *bat mitzvah* when she was a teenager. A short while later, another woman came into the section whom I knew, and then another women who had been my student, and then the mother of the former student who first said hello. A little circle began to close for me and around me. I had started out in an empty women's section all alone; then it started filling up and I felt at home.

I heard the rabbi's voice and saw him through the mechitzah. He was the rabbi who had performed my son's b'ris 20 years ago. We see each other from time to time. He still remembers me. How does he do that—remember the mothers of sons he has circumcised so long ago?

The mechitzah didn't bother me at all. There were enough little holes in it so I could see through. It was white and lacy, and actually it was a measure of relief. The women's section was like this huge support group. So instead of hiding us, the mechitzah was sort of like a protection—a little veil that enabled us to be ourselves.

Women weren't praying initially; they were singing or talking quietly among themselves. We were coming together and focusing on trivia at first—kids, day-to-day details. The women took a while to get involved with prayer. It took me years to adjust to men and women sitting together, and after I did I swore I would never go back to segregation. But there I was at Kol Nidrei in the women's section behind a mechitzah, and I was enjoying it. Not only enjoying it, but comforted by it. What kind of a Jew does that make me?

Everyone was dressed in white or pale, very pale colors. The light in the shul was very bright. As I looked through the mechitzah I saw the men all dressed in white, too—their white *tallitot* draped around their shoulders. They were adjusting them again and again; the blue stripes of the shawls waved with their continuous movements. You know how men do? The constant shrugging and adjusting of the tallit over their shoulders?

There was constant sound coming from their side: humming, singing, praying. The sound and the individual motions of the tallitot began to merge, and it looked like waves, sound waves, ocean waves. It was so hypnotizing, as if the men beneath their tallitot were no longer individual beings but interconnected parts of a greater whole. It was very pure, continual, steady. I began to depend on the constancy of it. I knew I could look away and look back and trust that it was still there—rhythmic, moving in unison, humming with waves of white wool and sound.

The service ended far sooner than I wanted it to. I wasn't ready to let go of the experience but wanted to linger on and stay within the safety and comfort that the women's section had given me. I hated the idea of leaving the shul, saying goodbye to my friend, getting back into my car and returning to the mundane.

So, what kind of Jew am I that I do not light candles every week but find comfort and protection in a mechitzah? Why do I seek Orthodoxy when I need connection? Still I do not understand this, but I'm glad that I have the way to connect when I need to. And even today, so many months after, I can call up the image of those white tallitot—waving, breathing almost with a life of their own—and be calmed. Why do we have to label the kind of Jew that we are? I am a Jew. That's all there is to it.

CHAPTER 8

By God's Design

The story of Robert Dov Tennenbaum

IT'S CLOSE TO lunch when I finish. I've been working since 6 a.m. or so and I'm exhausted. It's still dawn-quiet in my studio. No drone of radio or TV yet; no shouts of visiting grandchildren splashing in the pool; no clattering and whining from the garden crew's army of lawn mowers. The door is closed, and once I'm into my painting, once I've decided which sketch from my book is really speaking to me, my hand just takes over.

When I finally take a break, I feel like I've had an encounter with something or someone from above. Looking down at my easel, I marvel once again that a chance meeting with a *Chabad* rabbi opened up to me an entire world of self-expression that I thought was always forbidden to Jews. What I've learned from Hillel Baron, in the decade since we met, is that though the Second Commandment forbids Jews to worship images—printed, sculpted, drawn or otherwise—Jewish life is nevertheless rich with an artistic expression that goes back to the time of the Torah. Like Jacob, who struggled with the angel and awoke saying, "God was in this place and I did not know it," I have struggled with the creation of art, never realizing that God could be there, too.

As an architect, I've spent the greatest portion of my years shaping the urban environment. In recent years, I've been in charge of land acquisition, real-estate development, and campus beautification; transforming an inner city institution of higher learning into an oasis; balancing open spaces with the ever-expanding need for classrooms, research space, student housing and administration buildings. My vision for a beautiful urban environment is one that enables users to function efficiently, safely and comfortably.

Away from work, my creative energies took another path. I operated on the premise I had been taught in school—that art exists for its own sake, that it informs itself and doesn't have to refer to anything else. That philosophy carried me through years of experimentation with abstract photography. But somewhere along the way, creating nonobjective art became too easy. Photography ceased to answer the creative urge within. I wanted my art to be informed by something meaningful; I just didn't know how to find it.

Those longings coincided with two trips abroad—the first to Israel in '81 and the second, some years later, to Austria, from which my parents and I had fled in 1939. While in Austria we visited Mathausen. It was an intensely emotional experience to realize that had my parents not acted in time, Mathausen would have been our tomb instead of a terrifically sobering but nevertheless temporary stop on our journey. While there I took a series of photographs that I eventually combined with earlier photos from my trip to Israel. In these works, I juxtaposed images of Israeli survivors looking back at Mathausen. Judaism was creeping into my work of its own volition. Then Rabbi Baron laid a challenge upon my drafting table—to take a down-at-the-heels tract house and transform it into a synagogue and preschool. I was to create a place where Jews could connect with God. I had been involved for so long in the big picture that I was quite excited to be able to work on a more human scale, to focus on the needs of individuals and not an entire institution. It was a very special assignment, and I found myself electrified by the opportunity.

My first task was to go and study, to read up on ancient synagogue design and learn what the Torah had to say about the work of artistic creation. What I discovered was so creatively explosive for me that the dust has yet to settle. I don't think it ever will. I had no inkling of the rich tradition of illuminated manuscripts in Judaism. *Haggadot* and *ketubot*—medieval texts lavishly adorned with color and gold leaf, fanciful animals and intricate geometric patterns—I knew of none of these. My initial readings concentrated on the last two portions of the Book of Exodus—*Vayakhel* and *Pikudei*—which detail God's instructions to the Israelites for the construction of the Tabernacle and the Holy Ark.

"Let all among you who are skilled come and make all that the Lord has commanded, the Tabernacle, its tent and its covering, its clasps and its planks, its bars, its post and its sockets." The planks for the tabernacle were to be hewn of acacia wood 2 1/2 cubits long, 1 ½ cubits wide and 1 ½ cubits high. Slowly I realized that I was reading God's own blueprints for the first sanctuary in which His spirit was to reside. Rabbi Baron, unwittingly or not, had engaged me in a project in which I could combine a lifetime of experience with my dawning need to create something informed by meaning—art inspired by my own Jewish heritage. So like Judaism's first artisan, Bezalel, whom God chose above all others to do the work of making the Holy Tabernacle and whose name means "in the shadow of God," I, too, got down to the job of creating a space in which God's spirit would reside.

Because the building would serve two functions—worship and education—I reoriented the house so that the sanctuary was flanked by classrooms that could double during services as additional seating for the men's and women's sections. Rabbi Baron's vision to bring "holy light and beauty into our building" guided my sketches. Above a beautiful wooden ark donated by a

Maryland congregation that had closed, I installed two skylights to channel the sun's rays upon it. The doors of the ark are panels of a pale fruitwood richly carved with images of *shofarot*, an unfurled *Megillah* scroll, Sabbath candlesticks, and the like. The body of the ark itself is a dark mahogany framing the deeply-carved doors. When light hits the ark, the images from the door panels stand out in even greater relief.

As I got deeper into the project, I marveled that I was working with a rabbi, Chabad no less, who was committed to using art to bring people to God. Only now do I realize he was using art to bring me to God, too. He had me design a series of stained-glass windows featuring the 12 tribes and a second series featuring the matriarchs and patriarchs. The latter graces the women's and men's sections during services and they also are dominant features of the two classrooms. The building would not only be used to elevate the spirit but the mind as well. Rabbi Baron's plan was for teachers to use the windows as jumping-off points for stories and lessons about our earliest ancestors.

One day I was at the site talking with the engineer and a few of the construction guys. I'd had hundreds of such meetings, but this one was girded by a deeper awareness. On one level we were talking beams and trusses, wiring and insulation—the modern-day equivalent to acacia planks, tent poles, and silver lamps; but on an entirely different level we were talking about making a place in which God would reside. I'm always eager for the day I can enter a building whose design and construction I have overseen. As the synagogue took shape, I was even more anxious to see how our plans for this holy space would all come together.

Rabbi Baron was determined that we have *Kol Nidrei* services in the building, with or without a certificate of occupancy from the county inspectors. We didn't quite finish on time, but we didn't let that stop us. The floor was a concrete slab, and there was still a lot of detail work to be done, but the congregants of Ahavas Israel prayed Kol Nidrei in their new home, unconcerned that it didn't pass county inspection. That night we were focused on inspection by a higher source.

The acoustics were perfect, the light subdued and gentle. For the first time in my life I prayed in a space of my own making. It remains the most electrifying Kol Nidrei service ever—to have experienced a congregation praying in a space I had been asked to design, to see in their eyes appreciation for the work Rabbi Baron and I had done.

I thought of the Torah's Bezalel, God's appointed architect, and wondered how he and the children of Israel felt when all the work of creating the Holy Tabernacle was done. Did they look at their work and think to themselves, "*kee tov*, it is good," as God said in the Torah after each of the six days of creation?

A week or so after that service, a woman approached me and said that when she prayed in the sanctuary in the morning the stained-glass windows created "such a beautiful glow that she could feel God's presence." That right there made it all worth it. My experience as a synagogue architect hasn't changed me in that I've joined the ranks of Chabad. My wife and I are still what we call High Holiday Jews. But so much else has been transformed. I study the prayer books with a new understanding and a new energy and eagerness. As I read, I sketch and note page numbers containing translations that particularly interest me for future exploration in paintings.

There's a special verse that has snagged me right now. It's from the *Mussaf*: "Your cloud of glory is a holy utterance; with flames of fire with thunder and lightning you reveal yourself; at the sound of the shofar you reveal yourself."

My grandson saw my initial sketches for this verse during a recent visit. "That's a shofar, Grandpa," he said. "We blow it when we want to get God's attention." His words come back to me in the dawn quiet. Like Bezalel, I work in God's shadow. In the stillness of my studio I hear the trumpeting of God's shofar, calling to me. Calling me to creation and prayer. Calling me to create what I have come to call my own visual prayers.

PART 3

Shabbat

More than Israel has kept the Sabbath,
the Sabbath has kept Israel.

—*Ahad Ha-Am*

"REMEMBER THE SABBATH day and keep it holy." The Fourth Commandment makes clear the Divine intention that the Sabbath was to be a day of rest for the Children of Israel, and for their beasts and their servants as well. As God rested after His labors, so, too, are Jews commanded to refrain from the work of creation. The Sabbath, like every day and holiday on the Jewish calendar, begins at sunset. This is because in the Torah, the days of creation are delineated thus: "It was evening and it was morning, the first day."

Shabbat (or *Shabbos*) observance spans the gamut from strict adherence to loose interpretation. Jews who are *Shomer* Shabbat, strict observers of Sabbath regulations, do not use the telephone, drive their cars, or turn on lights or any cooking flame over the Sabbath. For others, the seventh day passes with little or no notice. And for others, a Shabbat celebration falls somewhere in between.

Shabbat is ushered into the home by the lighting and blessing of candles. A second blessing, *Kiddush*, is recited over wine. The Kiddush prayer sanctifies the Sabbath and offers thanks to God for "creating the fruit of the vine." *Motzi*, thanking God for "bringing bread forth from the earth," is then recited over the *challah*, a bread made by braiding together strands of dough. Some families incorporate ritual hand washing and blessing of their children as part of the prayers preceding the festive Sabbath meal. Some end the meal by singing "*Birkat HaMazon*," a prayer of thanksgiving.

The Sabbath has long been perceived in Judaism as an island of sacred time. Imagine stepping into a world where there's no laundry to fold, no work to do, no carpools or errands. Instead there is rest: worship in synagogue, reading a book, taking a nap, spending time with family in meaningful ways. Shabbat is considered the most sacred of all the Jewish holidays.

All denominations hold Sabbath services on Friday evenings and Saturday mornings. Many also hold a combined service that bridges Saturday afternoon and evening. As the Sabbath is greeted with ceremony, so, too, is it ushered out with ceremony; *Havdalah* ritually marks the end of the Sabbath and the beginning of the new week. When the ceremony is over, we reluctantly bid farewell to the Sabbath bride until the next week.

CHAPTER 9

Making Ten

The Story of Mark Alperin

I DON'T LIKE to talk a lot. My mom calls me a man of few words and many thoughts. It's not so much that words come hard for me, but with all those thoughts, who has time for words? Maybe that's why I like going to *minyan* on Friday nights. I pray, but I don't have to talk too much. I don't have to lead. What counts is my presence.

One Saturday during services, my mom heard that the congregation needed help making minyan before Shabbat. A minyan means 10 men, and without it, mourners cannot say *Kaddish*. When my mom came home and told me, I decided it was something I could do. I told my friend Joel, and he decided to come with me.

The first time we went, we were amazed at how rapidly everyone read. We were so lost; the rabbi helped us with the page numbers so we could keep up. It took us two or three months to feel comfortable. But we always felt welcomed, so we continued to go. From the beginning, the men were glad to see us and made all these comments about how young we were. That we brought the average age down by half was one of my favorite lines.

The next week I still felt pretty lost, but it wasn't as frustrating. We were having a good time and enjoying the company. We also knew we were helping out the congregation. That second Friday I counted the people and noticed that my friend and I made nine and 10.

Three people got up that evening to say Kaddish. Kaddish is said on the anniversary of the death of a loved one or if you are in active mourning. You say Kaddish to lift up the soul of the dead person. Kaddish is recited to reaffirm our faith in God despite the pain of our loss.

I know some places let you say Kaddish even if there aren't 10 men and a lot of *shuls* now count women in the minyan. Our shul is very conservative and, fair or not, we count only men.

The men are dependent on me, but I don't go just for that reason. I go because I enjoy it. I've begun to look forward to the minyan each week. I purposely don't make plans after school on Friday afternoons, and my friends know not to bug me to go anywhere with them. High school is filled with so much work; it's a nice way to relax at the end of the week. I feel closer to God now than I did before I started to go.

I take a *kippa* from a box at the *bimah*, grab a *siddur*, and sit in the second row. I enjoy the fact that the Friday evening service is short. You're not there for three hours or more like you are on a Saturday morning. I also like that the room is small. The rabbi and the cantor are more relaxed, and sometimes they joke around. It feels more like a close community.

A few weeks ago I didn't do well on a Spanish test and I'd blown a chemistry lab, too. It was an awful week. I was pretty down when I went into the little chapel where we pray. By the end of services, I felt better. I realized it was just one test, one lab. I could make up the grades later. That's what the minyan can do for you. Lighten the load.

One night after a big snowfall, Mr. Ralph needed to be walked home. Joel and I helped him. Mr. Ralph is one of the older guys who's always at services. He's smaller than me; he comes up about to my chest and he always has candy in his pocket to give you. Kids, grownups—it doesn't matter—he's always handing out Hershey's Kisses or butterscotch drops.

It took a while to walk him to his apartment. It was 20 minutes each way and it was cold. I went ahead and stamped down the snow with my boots while Joel followed holding on to Mr. Ralph so he wouldn't fall. He taught us Yiddish words on the way. I don't remember any of them. He thanked us a lot for getting him home. Too much thanks. It just felt good to get him back safely to his apartment.

I've been going to minyan for two years now, and it's really become a part of me. I was away over the summer, and when I went back in the fall it felt really good. Like I'd come home. I really hope I can find that kind of "home" feeling once I go to college. I don't know. I'll just have to see.

Author's note: Two years after this interview was conducted, Mark Alperin's shul voted to count women in the minyan.

CHAPTER 10

Of All Things, a Piano?

The Story of Michael Isaacson

"I HEAR YOU write music," my roommate Larry Kushner mentioned to me during the summer of '67. I was having my morning coffee before hitting my post as lifeguard at Kutz, the Union of American Hebrew Congregations' (UAHC) national leadership camp in Warwick, New York.

"Wrong!" I replied. "I'm the lifeguard, just the lifeguard," and I turned back to my cup to end the discussion before it could go any further. I'd recently graduated from Hunter College and had no interest in doing anything connected to music. Don't get me wrong. My degree from Hunter was in music education. I would go on to earn a Master of Arts in music composition from Brooklyn College and a Ph.D. in composition from the Eastman School of Music, with an interim at Juilliard for keyboard studies. But that summer I needed a break. I'd been a music and drama counselor for years, and all I wanted to do that summer was swim, get a tan, do some girl-watching, and keep the roughhousing North American Federation of Temple Youth

(NFTY-ites) and the rabbis' kids from drowning themselves or each other in the pool.

But Larry (today, he's the well-known writer and authority on American Jewish mysticism, Rabbi Lawrence Kushner) was insistent. "No, really. I hear you write music," he repeated, "and, well, we're having a jazz service this *Shabbat* and I'd like you to write some music for it." One look at his eyes, filled with optimism and whimsy—intense and confident behind his wire rims—and I knew I had to do this. Refusal was no longer an option. Resigning myself to the inevitable, I pushed away the cup quickly cooling off in front of me and motioned for Larry to sit down and tell me what he had in mind. Though I didn't know it then, the songs that were to come out of that summer changed the course of my personal Jewish odyssey and my approach to music as well.

And so the pattern of my days at Kutz evolved. Each morning Rabbi Gerry Brieger and I would find an intriguing text. Then I'd troop off to my post at the pool—hat, zinc oxide, whistle, and now a pencil and a pad of staff paper in hand so I could jot down ideas and any melodies that the text inspired. Across the road from the main house was a small shed where they kept sports equipment. There, squeezed in among volleyball nets and poles, balls and spare basketball rims, was an old, upright piano. During my breaks I'd steal a few minutes to play the morning's melodies and see if they sounded the same as I had heard them in my head.

It took me years to realize that I was re-creating, in part, my father's pattern of work. Louis Isaacson was a motion-picture projectionist and, before his union seniority enabled him to work with a partner, he spent his eight-hour shifts in total isolation—a sad irony for a man who loved being with people. That summer at Kutz was just the beginning for me—spending part of my days shut off from the sounds, textures and connections of the world.

One of the great frustrations of my life is that I never had enough of my father. Only a month before my *bar mitzvah*, he put a deposit down on the catering hall and as he signed the contract said, almost as an aside, "I hope I live to see this party." He didn't. My bar mitzvah party was a surreal Felliniesque affair—everyone's smiles were too big and too bright. They could not hide the fact that we were all crying inside. At 46, he was taken from us too soon.

In 1958, when my father first found out that he was losing the battle with lymphosarcoma, a cancer of the lymphatic system, he began to prepare for the inevitable by preoccupying himself in a nesting ritual of sorts—inspecting all the light fixtures and the electrical plugs. One day he came up to my mother and said, "What this house needs is a piano." And my mother, after a considered beat, said, "Okay, sweetie, let's go buy one." And they did—a honey-colored Kranich and Bach spinet. My mother hired a teacher, and for the two years my father was dying, I took lessons.

By the time he passed on, I had learned enough to be able to take refuge in that piano, playing it for hours at a time. It comforted me. It could accept my rage and despair, my anger and confusion. Each time I played, I was able to imagine that my father was still in the room, listening and appreciating my music as he had done not so long ago. Pounding those notes, attacking the arpeggios, banging out full-voiced chords, I dealt with my grief in a primal and cathartic way.

Mine wasn't a kosher way of mourning, but thank God my mother knew enough not to let the *rebbe's* restrictive teaching at the *yeshivah* I attended deny me this consolation. In my studio I keep a photo by Roman Vishniac on the wall above my piano. It is of a boy in *cheder* looking up at the sky as if to ask, "When will it begin? When will I know the larger world?" That's how I felt each day in yeshivah.

It was all Old World, my yeshivah education; the teachers were battered remnants of the Holocaust who had little interest in instructing a squirmy bunch of Brooklyn preteens. Their whole lives had been spent teaching *talmidim* (motivated students); what did they know from American baby boomers? And so they stood at the front of the classroom, smoking cigarettes, day after day droning on about this text or that. When we didn't respond to their questions, our ears were pulled. It was torture—being a right-brained creative kid in a classroom where left-brained repetition and rote translation was everything.

But one hour of the week, only one, we had choir—an island of joy in the tedium—and very quickly music became my salvation. I loved using a different part of my brain, and by the time I reached high school (a rebbe caught me reading a paperback called *The Nun's Story* and it was mutually decided that I leave *mesivta* for secular public high school), I was off and flying. That's where my successful life began.

Still, I couldn't walk away from the Jewish training that was the core of my formative years. My Jewish music comes from my mother's devotion to *Yiddishkeit* and my resolve to vindicate a belief system all but destroyed by those chain-smoking rebbes. "Never confuse Jews with Judaism," I later learned. If I hadn't gone to yeshivah, I don't think I would have been so motivated to find an alternative expression in the negative space, as it were, of what was presented to me.

When I compose Jewish music, I strive to create an alternative to that status quo which, for me, was numbing. Music is my way of dealing with the love/hate relationship I have with rote Judaism. It is the focal point—the path—that enables me to concentrate all that I am, all that I have experienced and all that I have learned. I never took the yeshivah assumption that there is only one way to do everything at face value. It seemed that there is always a greater truth and I had to find my way of knowing it.

According to a *Kabbalistic* legend, before birth, God gives each child all the answers and directions needed to lead a complete, blissful existence. Then just before the child passes through the birth canal, an angel touches him upon the upper lip, causing him to temporarily forget all of God's lessons. And so we spend the rest of our lives searching for and rediscovering the way. My summer at Kutz was the beginning of re-finding the answers in the negative spaces, bringing a new American creativity to Europe's tragedy.

I never thought of my songwriting as high culture, but those were the days when singing a song was an important event. It was magic. I've often struggled and anguished over orchestral pieces and choral works, but I've never struggled over songs. They always came easily to me, and I suppose that's why I never put much credence in them. It was simply summer fun.

After working out the melodies in that storage shack, I would teach the day's song to Doug Mishkin, the summer's song leader. He would teach it to the campers after lunch, and by nightfall it was an instant classic. I have never seen ideas move so fast in my entire life. *Ma Gadlu, Sh'ma, V'ahavta*, melodies still sung in congregations and youth camps to this day—all came out of that incredible summer. By the way, a camper named Debbie Friedman, now of blessed memory, was there in the early days. Years after she became a renowned performer, she told me those first songs of mine inspired her to write Jewish music of her own.

There was one evening late in August when I realized the scope of the need I was filling. The entire dining room was alive with campers stamping and clapping, standing on chairs and on tables, singing at the top of their lungs a song that I had written only days before. The electricity was palpable. When people embrace things to that degree, what you appreciate is the deep need they have for it. Their generation was calling for an authentic and new, joyful Judaism. They were losing themselves in music much the same way I had in the weeks, months and even years after my father's death. Their embrace was not born of grief, perhaps, but their souls' need was just as great.

There are times when in the process of making music I am in a zone where time and space cease to exist. During that timeless brain shift, I have often felt my father's spirit hovering around me. I recall his voice, what he said, how his eyes shone, his smile. And sometimes, even today, 40 years later, I sit alone in my studio and say, "Daddy, here we are together—you in your projection booth, me in my studio. We are alone." And then there are the glorious moments when I finally get to conduct my music in front of an orchestra. I take my bow and before I raise myself to face my audience I think, *Daddy, this is where you should have been.*

What if my mother had not acquiesced to my father's seemingly exotic idea? Of all things, a piano? A piano which I later learned from my mother cost $775—the balance of their entire life's savings. What would I have become had thrift and anxiety prevailed over love? Ultimately, God's plan for us triumphs.

CHAPTER 11

God? In a Parking Lot?

The Story of Batya Berlin

"WELL, YOU'RE NOT pretty, so you better be something. You better be real smart." Poignant to think that's what I told myself when I was a child, but I did. And now, at 75, as I look back on my life as a Jew, I'm happy with what I see. I'm rather glad that the little girl I was chose to pursue Jewish knowledge.

Over the years, I've sought out teachers the way other women might chase down plastic surgeons. I've learned Hebrew, explored Talmud, learned how to approach Torah text and apply it to my life at a time when my swan sisters were applying foundation and false eyelashes. When my children were young, as soon as I felt they could handle the time away from me, I enrolled in Judaica classes at the University of Detroit and later at Wayne State University. There was something driving me—you could almost call it a passion—to learn and to rejoice in my learning. I was determined not to be stupid about anything Jewish.

I grew up with good Jewish experiences—walking to *shul* with my *bubbe*, attending a Reform congregation in

Flushing, New York, with my parents. However at Bubbe's shul, learning Hebrew wasn't an option for females, and since Reform congregations of my day eschewed bar and bat mitzvah ceremonies altogether, there was no opportunity to learn Hebrew there, either. As an adult, capable of sailing my own ship, I promised myself that if there was something to learn, I was going to learn it.

Ultimately, the true joy in my learning came from sharing it with others. Nearly 15 years ago, the rabbis at my synagogue said they wanted to start a daily *minyan* and asked me if I would be interested in leading it one day a week. In those days it was not common for a Reform temple to hold regular morning *minyanim*, but our rabbis felt there was a congregational need for it and were casting about for lay leaders who could conduct them in their stead. And so they came to me, setting the course of my Tuesday mornings ever after.

It's my custom to arrive at the temple at 6:55 a.m. to make sure the custodial staff has arranged the chairs in the library where we daven. I've come to love the quiet anticipation of prayer as I put the *siddurs* on each of two dozen chairs in the room. I look over my notes of the *d'var* Torah I give each week and wait for my fellow prayer pals to arrive.

One day last spring, the custodian failed to show up. I arrived at my usual time, but the doors were locked. I went around to the other side—no go. I was getting nervous, not only because I felt responsible for my clutch of minyan buddies, but because we were to be joined that morning by a newcomer, a woman whose mother had died the week before. She wanted to say *Kaddish* for her, and I was loath to let her down at this crucial stage of Jewish mourning.

Cars started driving up, and still no custodian. Soon there were 22 of us there, milling around, not sure what to do, unwilling to leave, but unsure how long we should wait for someone to come and unlock the doors. We needed to pray, to do as we had done for months and even years. It was important to us all. As their minyan leader, I felt responsible to them and especially responsible to the woman joining us for the first time.

"Wait," someone said suddenly. "I have a prayer book in my trunk. It's been there forever. I don't know why, I just never took it out. Let's just do it here. Any objections?" Of course there were none, and so there among the Chevys and Pontiacs, in running clothes and jackets and ties, we got down to the business of praying. We shared the book, passing it around our circle one by one. Many of us didn't need to read or hear more than the first word or two of a phrase and we were on our way.

A line in the prayer book reads, "Lord, I love your house, the place where your glory dwells. So I would worship with humility, I would seek blessing in the presence of God my Maker." So often we think of houses of worship as synagogues, but they don't always feel like houses of God. There in a parking lot, bathed in the morning light, we were truly in God's house. The air was cool, ringing with that delicious Michigan caress on the skin that makes you forget slogging through snow and the long, dreary wait for blue skies.

Facing east for the *Bar'chu* was automatic. We merely turned toward the rising sun and read, "Praised be the Lord to whom our praise is due now and forever." Now, in Hebrew, the word Bar'chu comes from the word *berech*, meaning "knee." We are not so much praising God as kneeling before Him in gratitude. That morning our words took wing; they came to life as we blessed God; we praised God; we thanked God, if not physically kneeling, then spiritually and emotionally on our knees in gratitude for giving us a splendidly elegant half-hour of beauty and camaraderie.

When it was time for the *Sh'ma*, the book was passed to me by my friend Lucy, who is my Sunday counterpart. We began leading minyan at about the same time, and over the years I have come to treasure our post-minyan discussions and the sweet friendship that has grown between us. "Hear, O Israel: Adonai is our God, Adonai is One." I have repeated those words for as long as I can remember, but doing so on the cusp of a new day, it was impossible not to feel God's oneness. We all remarked later on how close we felt. No one said if it was a closeness to one another or to God, but I'm not sure if it isn't one and the same thing.

By the time we reached the *Mi Shebeirach*, the prayer for healing, the air had grown warmer. It was alive not only with our prayers and singing but with the calls of various birds and the first drone of a distant lawn mower. I was reminded of the time I'd been sick and the group told me that my name led the Mi Shebeirach list in my absence. Even our voices sounded good. Some mornings in the library I say a prayer of thanks to God for having the patience to listen to our gravelly notes. When we reached the Kaddish I was so glad we had persevered, so that a mourning daughter could be comforted on her first day of saying the mourner's prayer.

We learned a lot of things that day. We learned that we don't need a book, but we do need each other. We learned that we didn't need the comfort of chairs, that we had the strength to stand for the 30 minutes or so it took us to complete our prayers.

And I learned that I don't have to be in anything but a receptive mode to be there for God and for God to be there for me.

Each morning when minyan is over, I walk with a lighter step. My knees don't hurt as much. My fingers and shoulders move with greater ease. I am primed for what the day will bring. That morning last spring, it was even better. There, amidst the pitted asphalt and yellow parking-space striping, a divine exhalation and inhalation filled the expanse. Glory, oneness, peace, wonder, love. It was all there. Each of us walked away with a piece of God inside us. And that morning I left the parking lot feeling radiant with a beauty that has yet to fade.

CHAPTER 12

Shalom Aleichem

The Story of Alan May

NEARLY 50 YEARS ago, at 3 p.m. and 10 minutes outside of Dubrovnik, I fell asleep at the wheel and drove off a cliff. Miraculously, the car landed upright in a gravel pit just 10 feet below the road. You can bet that woke us up. While we were gathering our wits about us and assessing the situation, out of nowhere a group of students and their teacher materialized. They had been playing soccer on the outskirts of town and were returning from their practice. They saw us surveying what turned out to be minimal damage to our car. As a team, they positioned themselves around the car, hoisted it into the air and walked it up the embankment of the gravel incline. They set the car on the road toward Dubrovnik and, with a wave and a few unintelligible words of dialect, left. We changed the tire, drove on into the city, had dinner and checked into our hotel for much-needed sleep.

My friends and I had just graduated from college and were off to see Europe before entering law school. We purchased cheap airline tickets, bought a Ford Cortina in Belgium, and set out on a seven-country summer tour. Having seen the sights of Vienna, we were determined to drive straight through to Dubrovnik. In 1963, the AAA maps didn't really tell the whole story in a country like Yugoslavia. What appeared to be roads were actually unpaved paths so narrow that two cars going in the opposite direction couldn't pass each other unless one driver pulled into the side of the mountain while the other driver continued on.

It was quite common to see people walking their cows back and forth from the grazing pastures. We carried an extra can of gasoline with us, since filling stations were few and far between. The evening before we got to Dubrovnik, we had dinner at a small restaurant where the waiter took us into the field beside the restaurant and asked us to pick out which lamb we wanted to eat for dinner. The lamb was slaughtered in our presence and then cooked for us. The situation was rather quaint and the lamb, quite delicious.

If life was primitive, I was about to find out just how odd and serendipitous it was, too. Who would have thought I'd meet a Jew in Dubrovnik? At that point in my life I was accustomed to thinking about Judaism not as a common denominator but as something that separated us from the rest of the world. I came from a very assimilated Jewish family. I had been to two or three Seders in my life. A *Shabbos* dinner or two at a friend's house, but never in my parents' or grandparents' homes. We had menorahs but didn't light them; we had *mezuzahs* but didn't post them. At the time, assimilation was the antidote to anti-Semitism.

So there I was in Dubrovnik at six in the morning. I'd left my friends back in the motel to sleep off our adventure. I wanted to fill the tank and our empty can of gas. I also started to look around for a place to fix our tire, not wanting to venture too far on the spare. The man at the gas station (not a gas station really, just a single pump in front of a store) directed me to a place that might help with the tire repair.

Each time I entered a shop, I tried to find a common language. "*Sprechen Sie Deutsch? Russe? Español?*" I asked.

No one would even look at me. I later learned that no one in Dubrovnik would answer in German, because of their hatred of the Germans. They didn't particularly like the Russians much, either. I went from store to store trying to find someone who could help me repair the flat tire, when I finally entered a shop that looked to be selling nondescript machine parts. Again I tried, "Deutsch? Russe? Español?" Someone behind the counter began to make fun of me as if he thought I was putting on airs. "Montenegran?" he mocked me. "Serbian? Croatian?" Thoroughly disgusted, I turned around and left the store, men's laughter ringing in my ears.

I sat down on the front stoop. At my feet was a stone that had a vague triangle shape as part of its natural striations. It was about as big as my palm and, at a loss for anything better to do, I took out my pocket knife and began carving into the triangle motif that was part of the stone. Next, I superimposed a second triangle on top of it to make a Jewish star.

About a half-hour into this carving respite, the man who had mocked me came out of the store and stood behind me, looking over my shoulder as I carved. He knelt down beside me, put his arm around me, and said, "*Shalom aleichem*." I was stunned. And then in Spanish he said, "Come with me."

He took me to a little store where a man, who turned out to be a vulcanizer, put a tube into the tire and then patched it by pouring layer upon layer of molten rubber over the hole. Then he re-grooved the surface with some sort of implement and handed me back a perfectly usable tire. The repair bill was the equivalent of $2. I paid the workman and my new acquaintance and I left the shop.

I don't even remember his name, even though we spent the afternoon together. Call him Marko, if you will. He was about 5 feet 10 inches tall, a little heavyset, with dark, wild hair. His clothes were rough but neat. He spoke to me in Spanish, explaining that he also spoke Ladino, the Spanish equivalent of Yiddish.

I followed him into the old walled section of Dubrovnik and listened as he told me about his ancestors who had been driven from Spain during the Inquisition. During the early 16th century they settled in what was now Dubrovnik. Down one alley and up another we walked until we came to a small synagogue on the second floor of a small building. It was extremely rustic, but I recognized the *ner tamid* hanging from a slender chain at one end of the synagogue. I wouldn't say there was an *aron hakodesh*, but there was a Torah scroll resting in a little niche carved in the synagogue wall behind the ner tamid. My initial shock at being welcomed because of our shared Judaism gave way to understanding of the unity and fraternity among Jews.

Despite our very assimilated home life, my parents were committed Zionists. Dinnertime conversation was always filled with stories about Israel. My father, one of the few Jews to work for Ford Motor Company, helped place Ford in Israel in the '40s, even before statehood. He and a group of other Detroiters formed Rock Products, a company that helped build roads in Israel. It would be years before I understood my father's commitment to *achdut*, Jewish unity, but there in Dubrovnik, I was getting a glimmer of what it meant for one Jew to reach out and help another.

Marko and I had lunch together, and as he told me more about his family and their history, the Inquisition transformed itself in my consciousness from some abstract calamity that took up a few pages in a history book into something that was alive. Jewish history became Jewish feeling. Someone once said that Jews don't have history, they have memory. During our walks through the alleys of the old city, I felt as if I were tapping into collective Jewish memory in a way I never had before.

We ended up at his home, a small wooden building in which three or four generations lived together. Most of them spoke Ladino, so we could communicate on some level by using Spanish. My friend showed me a 16th century *Haggadah* that his family brought with them when they escaped during the Inquisition. The book didn't stir up waves of emotion-laden memories. I had only been to a Passover Seder or two growing up and thus didn't have a bank of experiences to be teased awake. I recognized the Hebrew letters for what they were but didn't know an "*Aleph*" from a "*Bet*." Only as an adult, when I became president of my temple, did I begin to study Hebrew in preparation for a belated bar mitzvah.

When Marko handed me his family's ancient Haggadah, something in me shifted. I didn't look at this book as a Gentile archeologist might have—dusting off a find with an air of intellectual expectation. The Haggadah became alive in my hands. It had been carried and cherished for close to 500 years. I felt its power to link generation to generation. As the sun began to set, the woman of the house lit and blessed the candles. Marko chanted *Kiddush*, then *Motzi*. I was on the other side of the world from home, about to eat dinner with total strangers. Nevertheless, they were Jewish, I was Jewish, and so I was home.

Dubrovnik was my first awakening to the universality of Jewish achdut. The word comes from *echad*, the Hebrew word for "one." A Jewish family's memories had become mine in one crazy-quilt afternoon of experiences. Now, whenever my wife and I travel, we always seek out Jewish life. Whether it's eating at Joe Goldenberg's in Paris, going to Dachau, or worshiping at Touro Synagogue in Newport, Rhode Island, we make time for Jewish exploration. Is the town a Federation town? How do the Jews fit in with the community? How do they help and support one another?

As Jews we have the opportunity and responsibility of acting upon two levels of achdut. Jew to Jew is certainly one. And there is the additional sense of achdut we must attend to—oneness with our fellow human beings. In Dubrovnik, the teens and their teacher helped us simply because we were in need. Their help was no less meaningful because we didn't connect on the plane of shared heritage.

Two decades after Dubrovnik, then-Governor Millikin asked me to serve on the Michigan Civil Rights Commission. He got a lot of heat for selecting me and not reappointing an African-

American whose term had just expired. The newspapers chose to headline my appointment thus: "**Jew Replaces Black.**" I was reminded from the start that the public was going to look at me as a Jew and I was going to have to act as one. That meant preserving the rights of everyone. It meant acting from an understanding of achdut in the broadest sense possible.

I have served many satisfying years on the NCCJ. Once called the National Conference of Christians and Jews, the acronym now stands for National Conference for Community and Justice. My civil-rights work comes from a place of sociological, intellectual and religious commitment to doing what is right on behalf of all human beings. If the Jew does not help those in the greater community, he will never be part of that community. This is, for me, Judaism's most important cornerstone. Only by helping anyone in need can we ever have *shalom aleinu*—peace upon us all.

CHAPTER 13

On the Doorposts of Your House and on Your Gates

The Story of Mark Isaacs

THE MOTIF THAT'S permeated my life? Doorways. Doorways and doorposts. As an architect, I've been trained to look at doorways as frames for vistas; they are the physical cues for transitions between various household activities. But these entries and exits signify more than movement through space, outside to in, kitchen to dining room. Old enough now to study *Kabbalah* (in my 40s and a family man), I am keenly aware that doorways and the doorposts that frame them also symbolize our transition between the holy and the mundane, between acknowledging God and being oblivious to God's ever presence. It's no coincidence that we are instructed to affix to our doorposts Judaism's proclamation of Adonai's oneness and the commandment to love God every moment of our lives.

Close to 20 years ago, I saw a film based on Abba Eban's book, *My People*. In one segment, a Moroccan housewife was shown preparing her family's pita bread. Standing at the edge of the wood-fired oven outside her modest home, she recited the *Sh'ma* as she patted and shaped the dough. By bringing God's presence into this daily chore, she elevated this most common act of bread-making into a sacred moment. In that one act she declared the absolute oneness of God in all things—in the bread and in herself as the maker of the bread present in the very moment of creation.

In my early 20s at the time, I was thunderstruck to realize that for this woman, the Sh'ma was as much of an ingredient as flour and water. She showed me that everyday moments can be made holy when we acknowledge God's presence in them. This takes practice. But I am convinced that the essence of our tradition is this: we can become steeped in the holy by the simple act of remembering to love God as we go about our daily lives. Loving God takes so many forms. It's kindness; it's appreciation. It's even summoning compassion for the unfortunates, such as the prostitute I once saw as I drove through an urban neighborhood. Loving God means recognizing that my sister is out there on the street, in my city, in my back yard, not someone else's. Seeing her, I know that something here is wrong. It is not possible to fix the entire world's pain, but I do have an obligation not to blind myself to another's misfortune.

Sh'ma and *V'ahavta* don't have a place in our lives only on Friday night or Saturday morning. "Hear, O Israel: the Lord is our God, the Lord is One!" and "You shall love the Lord your God with all your heart, with all your soul and with all your might" are prescriptions for living a life of meaning and significance, of connectedness and holiness. If we can hold on to this realization, we have the potential to transform each and every moment of our lives.

My quest to know and love God has taken me to Eastern meditation practices. Far from abandoning Judaism, I was drawn to meditation because of the chanting involved. I come from a chanting tradition. Sanskrit is no more alien a language to use than Hebrew. Years ago, as I meditated at the close of an all-day workshop, the conscious prayer of my heart was this: *God, give me a signal; give me a sign that you are there.*

I entered a place deeper than any I had ever been while meditating, and all of a sudden I had an inner vision of an elephant-headed deity. Think Babar—but up close and personal. This Babar character looks me in the eye, gets eyeball to eyeball with me, and winks. In Sanskrit this is called a moment of *darshan*, of seeing God in the other. In the moment when the elephant winked, I heard the words inside of me, "I am here, where are you? I am here, where are you?" When I later learned that this elephant deity is called Ganesh, the remover of obstacles, the opener of doors, I knew with absolute clarity that the darkness covering my heart had been removed. I felt as if there were an old-style preacher in my head shouting, ***GOD IS AT THE DOOR!*** *OPEN THE DOOR AND LET HIM IN!*

Months later I told my rabbi of this experience and he reminded me that the very first question God asks Adam, post-transgression, was just that, "Where are you?", as if to teach us that God isn't going anywhere. God's there. We, by virtue of our actions, can maintain the link or sever it. The problem is we don't take the time to let God in. God is always on the other side of the door. All we have to do is open it, not even open it but just reach toward the knob, and God will be there for us on the other side.

The V'ahavta tells us to write the words upon our hearts, upon our doorposts and upon our gates. Why? Because in the time it takes to move from our door to our gate, or in today's parlance, from the garage to the car, we forget about God. When we drive to work we can allow ourselves to get caught up in the traffic, or we can consciously and continually practice opening our hearts to the bliss of creation before us. We are commanded to love God and teach this to our children and speak of this in our homes, when we rise and when we lie down, because forgetfulness is pervasive.

And why is it written to "on" your heart and not "in" your heart? The rabbis teach that our hearts are often closed but if we put the words "on" our heart, they will be right there during those rare moments when our hearts open up. If we are truly fulfilling the commandment of loving the Lord moment to moment, then the act of loving that which is most holy will keep our hearts open. Keeping "the words upon our heart" will be like wrapping ourselves in *tallis* and *t'fillin*, protecting us with love, allowing us to project divine love and lovingkindness out into the world and transforming ourselves and our world in the process.

There is a story that comes to us from Rebbe Nachman of Breslov. He had a student who was always running from work to *minyan* to pray and back again. After watching him scurry mindlessly day after day, Rebbe Nachman asked, "Tell me, have you seen the sky today?" The disciple called back to him as he ran, "I haven't had time to see the sky; I've been working and now I'm running to pray." Of what use is prayer if we don't stop and find God in our midst? That midst can be the making of pita bread, or a telephone conversation, or a session in front of a computer screen. We've got to take a moment to see the sky, to acknowledge God's oneness in our lives.

When I was asked to design the Roth Family Center—a building to house Louisville's Jewish Family and Vocational Services—it was important to indicate to the community the Jewish content of the building. The work of an architect is to be involved in the co-creation of the physical world. In a commission of this kind, or when I am asked to design affordable housing for the poor, I am doing God's work. God is the ultimate architect, the senior partner, if you will; I'm just the apprentice.

The building's main elevation faces south, which enables passive solar energy and natural daylight to help illuminate and heat the building. In this way the building embodies good stewardship of God's resources. Mindful of Rebbe Nachman's disciple, I used windows liberally to imbue the structure with a strong sense of the outside. You can look up from nearly anywhere in the building and see the sky. Not only did I want the building flooded with natural light, I wanted the light to be a subtle reminder of the illumination that goes on in our hearts when we are transformed. This is the Divine spark at work that propels us to open the door to God. Wonderful things happen in this building, and I wanted to honor the hard work of transformation that occurs between our social workers and their clients.

Copper, molded in the form of a stylized letter *chet*, frames the building's main entrance. Worked into the copper is a freeform letter *yod*, so that the doorway spells out the word *chai*. The doorway is a subtle message to the community that the most precious of Jewish values—life—is very present here.

The interior of the building is designed to echo the public spaces and narrow pedestrian streets of Italian hill towns. Instead of impersonal lobbies connecting departments, inviting piazzas link individual neighborhoods. In place of dark hallways, there are light-filled streets. The entire building thus becomes a community where *tikkun olam*, the repair of God's world, is undertaken each and every day.

When I designed the green copper forms on the building's western side adjacent to the southern exposure, it was clear to me that I had used a shape that resonated loosely with Hebrew calligraphy. I couldn't make sense of the motif, but I knew on some level that it was inspired by the Hebrew alphabet. Little did I know that my spiritual intuition was hard at work inside me.

Only when the building was complete did I realize I had designed a *pei soffit* (the configuration of the letter pei that comes at the end of a word) into the copper that framed the corner of the west side of the building. Pei stands for the power of human speech. Curiously, it is the letter that begins the Hebrew word *petach*—doorway. But why this letter? What Hebrew word ends with this letter? As I stared at the side of the building, the answer came roaring at me from a place of deep understanding: "*Ein Sof*." That which is without end. Ein Sof is the term the *Kabbalists* used for the Almighty.

When I viewed the western and southern elevations as one element, the building revealed itself to me further. The copper chai and the copper pei soffit bracket the nine second-story windows that I had come to think of as a symbolic Chanukah menorah. All of a sudden I realized that I had physically represented life at one end and God's boundlessness at the other, and between the two there is nothing but light.

When clients come to the Roth Family Center, they are often in a leaden state of being. They come for counseling, for job retraining and placement, for help in making the transition from immigrant to citizen. It's not certain this building will reach out and heal them, but the potential is there. Perhaps they will look across a skylit ceiling and out a window and feel a ray of hope enter their hearts. Or perhaps as they move through the piazza doorways they will see the mezuzah and realize that God is near, that He has never left.

"Where are you?" God asks. "Where are you?" Now is the time to reach for the door. Open it. God is waiting on the other side.

CHAPTER 14

"And with Her the Angels of Peace and of Rest"

The Story of David Elcott

THE NAZIS DESTROYED my grandmother's house on Kristallnacht. My grandfather was a wealthy man and had built a four-story mansion and filled it with the best that money could buy for his wife, the wife he adored. Rugs, paintings, dishes, everything chosen for the house was a symbol of how my grandfather cared for the family he loved. My grandmother told me once that the beautiful furniture in the house the Nazis destroyed on Kristallnacht was designed to match the carved wainscoting on the dining room walls. My grandmother and my grandfather were to live in the house for the rest of their lives; it was built to withstand that much time. But it wasn't built to withstand Nazi marauders.

They came on November 9, 1938 and shattered all the windows of their four-story mansion—windows my grandfather had situated so that my grandmother would see beauty whenever she looked out. My grandparents' house was just one of hundreds of homes, synagogues and Jewish businesses attacked that night.

Because of all the Nazis did, my grandfather and grandmother picked up and left Germany within days. They left behind their mothers and fathers, brothers, sisters, nieces and nephews—planning to send for them when they got settled. In one way or another—by fire, by bullet and by beating—every last one of those left behind perished. Soon after their arrival in America, my grandfather died. Of a broken heart, I was always told. He saw his role in life as caring for his family and when he realized he couldn't save them, he died.

It was years before my grandmother had a home she loved again. In her late 80s she had a stroke, precipitated by a long bout with meningitis. She could no longer walk easily; her balance was off more than it was on. And so the whole family brainstormed and decided to build her a house at the back of our property. My wife, Shira, and I had four young children at the time. My mother lived nearby and could visit easily and often. We had the land and, selfishly, I was thrilled to have my *mutti* so close by.

We laid a brick path that led from the back of our house to the front of hers and situated the house amidst the fruit trees that grew in the back yard. When they were big enough, our kids would climb up onto her roof and pick plums, tangerines and grapefruit to have for breakfast with their mutti.

Moving day, my father and uncle carried my grandmother up and over the threshold. We were all there waiting: my mother and my aunt; my sister and brother and their kids; my wife and I and our four. My grandmother looked around and saw 20 of her descendants waiting for her, waiting for her reaction to her new home. She burst into tears. "When I was young," she said after composing herself, "my husband built me a house. But this that you have all built is the most beautiful house I have ever known. The house in Germany cannot compare."

Our life was so idyllic then. The kids would toddle over with their diapers hanging to have breakfast with their mutti; afternoons they would return to eat M&Ms and watch TV. Often, I would come home from work and find her and the kids sitting on her little patio playing cards or Candyland. She used a walker, and Noam, Yaron, Talia and Liore listened for the scraping of mutti's walker on the brick path that meant a visit from their great-grandma.

Then one day my wife said to me, "You know, if I had it to do over again, I'd be a rabbi." Shira comes from a long line of rabbis, and I turned to her and said, "Well, you can still be a rabbi—you can do it now."

"You mean that?" she asked. "You really mean it?"

"Sure." I had no idea what this would spell for our future, but I knew I did not want my wonderful wife to spend her life regretting roads not taken.

Our initial plan was for Shira to begin her rabbinic studies in California and commute to New York for the year she had to spend at the UAHC. I would keep my job in LA and we would cross the bicoastal bridge when we came to it. Our whole family was in California, remember, and it was inconceivable that we would move and leave it all behind. Then, at the last moment, a job at the National Jewish Center for Learning and Leadership (CLAL) opened up for me. We decided to take a one-year leave of absence so that I could work at CLAL and Shira could take her first year of rabbinic studies in New York.

For years it had been our custom to sing Chaim Bialik's poem "*Hachama Merosh*" each week as *Shabbat* approached. It begins with these words:

The sun on the treetops is no longer seen.
Come, gather to welcome the Sabbath, our queen!
Behold her descending, the holy, the blessed,
And with her the angels of peace and of rest.

The house would be reasonably straightened, the kids scrubbed clean. Playing the song's first notes on the piano was my signal to the family that the sun was setting and Shabbat was beginning.

"Hachama Merosh" is meaningful to Shira and me for reasons beyond our lives together. We had both learned the melody at Camp Ramah before meeting each other. Throughout my childhood, I heard it during Shabbat services. "Hachama Merosh" gives us constant connections to those times and places beyond our current reality and embodies for us the ceasing of the week's frenzy and entering together a place of calm and release.

My parents used to ask me why Shira and I had chosen to be *Shomer Shabbat*, and I told them that it was because it was so hard to be a parent. We are a high-energy family, and having a day of total rest was not a restriction but an incredible gift of rejuvenation. That awareness was in the song, too. Whatever chaos pulled at us during the week, "Hachama Merosh" was there to weave us all back together.

Our last night before the move to New York, the only thing left in the living room was the piano. Awaiting the movers, the refinished baby grand sat in an alcove in a bay window, framed outside, as it had been for years, by raspberry and boysenberry arbors. In those days, the piano was our proudest possession. Knowing we could not be without music in our home, a wonderful friend loaned us the money to buy it when we were newly married.

Empty of furniture save a bookcase and the piano, the living room had been a spur-of-the-minute gymnastics studio. I'd improvise aerobics music and the kids would do crazy exercises. My sister had donated a washing machine box to the cause and our kids and their cousins turned it into an indoor playhouse. Many a Passover saw the room transformed into a "Seder tent." All those years of fun and dancing and celebration thrummed in the air as we gathered around the piano now.

As I sat down to play, we were all keenly aware that this was the last time we would sing together for a year. There were 25 of us that night—my parents, mutti, my siblings and their kids, Shira's brother and family. We were singing so much more than "The sun on the treetops is no longer seen." We were singing of our world in California and what our life had been. Our memories resonated off the blank walls: the staccato motion of the kids' chubby feet as they went between our house and mutti's, adolescent strains of our lives before Shira and I met, the sad undertones of the life and loved ones mutti had left behind in Germany. We sang of mutti at Disneyland and all the memories we would carry to New York. We sang of loss and the uncertainty of future gains. Our song was tradition and permanence. It was continuity and wholeness. It was leaving and change. The chords of "Hachama Merosh" expanded to include it all.

Shira remembers our singing with more pathos and tears than I do. My style is, once the decision is made, that's it. I look ahead. It was a moment of great clarity for me to realize the incredible power and beauty a song can muster. That is the wonderful thing about being Jewish and having Shabbat in your life. You are not alone, not ever. You carry loved ones and experiences with you not just through space, but through time, too. It wasn't just me and my kids singing, but our ancestors and my descendants after me.

Still, after our picnic dinner on the patio (all the furniture was loaded into the U-Haul), my sister and I held each other, not knowing if we would really be back or not. One by one, all the family came over and we just stood there, holding each other, crying and gathering strength for the move.

We never did return to California to live. New York became our home. Mutti came to visit often. "Have wheelchair, will travel," was her unsaid motto. But we kept the house in California until she died. We wouldn't take her from the house she loved so much, the one she loved even more than the house my grandfather built for her in Germany. I knew it had always agonized mutti that she never knew when or how her mother had died. She said *Kaddish* on her mother's birthday and during *Yizkor* on Yom Kippur, but she grieved that she could never recite the prayer on her mother's actual date of death. In 1990, Shira, the kids and I traveled to Czechoslovakia and Hungary. When we got to Prague, I visited Theresienstadt's archives. The information was surprisingly simple to find. I learned that on Yom Kippur of 1942 my great-grandmother Theresa was put on a truck, taken to the Polish border, thrown into a pit and murdered. Finally I knew the date, and soon mutti would, too. Would she be comforted to learn she had been saying Kaddish on her mother's actual *yahrzeit* after all?

I called from Budapest. "Mutti," I told her, "I've got it all. I know the date of your mother's death. When I get back to the States, I will come and tell you everything."

"Good, good," she said. "Now put the children on so I can tell them I love them and can't wait to see them."

Mutti died before she could see the kids again, before I could tell her what I learned in Budapest. We figured out later that she died just about the time our plane touched down in New York. It was as if she had been waiting to resolve this one piece of her life and as long as someone knew and could pull her mother's date of death from the oblivion of the Holocaust, that was enough.

The Friday night after our return, we withdrew from *shivah* to celebrate Shabbat. And we sang "Hachama Merosh." The melody expanded once again, large enough this time to echo our grief. Our song reverberated with countless memories of mutti and our everlasting love of the mother, grandmother and great-grandmother whose own song had begun with the shattering of glass and ended with the quiet coda of an answered unknown.

CHAPTER 15

Should War Beset Me, Still Would I Be Confident

The story of Judith Kaplan

LOOKING OUT MY roommate's window, I could see the black smoke as the twin towers of the World Trade Center burned and then collapsed 60 blocks away. I've lived in New York all my life, and it took only a second or two to realize that people I knew who worked in the towers might already have died. This is my city. That was my skyline, my buildings. The lobby of our apartment house was complete pandemonium. Some of our building's residents had run the three miles north, covered in ash, crying hysterically. We live quite close to the Empire State Building and we were terrified it would be next. Out on the street all we could do was watch. Can you imagine military vehicles lumbering down Lexington Avenue? It became so difficult to breathe that we had to cover our faces when we walked outside. A distinct smell permeated the air. It was completely different from the burning odor we're all familiar with and lasted for months after the attacks.

My roommate and I were desperate to help in some way. We gathered food and socks and towels for the Red Cross, but it seemed like such a small thing. Hundreds had already shown up to give blood, but that wasn't an option for me.

There was little to do, and it hurt to be unable to aid the city or the hundreds, even thousands of people affected. I didn't know it at the time, but an opportunity to help was about to present itself.

When a Jew dies, the *Chevra Kedisha*, the Jewish burial society, washes and dresses the body, and then a person called a *shomer* (*shomeret* in the feminine) begins what is called *shmira*—watching over the body until it is buried. During this time of guarding the body, the shomer also recites Psalms. Shmira is not only a gesture of protection, it is also one of respect. The human body once held a soul, and you want to treat it with the utmost dignity. Within hours of the attack, Armand Osgood from Congregation Ohab Zedek in Manhattan began organizing scores of volunteers to perform shmira. They began on September 12 with the arrival of the first remains, which, until they could be identified, could not be buried.

We believe that the soul doesn't leave the physical world until the deceased is buried. Until that time, the soul is in limbo and in pain, no longer animating a human body, but not yet free to return to God. The recitation of *Tehillim*, or Psalms, not only eases the soul's pain but helps the deceased return to God.

About a month after the attack, a close friend, Jessica Russack, called and said they were having trouble getting people to do shmira over the Sabbath. Because observant Jews do not travel on the Sabbath and none of those reciting Psalms lived within walking distance of the temporary morgue that had been set up adjacent to the Chief Medical Examiner's Office, no one was reciting Psalms on the holiest day of the week. Within a few hours we got eight girls, classmates of ours from Stern College, the women's school of Yeshiva University, to commit to this *mitzvah*. I took the midnight–4 a.m. shift.

The length of Thirtieth Street, from First Avenue down to the FDR Drive, had been converted into the aforementioned temporary morgue. The police and fire departments and the

Red Cross were all a part of the rescue and recovery efforts and had stations. The Salvation Army undertook the ongoing responsibility of feeding the volunteers, and the Red Cross also continued to provide chaplains.

I was very nervous the first night. How much would I see? Who would be there with me? Would I burst into tears? I was already so emotionally spent, so nervous and on edge. But when I entered the tent where I would be praying, a sense of duty and spirituality came over me. None of my fears were realized. I opened up my Tehillim, my book of Psalms, and just started to sing. It felt so good. I wasn't sad and I wasn't scared. I was surrounded by a feeling of purpose.

I've come to be known as "the singing girl." There are 150 psalms, and I sing each one. Some have their own melodies and sometimes I use the tunes from Lamentations. Melodies come to me from unknown places, too. One evening I realized that I had incorporated the melody to a Rosh HaShanah prayer my grandfather had been teaching my father before September 11. For weeks before the High Holidays I had heard them practicing together.

At first people were skeptical of us. They had grown accustomed to the volunteers from the Upper West Side praying at the morgue site for a month. I am pretty small, and one *Shabbat* I heard someone say, "What's this little girl doing here?" Their attitude didn't bother me. I was there for a purpose; it was me and the prayers and the souls. I just smiled and waved, and as time went on I became a regular on Friday night. Some nights the on-duty police officers talked with me about their experiences at the World Trade Center. Occasionally people would ask for the singing girl so they could thank me. "You don't know how much this means to know that someone is out here praying," one said. We don't just say prayers for the Jewish souls, but for everyone. This calamity transcended all boundaries. A soul is a soul.

After five months of these Friday nights, I needed a "real" Shabbat at home, a full night's sleep, and time with my family.

But I missed praying. I was back the next week, rested and eager to begin again. It's sad, but it's what we do. It's a *chesed shel emet*, a kindness that cannot be repaid. It's the biggest help, the biggest mitzvah you can do. It doesn't ruin Shabbat for me but adds an extra spiritual layer. In a way I leave the world and all my worries behind. Singing Tehillim one after the other is magnetizing. It's wonderful. I can't sit by and let pass this opportunity to help. Neither could my sister, who often does shmira during the week. In 20 years, when it's rebuilt, I can tell my children: "This is what happened and this is what I did. This is what the Jewish people did as a community."

During those first weeks and months, the air was heavy with souls of the dead. It sounds crazy, but I felt their presence. As I prayed I could feel them getting better. After talking with a policeman, I knew it wasn't my imagination. He's been around enough dead bodies to know the feel of a soul nearby. I feel them, too, and as the months have gone on and bodies have been buried, I also feel the air thinning. It feels lighter.

Reciting Tehillim at the morgue each Shabbat has transformed my attitude toward prayer. Tehillim are not unfamiliar to me. I'd been taught long ago to recite Psalms in times of crisis. Before September 11, I prayed, but the words weren't my words. They stayed on the page. Now I am connecting with the Psalms as never before. I know what it is to pray with my heart, not just my head. I have taken these words that King David wrote 3,000 years ago and made them my own. Each week I see the effect these Psalms have on people. Prayer has power. I've seen it. I've felt it. It's real.

By coincidence, the first assignment in our oral interpretation of literature class was to recite a Psalm that held particular meaning for us. The assignment was due September 12. Although I'd recited psalms all my life, I had no idea which one I would pick. On the evening of September 11, my roommate and I were particularly struck by Psalm 27:

The Lord is my light and my help;
whom should I fear?

The Lord is the stronghold of my life;
whom should I dread?
When evil men assail me
to devour my flesh,
it is they, my foes and my enemies,
who stumble and fall.
Should an army besiege me,
my heart would have no fear;
should war beset me,
still would I be confident.

That first week I was to do shmira, my mom asked me if that was really how I wanted to spend my Shabbat. I told her that it was the most meaningful way I could possibly spend it. Right after the attack, everything seemed incredibly bleak; I tried so hard to focus on the positive. In the subsequent weeks I've realized that good has come out of this tragedy. The unity of the people of New York is unbelievable. Their goodness cannot be matched. That goodness is our strength; that is what will beat the terrorists. That goodness teaches us to love and accept everyone regardless of their faith, skin color or nationality. This is the exact opposite of what terrorism is. Psalm 27 closes with these words: "*Wait upon the Lord, remain strong. Let your heart give you courage; wait upon the Lord.*" September 11 was the most awful day of my life. Doing shmira each Shabbat allows me to remain strong, giving courage to my heart, urging me to wait upon God.

CHAPTER 16

Transition

The Story of Janelle McCammon

IT'S A UNIQUE sound, that sharp hiss of a *Havdallah* candle being extinguished in a little spill of wine. The sound is biting and somehow creates a fitting final moment in the ceremony that separates us from *Shabbat* and transitions us back into the week. I can't say why exactly, but performing the Havdallah service is probably my favorite Jewish ritual. Havdallah connotes the same kinds of emotions that I imagine one has at a Jewish summer camp—that strong sense of shared community and intimacy. You're with people with whom you share values and fondness. You're in the position of acknowledging God, the Sabbath, and the relationship between God and man.

I am a child of the parsonage and while I have been out of my parsonage home many more years than I was in it, those were formative years nevertheless. My father was a Methodist minister and when I was growing up it was common for us to have people in our home for meals on a regular basis. Many times people would sing together after dinner. There is nothing in Christian life that is a counterpoint to Havdallah, no ritual acknowledging

Sabbath's end, but I remember from childhood a unique rhythm to the Sundays that anchored our week: religious school followed by the worship service; a special Sunday dinner in our home or with a congregant's family; visiting with church members and friends; and then the return to church for evening worship.

Being a child of the parsonage also meant that I grew up surrounded by an inescapable emphasis on God's role in the world and in our lives. It has been my experience that for many Jews, there doesn't seem to be that same dimension of a personal God that I felt was part of my life as a child. Maybe that is why I am so drawn to Havdallah. It reminds us that there is indeed a relationship between us and God; and that when we move back into the week, we do so with God's mandate to make this world a better place—to be a vehicle of gladness and joy and peace.

For me, those things come primarily through acts of kindness. Havdallah is our reminder to go into the new week with the idea of performing kindnesses at the forefront.

Havdallah literally means separation and in many ways, because I married a Jewish man and we have raised our children as Jews, I have been separated from the religion of my childhood. We waited many years to have children while we weighed how we would handle religion in our house. Ultimately it came down to one of us giving up our preferences for the good of the family. I moved into Jewish life doing all the "normal things"—going to services, attending classes and becoming involved in many aspects of temple life. When our children were born there was a *b'ris* and special baby-naming ceremonies. My children's bar and bat mitzvah ceremonies are cherished memories. It was very affirming for me because I had assumed the responsibility of raising Jewish children. I take great pride in my son's and daughter's comfort and sense of belonging within the Jewish community.

My own life has been greatly enriched by living Jewishly. The prophets have always been my favorite characters from scripture because they deal so beautifully with how to live. There is such a strong thread of social justice in Judaism. Taking care of those less fortunate is explicit; it's not just something you are supposed to do out of love as it is in Christian theology, it is commanded—whether you feel drawn to help others or not is immaterial. It is through people that God works in this world. This was how my father and my mother lived each day of their lives. Their example is probably one more reason why Havdallah has resonated with me so much over the years. Havdallah separates us from the beauty of Shabbat, all the while sending us forward with a keen reminder of God's mandate in our lives. At the moment of that biting sound when flame hits liquid and is extinguished, I am moved into the new week. Perhaps, subliminally, I do so linked to the parsonage and to the relationship with God I have carried with me since childhood.

PART 4

Sukkot and Simchat Torah

Ye shall dwell in booths seven days.

—***Leviticus 23:42***

Simchat Torah means the Torah's joy and implies that it is not enough for a Jew to find joy in the Torah, but the Torah should also find joy in him.

—***Jose-Ber of Brisk***

FOUR DAYS AFTER Yom Kippur, another pair of holidays appears on the horizon. *Sukkot*, literally, booths, and *Simchat Torah*, Rejoicing of the Torah, are a lighthearted and exuberantly joyous counterpoint to the seriousness of the prior 10 days. With the physically and spiritually arduous High Holidays at an end, Sukkot initiates eight days of festivities that culminate in the holiday of Simchat Torah.

The *sukkah* is reminiscent of the temporary structures built by the Children of Israel during their 40-years' trek through the desert. Sukkot celebrates the gathering of the fall harvest festival, and thus on Sukkot the booths also call to mind the huts early Jews would construct in the fields during the fall harvest. Some scholars say the booths recall those used by vintners during the grape harvest.

A sukkah may be any size but must have three walls (the fourth side may be left open.) It can be made of most anything—wood, lattice panels, PVC piping and canvas. What makes a sukkah temporary is its roof, which consists of tree branches, bamboo, corn stalks, or any other plant material that has "grown up from the ground" or has been "cut off from the ground." The roof must be open enough to allow rain to penetrate. One should be able to see the sky and the stars, although this is not a requirement. A sukkah provides a prime opportunity for decorating. Children's artwork, paper chains and strands of fall gourds all make for great embellishments. Some families sleep in their sukkah; others simply take their meals in it, weather permitting.

There are two other elements associated with Sukkot. Called the four species, they consist of the *etrog*, or citron and the *lulav*, which is in actuality three branches—myrtle, willow and palm–bound together. Taken together, the etrog and the lulav are shaken east, south, west, and north as well as toward the sky and the ground to symbolize God's presence everywhere.

Sukkot, observed for seven days, is followed by *Shemini Atzeret*, a day marking the conclusion of the Sukkot observance. Simchat Torah is celebrated at the end of Sukkot and Shemini Atzeret and is the climax of nearly a month of fall holidays.

The Torah scroll, *Sefer Torah*, is the holiest object in Jewish life because the words written upon its parchment are God's words. For some, these words are understood to have been divinely given; for others, divinely inspired. The love and joy Jews feel toward the Sefer Torah reaches its peak each year at Simchat Torah. The scrolls are removed from the ark and are marched, and even danced, around the synagogue for all to see and hold.

In the Ashkenazi tradition, Torahs are dressed in coverings reminiscent of the priestly garments worn in the time of the First and Second Temples. The parchments upon which the text is written are attached to two poles called *atzei chayim*, trees of life. Indeed, the entire Torah itself is also called an *etz* chayim, a tree of life. The parchments are rolled around the atzei chayim and are held together with a *gartle*, or binding. Next comes a mantle, often made of velvet or canvas that has been artfully decorated with embroidery or other needlework. A breastplate, usually silver, is placed over the dressed Torah. In the Sephardic tradition, the Torah is housed in a casing made of wood or silver.

Since the Torah is Judaism's holiest object, it is often crowned as one would royalty. This crown, called a *keter* Torah, is also made of silver, as are the *rimonim*, smaller decorative crowns that are placed over the top of each Torah pole. Bells frequently hang from the rimonim. A special pointer, called a *yad*, literally a hand, is used during the Torah reading. The yad is suspended over one of the poles, ready for use when the Torah is read each Monday, Thursday and Saturday.

The Torah is divided into 54 sections called *parshiyot* (singular *parsha*). One portion is read each week, with two weeks of the year having a double portion. On Simchat Torah the very last section of the book *D'varim*, Deuteronomy, is read and then, without taking a breath the *bal kriah*, Torah reader, immediately begins reading from *B'reishit*, Genesis, again.

A Torah scroll is written by a *sofer*, scribe, who trains many years before being given the responsibility of writing a holy scroll. Each word must be perfectly rendered using a quill from a kosher fowl—usually a goose or a turkey—and special ink derived from vegetable matter. The parchment itself comes from the skin of a kosher animal, usually a sheep.

CHAPTER 17

The Time of Our Joy

The Story of Deena S. Borzak

IT'S NOTHING I'M proud of saying, but I never got it—the wow of birth that everyone talks about; the gratefulness and awe. I thought I did, but I really didn't. The babies came. It was great, but I really didn't get what it was all about. Not until Maya. Maya Dorielle Shuva. Our fourth daughter was born on *Shabbat Shuva*, between Rosh HaShanah and Yom Kippur, the time when you do *t'shuva*, return to a state of repair by repenting. Dorielle for "generation of God." And Maya, which in Aramaic means "waters from God." If nothing else, Maya's birth was that. She was awash in waters from God.

My amniotic sac broke at 26 weeks, and at first I had no idea what it was. This was my fourth kid—you'd think I would have known, but I didn't put it together. I thought I had suddenly become incontinent. I figured it out in one oh-my-God moment and I freaked out. I paged my husband. I paged the doctor, who told me to get to the hospital immediately. One kid was at a birthday party, a second was out on a bike ride, the third was with me and there I was, pouring amniotic fluid all over the place and out of my mind with panic that I'd be giving birth by midnight.

My husband found me huddled in a fetal position, crying, "Let's go back in time. I can't deal with this. I want my mom." Which was dumb, because my mother had been dead for 13 years.

"We'll deal with it," my husband said. "Let's get going." A neighbor came to hold the fort and we raced to the hospital.

The orderly in triage asked if we were having a baby.

"*No*!" I shouted. "I'm not having a baby."

"We don't know," my husband answered. (He's a physician. He's trained to stay calm.)

"Well," the orderly said, "my hopes and prayers are with you."

The first thing they did was establish that my water had broken, like there was any doubt, and then asked me if I knew what I was having. I didn't. Turns out girls do a lot better than boys being born this early. Having come from four sisters and having three girls of my own, I couldn't believe that God would throw me into premature labor and then stack the deck against us by giving me a boy.

The nurses stuck me everywhere with IVs and then gave me the world's most horrible shot to develop the baby's lungs. All through this I was asking them, challenging them, to tell me what it would mean, delivering a baby this early. I knew there were no lungs, no eyes. I'm not one of those people who say Down syndrome babies are God's angels given to us because we are strong enough for the burden. I didn't want to be in any record books for delivering the world's earliest surviving fetus.

"You have a 98 percent chance of delivering before morning," the head nurse said to my husband and me before he left to relieve the neighbor who was caring for our girls. "Most moms don't hold their pregnancy through the night, but if you do, we'll give you all the books you want to read." And then they gave me a sleeping pill. Can you believe it? After all those months of no wine, no caffeine, here they were giving me aspirin, Advil, espresso, whatever I wanted. I think they figured at that point it was anything to keep my sanity, which was actually back home on the bathroom floor in a puddle of amniotic fluid.

I went to sleep and awoke still pregnant. My husband returned soon after breakfast. "You've beaten the odds. Here are the statistics. If you make it this many days, the baby can breathe on her own; make it this many days and no feeding tubes." Every day tipped the scales in favor of the baby's survival.

We were in this incredible race against time. We knew from all the picture books what the baby looked like. Eyes sealed, no fingernails, translucent from head to toe. All I could do was lie there and hope that I wouldn't go into labor. With the other three, my water had broken and labor never began. I had to be induced each time. It occurred to me that maybe that's why God gave me the body He did.

For 21 days I lay in my baby's urine while the world went on around me. The amniotic fluid kept leaking out and replenishing itself, so we knew we had a healthy little person in there. I was constantly soaked. My dad went out and bought 50 pairs of underwear for me. Every night he took away the wet ones, washed them and brought them back. That's how needy I was.

Erev Rosh HaShanah arrived. We are *Shomer Shabbos*; we do not drive on the Sabbath or on holidays. I knew I wouldn't see my husband or the girls for three days, since Shabbos came right after Rosh HaShanah. It was unbearable. I was crying; amniotic fluid was still leaking from between my legs. I was just a big puddle of saltwater and didn't know how I would make it through the next 72 hours.

The first day someone came to blow the *shofar* for me. My husband's friend had asked him to and he walked four miles to get to me. It was such a wonderful sound. The whole point of blowing the ram's horn on Rosh HaShanah is to wake God up and say, "Hey, God? Remember us? We're the children of Abraham. The ones you promised eternal protection to. Are you listening to our prayers? Do you hear our repentance? Protect us." If ever two beings needed protecting, it was my baby and me. I read the prayer book like I never had before in my life.

By the second day of Rosh HaShanah, the amniotic fluid was decreasing and we all knew the next stage, whatever it was, was coming. I waited as long as I could to call my husband. When he got to the hospital I was in full-blown labor and total denial.

The delivery scene was surreal. I was hysterically crying that I couldn't go through with the birth. My husband had the nurse plug in candles for Shabbat, since we couldn't light real candles, and then he started to chant *Kiddush*, the blessing over wine—silver wine goblet, Manischewitz, the whole thing. It was the most bizarre experience of my life. We were on the brink of so much—poised between the new year and the old; between Shabbat and regular time; teetering as close as you ever want to be between life and death. All of us—the OB, nurses, anesthesiologist, ICU pediatrician, my husband, Maya and me—we were right there dancing on the tension of all those edges.

Suddenly, I felt it. That urge to push that everyone talks about. I had never felt it with my other three. My babies were always taken from me, but I felt Maya. For the first time in my life, I felt what it was like to push a baby out and feel it come through you. I pushed once more and the OB shouted: "**Mazel tov! You have a girl! A beautiful baby girl!**" And I thought: *Beautiful? What can she be thinking? She wasn't even three pounds. I had chickens bigger than that in my freezer.*

Then Maya cried. She screamed for all she was worth. Maya had lungs, and they were working. They took her picture, put her on a ventilator and took her away. The camera's there as insurance. Sometimes it's the only picture parents have of their child. I went home two days later and left Maya behind.

Yom Kippur was somewhere in that awful postpartum cycle of pumping breast milk, getting the girls off to school and then rushing to the hospital to be with Maya. She was hooked up to 96 tubes, wires and monitors; there were brain bleeds and seizures. The nurses thought I was nuts because I refused to change her diaper. How do you change a diaper the size of a gauze pad? How do you bond with something that seems to have more wires attached to her than veins? I was so afraid. They called in a social worker to "talk sense into me."

"Take me to bad mother land," I told them. "I'm entitled to my reactions."

Maya was born with down all over her like a baby chick and we watched her develop outside the womb. We saw her skin lose its translucence. Next, her eyes opened and finger- and toenails developed. I felt like she was one of those exhibits from the Museum of Science and Industry in Chicago.

Sukkot rolled around. Of all the holidays, it's my favorite. Also called *zman simchateinu*—time of our joy—Sukkot is a week of partying, of welcoming people into your home and being welcomed into theirs. The kids are off school and you don't have daylong services to wade through. You eat on paper plates and do a lot of casual, child-oriented entertaining. It's just what the name says—a time of joy.

Because the two days of Sukkot were then followed by Shabbat, we faced three days during which we couldn't drive to the hospital to be with Maya. We live 12 miles from the hospital, an impossible distance to walk. The community near the hospital caught wind of our predicament and took all of us in, welcomed us in the truest sense of the holiday. Someone's in-laws were in Pittsburgh and gave us their house. Another couple called and said, "Use our *sukkah* whenever you want." Each day our kids ate and played with different families. I was still unable to walk the two or three miles to the hospital, but for two of the three days it was permissible for my husband to push me in a wheelchair. So that's what we did.

On one of our treks I asked my husband why he insisted on saying Kiddush the night Maya was born. He was so calm, so deliberate while all hell was breaking loose. "How would we ever forgive ourselves if we didn't light candles and do Kiddush while she was being born?" he asked. "If something had gone wrong, how could we face each other in the morning?" So much had gone wrong, I thought to myself, but our daughter was alive and growing.

We made so many friends that Sukkot week. Everyone was praying for Maya. Her survival became a community project. My older three learned a lot after their baby sister's birth. They've learned how to stand up for her and pray for her. They saw how dozens and dozens of people banded together to help us. We were never alone in this crisis. That's what community is.

Maya learned to sit up at one year. She is speech-delayed, but she is also a wonderful, totally pain-in-the-neck toddler. She has learned to say, "No!" This year she decorated her first sukkah. We have a picture of her holding a paper chain in one hand and a bright orange gourd in the other. She is smiling a great big, normal-toddler smile. What a difference from that first picture snapped in the delivery room.

Sukkot is still my favorite holiday. But it means a whole lot more to me now. Sukkot is the time I learned what it really, truly means to welcome a baby into the world. It is forever a reminder of the time of our greatest joy—when we hovered on the brink between life and death and, miraculously, life won.

CHAPTER 18

It Is a Tree of Life

The Story of Jules Doneson

"I WANT YOU to carry one of the Torah scrolls," Chaplain Major Naditch said to me as I approached the *bimah*. I shifted my weapon to my left side and prepared to shoulder the Torah on my right. Was it sacrilegious to hold an instrument of death in one hand and the tree of life in the other? Given the circumstances, I didn't think so.

Somehow I had known as I made my way through the mobs of people crowding the Great Synagogue's courtyard that morning that I would be given a Torah honor. Not because I was such a hero. I just figured that if I were organizing the event it would make sense to give the *kavod*, the honor of carrying the Torah scrolls to Jewish soldiers representing the Allied nations.

Despite the fact that announcement of this service for Jewish soldiers had been hush-hush, it seemed as if every Jew in Paris caught wind of it. When I approached the synagogue, police officers were still removing the boards that had covered the ornate doors and windows of the Rothschild Synagogue during the four years of Nazi occupation. The courtyard outside the synagogue was mobbed—men, women, children, mothers pushing their babies in perambulators—all wanting to enter. Everyone in a uniform was allowed entry first, and then as many in the courtyard as could squeeze in, did.

When I finally made my way into the synagogue, I immediately heard "*Shalom aleichem*" echoing from every corner of that magnificent building. Tears of joy streamed down the cheeks of all who could cry. Not only was France free, but the entire Jewish population of Paris was liberated, too. I had never been to the Wailing Wall, but I imagined that the emotions filling the sanctuary couldn't have been much different than if we were gathered in Jerusalem itself.

The crowds had been fairly quiet during the service and Chaplain Naditch's sermon. But when Rabbi Kaplan, the chief rabbi of France, opened the ark and began taking the Torahs out, bedlam broke loose. It was total pandemonium. Tears. Shouting. The applause reverberated from the floorboards into the soles of my shoes. I have never seen anything like it before or since.

Rabbi Kaplan handed a Torah to me and one each to soldiers from the Free French, Great Britain and Free Polish forces. Then he took the fifth and final Torah for himself. It was time for the *hakafah* to begin. Hakafah means "to march around," but inching around better describes what we did that morning through what seemed like thousands of people.

The women who had been sitting in the upper balconies came down in waves, shrieking and crying. Imagine the joy of seeing a loved one you thought was lost to you, how you would touch her, hold her, to know all was okay. Everyone wanted to touch the Torah scrolls. Kiss them. For nearly four years this synagogue had been boarded up, completely inaccessible. On Rue de la Victoire that September morning, was a family reunion of the most emotional kind possible.

The Torah is not an artifact. We chant from it every week. We study from it. Kids prepare for their bar and bat mitzvahs using it. Old men have *aliyahs* over it. The Torahs of the Rothschild Synagogue in Paris had lain mute in a state of suspended animation—and now we were celebrating with the most profound joy possible. We were literally bringing the scrolls back to life.

There is something very electric about carrying a Torah. You can't help but realize in the pit of your soul that when you carry a Torah, the essence of the Jewish people, the entire history of the Jewish people, is in your arms—Abraham and Isaac, Moses on Mount Sinai, Sarah entering motherhood so late in life—it's all there cradled against your shoulder.

I had no idea as I inched through the synagogue that I would soon meet a soldier who would change the direction of my life. I had no idea that Marcel Berger was rescuing Jewish children and transporting them to Palestine or that I would join him, unasked, in his mission. Holding one of the Rothschild Synagogue Torahs, I had no inkling that I would soon journey to Palestine in '45 and again in '46, or that from '48 to '50 I would serve in the Israeli army. All I knew at that moment was that I was crying along with everyone else. Paris was liberated. The tide was turning.

And then, during our final turn, a young girl approached me. She couldn't have been more than 15 years old. She tore from her coat the beige six-pointed star with *Juif*, "Jew," painted on it in blue ink. "*C'est pour toi*," she said. "This is for you." Then she kissed me on the cheek and pressed the star into my hand. I watched her melt back into the crowd, her rough cotton badge of honor grasped between my fingers. Before my eyes, in the form of one slender girl who had suffered unimaginable cruelty, was the value of liberty, the price paid for freedom.

I have carried many Torahs in my life. It's an honor I have never refused, not even when I was in Singapore and was asked to carry a Torah whose ornate silver case alone weighed a knee-buckling 100 pounds. When you are asked to carry a Torah, you are given the honor of being part of the jubilation. You become a messenger of joy.

It's been 57 years since that morning celebration in Paris—57 years since I experienced the power our Torah has over her people. Each Sabbath after the Torah is read we sing "*Etz Chaim*

He"—"It is a tree of life to those who hold fast to it and all who cling to it find happiness." This is an amazing thing—a people who dance with a book. Cling to it. Hold it fast. Find happiness.

CHAPTER 19

We Are Your Ancestors; You Are Our Children

The Story of Neil Yerman

EVERY TORAH SCROLL is imbued with its own personality. Some are written in a cramped and anxious hand as if the *sofer*, Torah scribe, has embedded the fear and narrowness of *shtetl* life right into the Torah parchment. Others, their letters angular and precise, bespeak a world of rigidity and lack of ease. The Torah on my work table, one of the few restorable Czechoslovakian memorial Torah scrolls, came with a great sense of life and lyricism. Written in a Sephardic Italian hand, it had been created with a wonderful *kavanah*, or spiritual intention. Nearly 250 years old, the scroll flowed with slender and elegant letters. Little did I know how the parchment would fight me, how it would challenge my efforts to make the Torah fit for use.

This particular scroll had a five-column parchment piece that needed replacing. My task involved removing the damaged section, setting it aside for burial, and then matching the writing and inserting the replacement section so seamlessly that it would be indistinguishable from the rest of the scroll.

Working on Torah scrolls, both the restoring and the writing of them, was a calling I always felt within me; it just took me 36 years to claim it. In my early childhood years, as soon as I was able to hold a crayon, I scribbled on anything and everything in sight—the radiator, the walls, my mother's new curtains. I felt most at peace in school when we studied penmanship. The day my teacher said to me, "Neil, you write just like a typewriter!" I was in absolute heaven.

Forever in love with the form and shape of each letter of the alphabet, I doodled continually in my notebooks, extending the lines and loops of the letters into the margins of each blue-lined page. I saw life in the letters; each one had an association to something in my day-to-day existence. I drew creatures of fantasy and also well-known cartoon characters. By the fourth grade, my notebooks looked more like medieval illuminated manuscripts than the product of grade school class work.

Not until I was in my 30s did I finally return to this first love. I began supporting myself by creating *ketubot* and original bar and bat mitzvah invitations. I addressed envelopes—hundreds of thousands of envelopes. I began doing one-of-a-kind family trees and commissioned Judaic art inspired by my wonderful rabbis' Talmud and Torah *chevrutot*, study groups. Along the way I met and studied with bookbinders and scribes. I met manuscript restorers who taught me invaluable techniques of parchment and vellum restoration. I visited scribes from the Lower East Side of Manhattan to Crown Heights, Brooklyn, to Great Neck, Long Island. One day, several years into this professional world that I had chosen (or that had chosen me), the memorial Torah came my way for restoration.

It was late at night when I sat down to complete the final step in restoring this Torah—removing the section of parchment with its chipped, cracked and faded lettering—and stitching in its place the new parchment upon which I had written the same five columns of text. I had my specialized tools at the ready: scalpels, scissors, pliers, needles and thread made from the leg sinews and tendons of a kosher animal.

I looked over the restored portion again, a segment from the reading called "Balak." It's a noisy portion. Balak, King of Moab, calls upon the sorcerer, Balaam, to curse Israel. The children of Israel have grown so numerous and successful that Balak feels threatened. Three times, Balaam attempts to curse the children of Israel. But each time, instead of curses, God's blessings upon His people issue from the sorcerer's mouth.

God speaks through Balaam with a pronouncement that forms the basis for the *Ma Tovu* song. "How goodly are your tents, O Jacob, your dwelling places, O Israel." In his commentary, the great Jewish scholar Rashi writes that Balaam's proclamation is related to the balance between community and privacy preserved in the traditional arrangement of each family's tents. This multitudinous clan of *B'nai Yisrael* was made up of individual families each needing their privacy and singular dignity. Rashi teaches us that a community is healthiest when the rights of individuals it comprises are maintained and not entirely subsumed into the larger realm. This was the beauty that God/Balaam praised in Jacob's tents—their unique placement in relation to one another enabled both privacy and community.

Before inserting the new panel of text, I took up my pliers to remove the old *giddin*, the sinews attaching the panels one to the other. As I tugged at the threads I began to hear voices inside my mind, as if the giddin were pleading, "Don't take us out! We've been here too long. What are you doing?" I was startled, to say the least. I laughed and said to myself, *The threads are talking to me?* But the cries of protest persisted. My pliers were useless. It was as if the giddin were rusted into the skin itself; they wouldn't budge. I might as well have tried to pull up from the ocean floor an anchor from a sunken galleon. I got out a different set of pliers and then a scalpel and set to work again. This time the giddin slid right out. An eerie silence filled my work room. "I'm sorry," I said to the brittle curls of sinew scattered on my table and the floor below. "I'm sorry."

When I began sewing in the new parchment, the ruckus started up again. It was like it was coming right from the letters.

"What are you doing? We don't want these people here with us. We don't know them," cried the old letters.

And the letters from the new parchment argued back: "Well we don't want to be with you, either. We don't know who you are. You are strangers to us!"

And then it hit me. I was working on a scroll that originated somewhere in Italy in the 1760s and was attempting to insert a parchment produced in America nearly 250 years later. No wonder the letters were hollering. The lives they represented were being violated, cast aside and replaced with total foreigners! How could they welcome these "strangers" into their midst without protest? The original Torah represented the village, as it was two and a half centuries ago and there I was trying to insert an entire new village, as it were.

The sages have had many things to say about the letters of the Torah:

> There are nine worlds of understanding in every letter.
> Every letter is a life.
> Every letter is a complete world.

The night I struggled to make the Italian Torah whole, the phrases took on entirely new meaning. These ancient observations were born from literal truth.

After a while the din was so loud that "*Bet*," the Torah's first letter, and "*Lamed*," the Torah's last, came to calm everyone down. "Why are you making so much noise?" Bet asked.

"They're not from our village," said the old letters. "What happened to our people? Where did they go?"

"They weren't well and couldn't live here anymore," said Bet gently. "Tell the new ones who you are."

"We are the people of this village."

"Well," said the new letters, "We must be your great-great-grandchildren. You must be our great-great-grandparents."

"That's right," said Lamed. "That's exactly what you are to each other. These letters have come to live with you. Embrace one another." And they did.

A sudden calm settled over my work table. The scroll, which had been so difficult to unfurl, lay flat; the giddin felt supple in my hand and smooth as silk as I stitched the two parchments, old and new, ancestors and descendants, together. As Rashi taught, the individuals in a community must be recognized before the community can live in harmony.

The Italian Torah taught me that every letter is truly a life. Most of us don't know individuals on our family trees back more than a few generations. But the Torah scrolls that live in the *aron hakodesh*, the Holy Ark, are our ancestors. The letters contained in Torah scrolls represent the names of all of our ancestors who lived in shtetls, villages, farms and cities throughout the world. A "*Mem*" for Malka, a "*Yod*" for Yuhuda, a "*Shin*" for Shmuel. Their names, and the names of their ancestors and descendants, live on in the Torah. Life after life of fulfilling the commandments; blessing after blessing; prayer after prayer. Every letter is a complete world.

When a synagogue creates a new Torah and a small child places a hand over mine as I write a letter, that child and that child's prayer and sweetness live in the form of that letter in the scroll. Then that child becomes a bar or bat mitzvah and connects to that letter and the experience of writing it once again. The Torah is forever witness to these passages of the child's Jewish life.

I'm not a psychic or a channeller or a mystic. This is the work I do. But there is so much in life that we do not understand; we become so skeptical when we hear things that are outside our normal expectations. Who knows how the spirit of a loved one travels? Through memory? The instructions in the Torah are given to us straight from the lips of our parents and grandparents:

Love your neighbor as yourself.
Feed the hungry.
Clothe the needy.

These are Torah's words, spoken to us by our ancestors in an unbroken chain. A Torah can live a thousand years; it is a time capsule and you can go anywhere in it. I'm not suggesting that millions of souls live in the physical ink and parchment. What I am suggesting is that when you recognize the symbol represented by each letter, this realization has the power to teach you that which you cannot see, smell, touch or hear. The symbol has the power to awaken worlds of Jewish life within you.

PART 5

Mitzvot

The purpose of the laws of the Torah is ... to promote compassion, lovingkindness and peace in the world.

—Maimonides

TWO CONCEPTS CRUCIAL to Judaism's ethical tenets are frequently mistranslated, thus misconstruing the rationale behind their formation. *Mitzvah* (in the plural, *mitzvot*) is frequently understood to mean "a good deed." People often say, "It would be a mitzvah if you do this," or, "What a mitzvah you have done!"

In actuality, mitzvah means commandment. Judaism teaches us to do good deeds not because we want to be nice or because it feels good to help out. God commands us to do good because that is the path to a peaceful world. Humans can be weak of flesh; selflessness and altruism might not always be the chosen course of action. The structure of mitzvot, which command each Jew to do the right thing and refrain from the wrong action, ensures that at least some of the time, the high road is taken.

The word *tzedakah* is commonly understood to mean charity, which comes from the Latin word *caritas*, or love. Tzedakah, however, comes from the Hebrew word *tzedek*, or justice. Giving to the needy is not an option. It's not dependent on how one might feel on any given day. Judaism holds that those in need must be helped. Whether one's heart is inclined to help or not is irrelevant.

CHAPTER 20

If the Mitzvah Fits

The Story of Lisa Katzman

I LOVE TO read magazines. With three kids under five, it's hard to finish a novel. But I can read magazines while the baby naps or when I'm waiting in the nursery school carpool line. During one of my magazine breaks, I read about Shoes That Fit. I never thought something as simple as a pair of shoes could make a big difference in a child's outlook. But it does. It really, really does.

Shoes That Fit is a program in which volunteers adopt a school whose students are in need of new shoes. It was started by happenstance when a woman named Elodie Silva heard the story of a young student who complained to the school secretary that his feet hurt. The secretary (who is also Elodie's friend) removed the boy's shoes to see if a pebble or something similar was causing his discomfort and discovered that the sneakers were so small the boy's toes were curling under. When Elodie heard this story from her friend, she posted a notice at work: **Would anyone be willing to buy a pair of sneakers for a little boy whose shoes are too tight?** Within days, Elodie's cubicle was flooded with brand new shoes. That was the start of the national endeavor now known as Shoes That Fit.

I tore out the article, figuring there must be a similar need somewhere in my community. In addition to saving the Shoes That Fit article, I had clipped a story about a local man who had links to the Jewish community and New Detroit, an organization committed to rejuvenating and strengthening the inner city.

I was on the verge of resigning as my *shul's Tikkun Olam* committee chair, since I hadn't been able to get much off the ground. Then I got word that a woman was interested in chairing the committee, but only if I would stay on and work with her. I knew Lisa from our volunteering at an organic food co-op here and figured she'd be a safe bet. She loved the idea of bringing the Shoes That Fit program to our area, and we agreed that she'd attend the meetings if I would find a school in need and do the publicity.

I called the man with the New Detroit connections and explained our idea. Within a week, he set me up with a school to contact. "I have no idea what to expect from this program," I said to the teacher after describing our mission, "but I'm willing to try if you are. Would you send me a list of 10 kids who you know could use a new pair of shoes? I'll send you background material which includes the cardboard form to measure their feet; then give me their names and shoe sizes and we'll do the rest."

Sheryl faxed me a list of 10 kids. Lisa and I made a bulletin board describing the Shoes That Fit program and attached index cards to the board with each child's name and shoe or clothing sizes. The cards said things like, "Andra needs size four party shoes" and "Jamal needs size nine sneakers." We made five cards for each child, writing the shoe size on one and clothing sizes for underwear, socks, shirts or pants on the others. I also stapled pictures of kids to the board who had received clothing through the program in other communities and beautiful, very moving letters of thanks from the kids and their teachers. The word "self-esteem" kept popping up in the teachers' letters—how the students' self-esteem had skyrocketed from receiving a pair of new shoes. At the time I don't know that I totally believed it—part of me thought that's what the teachers had been told to say. Soon I would learn for myself how true this was.

We had the board ready in time for Rosh HaShanah, and within an hour of the start of services, all 50 cards were gone. That was good. What wasn't good was that we had no idea who had taken the cards or how we could follow up. Since it was *yontiff*, we couldn't leave out a sign-in sheet to have people write whom they were buying for. Come Yom Kippur we were in a panic. We didn't want to ask Sheryl for more names, since no donations had come in yet, but we didn't want to lose the momentum of the congregants' apparent eagerness to get involved. So we made up names and duplicated the original size and clothing information. Again within an hour or so of *Kol Nidrei* services, all the cards were gone. A few days after Yom Kippur, people started dropping off their shopping bags to the shul office and we realized this was beginning to snowball. We called Sheryl and said, "Measure more kids and send us their names! Fast!" We wanted to get new cards up in time for *Simchat* Torah.

People's capacity for giving just blew me away. If someone took a card to buy shoes, they would also buy a few pairs of socks or tights and barrettes. They made care packages of Halloween candy. And not just one or two people. Every single person who took a card brought back so much more than we'd asked for. Some people asked to "adopt" their kid and told us they would buy a new pair of shoes in three months or whenever "their" child outgrew the shoes. Lisa and I couldn't believe the generosity. We had had one meeting. *One meeting*. Do you know how many meetings committees usually have before they get anything done? In a few short weeks we had gone from helping 10 kids to helping 40. No one gave hand-me-downs; everyone left on the price tags and included sales slips so we could exchange if we felt we had to. My van was so full there wasn't even room for the stroller!

After the holidays we spoke with the nursery school director and she sent home a letter in the kids' backpacks. That fueled us up for another month. Just as we were wondering what new source to tap for donations, a check for $500 arrived in the mail for us to "buy the kids what they need." Each month the bounty just comes to us. It's like rain or manna. We ask and there it is. The shul has been a terrific help. We said, "We want to do this," and they said, "Fantastic, here is some money to get you started printing your posters, for postage or whatever."

The effect this has on the kids is stunning. These children have never had new clothes. They can't believe that someone cared enough about them to do this. When we got to the school the first time, we met with each child and had them try on the clothes. Then we took pictures of them. You should see how they smiled and posed for the camera. These children know when their clothes are stained and torn. They know. When they put on the new clothes, they insist on keeping the box and the bag—anything, even crumpled, white tissue paper—that proves they have gotten something new to wear.

Sheryl told me about a child who always hung back on the playground and never got involved with the other kids. Now she is out there every recess, playing and laughing. Those teachers' letters I got in the Shoes That Fit packet were right on. New clothes and these kids' self-esteem go hand in hand. I saw it when my daughter's kindergarten teacher specifically asked me to give her the name of a hard-to-fit child. Sure enough, we had a heavier girl on our list. Mrs. F bought her a beautiful blue sweat outfit—pants and a top, hair bows, and socks and shoes. When the child posed for her picture, she just glowed. In her thank you note she wrote, "Thank you thank you thank you. You are the sunshine shining down on me." I never would have believed the enormous difference this makes in the kids' lives. Nor would I ever have imagined how rewarding it's been for me. It fuels me. Working on this project, organizing the clothes, making up the packages, coordinating people's donations for the individual children literally warms me up. It is the most unexpected thing.

It takes me away from the mundane and makes me feel lighter. When I do Shoes That Fit, I feel like I am not walking on the same pavement as everyone else. If the kids are settled, drawing or watching TV, I know I could be doing the dishes or keeping up with the laundry, but I do Shoes That Fit instead. It gives me such a boost. I look at all the gifts that people have bought and I know how much the kids are going to appreciate it.

I've discovered something else, too. You'd think the kids would be very territorial with their clothes. But they're not. If a child gets two sweaters or two pairs of socks, they invariably ask: "Can I share this with my sister?" or "Can I give my brother the other one?" They don't hog their clothes. Their first thought is of their siblings.

I'd always heard that expression "doing God's work," but I never really thought about it. Now I know what it means. It's when you are doing something that has absolutely nothing to do with your benefit or the benefit of your family or anyone you know. As a mom, I spend nearly every waking hour doing for others. But Shoes That Fit is for those who aren't my own. I am filling a vacuum that no one else has filled. These kids are born like everyone else. They learn to read by second grade, they write and draw pictures—a triangle for a skirt, little sticks with ovals facing left and right for legs and feet. They try and they try, despite the hurdles they have to overcome each day. They are great kids and they don't give up.

For years, every night before I fall asleep, I have thanked God for my beautiful children, for my sweet husband, for my home, for my shul and my wonderful community. Working with these kids, I feel that I am showing God that I understand all He has given me. In my own small way I want to extend my thanks beyond the gratitude of my nightly prayer. I didn't frame it this way when I began, but more and more, this is what motivates me—acknowledging God's gifts to me by helping others.

I had always thought it would be nice to be a Big Sister, but I hesitated because I knew I couldn't devote such a solid block of time. This I can do. I can help a child in need. It doesn't matter what else is going on in their lives. For the time we are together—trying on their clothes, fixing their hair, taking a photograph and helping them write their thank you notes—time stops and they are transformed.

What we are doing is special, but I don't think that I am so special for doing it. I am simply a cog in the wheel of a group effort. We put up cards. People take them and return gifts for needy children. We organize their gifts and take them to the school. The kids put the clothes on and they hug us. They thank us and tell us we are the sun shining down on them. They feel sunshine. I feel God—His gratitude and love shining down on us both.

CHAPTER 21

Chosen Schmosen

The Story of Arthur Ost

I DON'T BELIEVE we are a chosen people. I think that's bullshit. Pure bullshit. We are not chosen. We Jews are just people. We should learn from our heritage that we must choose to be charitable. The Bible tells us to be good. We learn that from our history; it's in our bones. You gotta be good to people. Plain and simple. Jews have been oppressed, driven out of Egypt, stoned, ridiculed, thrown into concentration camps and slaughtered. But chosen? That's bullshit.

I feel connected to the Jewish people, but my connection is akin to what Paul Robeson said one morning at the Abyssinian Baptist Church in Harlem, after the Peekskill riots in the late '40s. "Blacks and Jews have similar histories of oppression and rising above their persecutors," he said. "We Negroes owe a great debt of gratitude to those who stood by the hundreds and defended me and all of us earlier this week."

Yeah, I know relations between Jews and blacks are not what they used to be, but I still think we can stand as one people. If you have common sense, then you think: *We have common enemies. We are natural allies. Anyone who has been oppressed can stand together.* At least that night in Peekskill we did.

Robeson had given a concert up in Peekskill on August 28, 1949. He was the son of a runaway slave, a Progressive and a peace activist in addition to everything else—football hero, singer, actor. I saw him play Othello with Uta Hagen. He was overpowering. You never saw anything like it. But it was the Progressive Party stuff that got him into trouble with the House Un-American Activities Committee. He was a radical, went to the Soviet Union and praised it; and so he was arrested and brought up on charges by McCarthy and all those idiots. Robeson just told 'em, "It's none of your business," and I gotta respect him for that.

Well, we read all about the Peekskill concert riots the morning after it happened. Halfway through the performance, goons from the American Legion stormed the stage and attacked Robeson—stoned him and beat him and the concertgoers. The legionnaires said, "We hate him because he's a Negro and a Communist." Now, was he a Communist? I don't know. Yeah, he did have leanings. But does that give someone the right to beat another human being?

A lot of us Jews were Progressives back then, and Robeson identified with the party. It wasn't Communism as much as Socialism. We were democratic, but with a small "d." Today, McCarthy seems ridiculous. Any party can espouse any "ism," and that's that. But back then, people were put on trial for their ideas; and Robeson and Jews like myself were outraged.

Robeson was determined to stage a second concert. I got a call from some guys I knew in the fur union to come to a meeting at author Howard Fast's house in Manhattan. Pete Seeger was there with about 30 union members. Of course, Robeson was there, too. You could still see the welts on his face and hands, and he said to us, "I don't want to admit defeat. I am going to sing again. Would you people come and support me?" He didn't even have to ask. How many times can you let the oppressors win?

The second concert was set for a week later on Sept. 4. Our plan was for union members to travel to Peekskill for the concert and be ready to defend Robeson and anyone else who might be attacked. Seven of us would remain nearby at the home of Dr. Sam and Helen Rosen, wealthy Progressive people who had invited Robeson and his men to stay with them overnight after the concert.

During the day we relaxed a bit; the Rosens had a pool, and it was still hot. This was early September, remember, and there was no air-conditioning yet. Finally, it was time for them to leave for the concert. The 30 union members would already be there. We didn't know what would happen, but we assumed a repeat performance from the American Legion. Sure enough, we heard on the radio that there had been another riot. People were injured, but this time the union guys fought back and the legionnaires got as good as they gave. Robeson and his bodyguards made it safely up to the Rosens' home at about midnight. "The concert was a success," he said when we got him into the house. "I will not be deterred by racism and the American Legion."

Seven of us stayed up the whole night, keeping watch on the Rosens' porch. We were scared, and even though we knew the goons could have followed him to the Rosens', we were young guys and we were thrilled to do what we were doing. We had no guns, just clubs. What's a club gonna do against a bullet? But nothing happened. It was quiet all night. I guarded Paul Robeson till morning.

Standing watch took me back to my high school days. I went to Boys High in Bedford Stuyvesant in Brooklyn. I was a Jewish kid in a mostly-black school, and the boys were friendly to me. The school turned out very smart people in those days. There was none of the mistrust you have today. None of that at all. We were kids, and we basically got along. Paul Robeson was my hero. Next to Martin Luther King, Jr., I think he is the most important black man of our century.

Morning came and Robeson's guards drove him back down to New York; word came to us through friends about the church service the following Sunday. During the service he gave his thanks to us and then he cried. We all did. I felt proud to be a Jew that morning in the Abyssinian Baptist Church. That's what it is to be Jewish. You don't have to pray at the Wailing Wall. You have to act in the spirit of *tzedakah*, of righteousness. It's not charity that you do because you want to feel good inside or because you have pity on the less fortunate. You do it because you have to. Because you are commanded to repair the world. That's what it's all about.

I never saw Paul Robeson after that. He moved to England, to Russia. He had a wife or two, and if I remember right, one was Jewish. He deserved a medal for being voted an All-American football player at Rutgers. Attended Columbia law, too. They took his sports record out of the record book. Denied him his medal. That's how far they went to excise facts. Some people are still trying to get the U.S. to issue a stamp with him on it, but I don't think it will happen because of his Communist activities. I think Robeson died sad and sick because he had been maligned. At the end of his life I don't think he was happy. But what a man he was! *What a man!* I still think about that night every once in a while.

Nowadays, I get up early in the morning, form a line with 30 people and put food into 200 bags at the Martin Luther King Senior Center. We're black, white, Rainbow, shmaynbow. We're people—human beings helping other human beings. When we're done at the center, I take bags of food to homebound seniors. On Tuesdays I go to another community center and teach Spanish to Americans and English to foreigners from Iran, China and Japan. It's all volunteer. That's my do-gooding.

I wouldn't think of stepping into a *shul* and praying. I'm 84 years old, and every day I do what I do and do it as a Jew. In the spirit of tzedakah. We are a giving people. Well, we're supposed to be anyway. We've been oppressed, and because of that you have to help the poor. I learned that as a kid. "There are poor people all over the world," my dad told me, "so eat everything on your plate and be glad you have food."

I still think it's bullshit that the Jews are a chosen people. But that night with Paul Robeson, I was chosen to guard him, and I did it. Guarded him like he was my brother. That's what it is to be a Jew. To guard those who need guarding and do it like they're your brothers. That's what Jews gotta choose to do. Every day, I tell you, *every day*.

CHAPTER 22

Addiction's Gift

The Story of Carol Y

PEOPLE COMPLAIN THAT temple dues are so high. I say it's the best money my husband and I have ever spent. Without the caring support of our temple community—while I underwent treatment and up until this very day—I doubt I would ever have had the strength to confront my addiction and enter recovery.

A nice Jewish wife, mother and nurse addicted to narcotics? Shooting up? Diverting medication to support her habit? You say this doesn't happen in the Jewish community? That Alcoholics Anonymous and Narcotics Anonymous meetings are always held in church basements and not temple boardrooms because only non-Jews have these problems? The truth is: Jews have these problems too.

I grew up in your typical American Jewish family. My parents were second generation, and as they gained a foothold on the American dream, they became increasingly preoccupied with how things looked from the outside rather than how they really were within our four walls. Pools, furs and Cadillacs were important. Unconditional love was not. My parents loved me because I was an A student and because I married a Jewish lawyer and lived in a nice house. I was their proof to the world that they were OK people and good parents. I sensed early on that if I made one false move, I could lose their love.

Drug use was part of our family's culture. When I became ill as a child, my mother would give me codeine-laced cough syrups and hot toddies with liquor. That was an accepted pediatric cold and flu treatment of the day. Today I know better. My earliest memory is of an argument between my parents over my mother's addiction to sleeping pills. These patterns, combined with the tenuous hold I had on my parents' love, set the stage for my own struggle years into the future.

At 25, I developed asthma and my doctor gave me codeine-laced cough syrups to manage it. My very first dose really hit the spot. It made me feel the way I thought other people felt all the time—relaxed, confident, and able to socialize at parties. It gave me guts enough to tell my husband, Steven, how I really felt about things. Today I realize that everyone suffers from social anxiety to some degree and that airing dissatisfaction to my spouse doesn't render me unlovable. I didn't then. All I knew was I didn't need a prescription to get these cough syrups that made me feel like I could handle anything. I had the perfect cover, too: I was treating my asthma.

My addiction began very innocently. First just a teaspoon at a time, and then two. Then a tablespoon. Then three or four ounces once or twice a day. By the time I was drinking a six-ounce bottle at one sitting, I knew I was hooked and on the road to something bad. I told Steven I thought I was in over my head, but he didn't understand what was happening any better than I did. "Deal with it," he said.

Well, I dealt with my addiction by progressing from codeine to other narcotics. My kids were young; I was working as a clinical nurse specialist. Steven was a new attorney, which meant that even though he made an effort to be home as often as possible, I was still alone He was home more than some husbands, but he was still gone much of the time. I was feeling depressed—and felt guilty for feeling depressed. What right did I have to be depressed? I had two beautiful toddlers 19 months apart, a lovely house and a wonderful husband. Outwardly, everything was perfect. I had been taught that that was all that mattered. Narcotics silenced nagging feelings of incompetence and guilt.

Over the years I held a succession of jobs, always quitting before my addiction could be discovered. Then someone at the hospital where I worked got caught stealing narcotics. An intervention was done on me as well when they discovered I was working under the influence. I entered intensive outpatient treatment (IOP) which requires a family member to accompany the addict to treatment.

I took my mother, since Steven and I both believed he should be home with the kids—a fact that speaks to how ignorant we were about addiction and my husband's codependency. He didn't see that my addiction had anything to do with him or that he was part of the problem and part of the solution. Neither did I.

I completed my treatment, although I continued to use all the way through. My counselor knew what was going on and finally threatened to put me in the country's premier treatment center for health care professionals. The threat of being separated from my family and being forced to face my demons completely unglued me.

I had reached a point of utter hopelessness. I felt I no longer had anything to offer life, and in this state I believed my family would be better off without me. I didn't want to die. I just wanted to stop my pain. I was in no position to grasp that my death would hurt my family irrevocably. When you have no sense of self-worth, no capacity for hope, you can summon no reason to go on.

On the night before my daughter Rebecca's ninth birthday, I took an overdose of antidepressants and lay down in my husband's study. Rebecca found me on the floor the next morning. That was my ninth-birthday present to her. Even this was not enough to make me quit. However, after my suicide attempt, I did enter psychiatric therapy.

About this time I was beginning to have nightmares and vague flashes of memory that left me with the edgy feeling that something in my childhood was very wrong. Working with Dr. M, the uneasy flashes of memory crystallized into total recall. When I was 10 years old, my father's brother-in-law had raped me. Rebecca's closing in on this age in her own life set off a crisis of psychological ricochet that forced me to face this long-repressed violation. When I gathered the courage to tell my parents, my father said I had taken one of his best friends from him. My mother only wanted to know if it had been one of her brothers; if so, she was prepared to defend him to the death.

I was in therapy with Dr. M for seven years, during which time I continued using. He was trying to relieve the pain of my rape trauma and depression on the assumption that I'd stop using drugs. It doesn't work that way. You have to stop using before psychotherapy can help the depression and the substance abuse. I am not faulting my psychiatrist. I credit him with helping me to raise both Rebecca and my other daughter, Heather, into the wonderful young women they are today. He was trained as a Freudian to use talk therapy. Talk therapy alone is an inadequate agent to combat addiction.

I also think that Dr. M couldn't face the fact that I was still using. Perhaps he couldn't admit to himself that I was sabotaging his treatment. Perhaps he was buying into that old lie that upper-middle-class, well-dressed Jewish ladies aren't out-of-control junkies. I was. My husband knew I was using but couldn't catch me at it. Ultimately, my employer discovered that I was still using drugs. On the verge of suicide again, I admitted myself to the hospital. My daughter brought me to admitting, where Dr. M was waiting for us.

Rebecca confronted my psychiatrist. "Look at her hands!" she shouted. "Don't you see how swollen her hands are? She's shooting up into her hands!" There was no longer any place to run or hide. I realized that if didn't get myself straight I'd end up dead. I went home overnight and the next morning entered the Mayo Clinic for 21 days. That was the beginning of my recovery.

I was afraid of so many things: that my husband wouldn't want me when I came home; that my children would hate me because I had left them; that my friends and my temple would reject me; that I would have no place to come back to when I finished my treatment at Mayo.

"What can I do to help?" my rabbi asked.

"Make sure my family is OK while I am gone," I said.

Instead of sending me flowers at Mayo, Rabbi Syme sent each of my girls flowers and a teddy bear. A therapist friend stayed in close contact with Steven. Rabbi Castiglione took him out to lunch many times over those three weeks. The entire Married Group at temple supported Steven, and the Young People's Society supported my girls. We couldn't have made it as a family without our temple.

I returned from Mayo *erev Purim*. In years past I had designed the sets for the Married Group's Purim play. That year it took everything I had just to show up. I considered wearing a Purim disguise but realized that I had worked too hard at Mayo relinquishing the mask of my addiction. It was come-as-you-are or nothing.

The cantor looked down at me from the *bimah*, gave me the biggest smile and told me how welcome I was. I knew then and there that no matter what had happened I would always be accepted at Beth El for who and what I was. No one was going to reject me because of my addiction. They were only going to embrace me. From that moment on, temple became a constant source of stability and support. My kids knew they could go to Rabbi Danny or Rabbi David any day, any time; my husband had a shoulder to lean on in confidence.

Throughout my addiction I had been attending AA and NA meetings and struggled with the fact that the meetings were always held in church basements. I wondered time and again, was AA Jewish? This question led me to study the Torah and Judaism and I found out that AA is indeed very Jewish.

AA says that you put your faith in a higher power of your own understanding. This is a Jewish concept. We don't define God as a specific entity. In Judaism we are given the freedom to understand God in whatever way we need to.

AA tells you how to behave toward yourself and your fellow man. This, too, is a Jewish concept. Judaism doesn't tell us what to believe, but how to behave.

AA teaches that you must not only ask God for forgiveness, you must also ask forgiveness from those whom you have hurt. You must go to the person you have injured and make amends, again a quintessential Jewish notion. What else is Yom Kippur but this?

Judaism has come to mean community for me. My childhood had been devoid of many family rituals and regular celebrations. In the years I struggled with my addiction, I worked hard to create memory makers—celebrations and rituals for my children. My Jewish study hasn't necessarily led to strict observance, but it has led me to being a strong member of the Jewish community. Reaching out to others in need is a big part of my recovery. Creating spiritually nurturing memories for myself and those I love is paramount. There's a reason alcohol is called "spirits": addiction is a spiritual hollowness, and we pour liquor and drugs into ourselves to fill that spiritual void. I have Judaism for that now.

I've adopted a family as well—the parents of close friends of ours. I have told Sam and Sylvia that they are my parents and my kids' de facto grandparents. They know all about me and still they love me. That was so hard for me to accept. That I could still be lovable. When I told my own mother the truth about my addiction and my commitment to sobriety, she said that she liked me better when I was addicted.

Sam and Sylvia loved me and kept on loving me. Over time, I started loving myself. There are times when they come to dinner and I go up to our second floor and look down at my dining room. Friends and family around my table are laughing and enjoying themselves. They are there because of me. I look down on them and I can't believe I finally have the life that I fantasized about when I was a kid. I have more friends than most people have in a lifetime.

I have come to accept the love of friends and family and I know that God loves me, too. King David has been a role model for me. He made lots and lots of mistakes, yet God loved him. He did some doozies. What David did makes what I've done look like small potatoes. Still, God loved him. Part of my recovery has been learning to accept myself, warts and all. I no longer expect perfection; it's an illusion, a one-way ticket to self-destruction.

My road to recovery has not been a straight shot by any means. I have relapsed along the way. The past year has been terrific. I take medication that blocks the cravings by inhibiting the effect of opiates. Even if I used I couldn't get high. The physical cravings will always be there. My medication doesn't allow me to escape into drugs and run from the everyday conflicts and stresses that are a part of life.

I counsel addicts in a methadone clinic now. The job is a huge part of my staying clean and staying in recovery. Every day I deal with the consequences of drug use. I see the pain, the destruction, the broken relationships and estranged children. I see the lost jobs and the lost money. I see the physical damage people do to their bodies, and it reminds me day in and day out why I decided to go into recovery.

My husband recently gave me a diamond tennis bracelet for my birthday. It's a replacement for one that was stolen from me during that 36-hour haze before leaving for Mayo. In giving me this bracelet, Steven was telling me that we were putting an end to that chapter of our lives. He no longer has to worry about setting aside money to cover a future stay in a treatment center. He was telling me that I have his trust back. Not all of it perhaps, but most of it. That means more to me than diamonds.

Steven and I are a lot closer than we ever have been. I learned in recovery not to take anything for granted. I've learned that I can't go through life on autopilot. This is the gift of my addiction. My faith, my relationship with God, is the gift of my addiction. Not of my recovery, but of my addiction. AA taught me to accept life on life's terms, to cope with anxiety, sadness and anger instead of using drugs to mask them.

I'm not advocating addiction as a character builder, but the person I am is the result of what I have lived through. I am happy with who I am now. And if I am happy with who I am now, I have to be grateful for all the things that led me there, including my addiction. If it took addiction to get here, then so be it. If it means realizing that I will always be in recovery, then that's just how it is. I take it one day at a time.

Author's Note: The names of the narrator and her family have been changed to protect their privacy.

CHAPTER 23

Hugs from Home

The Story of Susan Mandelbaum

I LIKE TO say I have three children and 220 other kids. The 220 others are the ones who get care packages and other mailings from our temple's College Connection Committee. I joined the committee when my oldest son went away to school. The program was small—just 18 kids—yet I thought it was important to reach all the kids from our *shul* who were away at college, not just the ones whose parents had put their names on our list.

After two years of listening to my suggestions about expanding the program, the president of our synagogue made my husband and me chairpersons. We formed a committee and immediately began gathering the names of every college student in our synagogue.

We operate on the premise that kids will open any package sent to them at college. I believe that Judaism can be fun. So many times it isn't and it just doesn't have to be that way. These packages reinforce our kids' Jewish identities and help them feel close to Judaism. If they feel close to being Jewish, maybe they'll think twice about the kind of Jews they want to be. Keep kids smiling when it comes to Judaism, build on the good feelings they may have and you've harnessed the power to change the world.

Along with the monthly temple bulletins and a subscription to *Moment* magazine, we send five packages a year: for Rosh HaShanah, Chanukah, *Tu B'Shevat*, *Purim*, and *Pesach*. Five times we reach out—five chances to slip in a little knowledge along with the fun. I love shopping for the care-package goodies and get as creative and innovative as I can. It buoys me to know that when the kids open our packages, they will smile and maybe even laugh.

The theme of the Rosh HaShanah mailing is apples and honey. We put in Bit-O-Honey candies for a sweet year and foam "stress apples." When December rolls in, our kids know the Chanukah package—complete with candles, menorah, lots of chocolate *gelt*, and *dreidels*—is on its way. Our Tu B'Shevat care package is the biggest hit of all. We send out the soft-sculpture people that grow grass hair. The kids keep them watered, and for six weeks they have a daily reminder of their Jewish heritage's concern for the environment. When March arrives, so does the Purim package, with zany masks and *groggers*, Laffy Taffy and other silly things. For Pesach we make up plague bags—little erasers in the shape of cows, sunglasses for darkness, Styrofoam for hail, and plastic bugs. We always enclose a *Haggadah* and a variety of kosher-for-Passover goodies, including chewing gum.

The packages have an additional value with respect to non-Jewish students who see them. If students have grown up in Utah, for instance, and have never met a Jew, this might be the first time they witness a menorah being lit and blessed. They eat some chocolate gelt. One day they might write or call home and tell about their roommate's interesting holiday, elevating the awareness level of an entire family. Jews cease to be aliens, becoming people with their own holy customs.

While the kids operate on college time, with exams, weekend film festivals, and frat parties, our care packages subtly remind them of their link to Jewish times. Along with the fun items, we always include educational information—flyers on student study/travel to Israel, scholarships for Judaic studies, or United Synagogue *Koach* activities. Our rabbis and cantors get in on the act, too. One year the rabbi wrote the kids about education being the process by which we become human beings. Often, the literature we enclose is not much different than what a parent might send, but because it's from a neutral source, the kids can approach it without all that static they may have toward home.

The cantor's tapes have been a big hit. The first one was a Chanukah audiotape we called "Songs and Banter with Love from Cantor." It contained the blessings for the candles and some Chanukah songs. We got such great feedback that we followed it up with "Cantor Sings All Year," which is a compilation of melodies linked to all the holidays, with some Jewish historical tidbits thrown in for good measure. Always, our goal is to keep it light yet meaningful.

One December break I was in synagogue and bumped into one of our students. "I just wanted to thank the temple, you, the rabbi and the cantor for the great packages," he told me. He mentioned that he had listened to the cantor's tape over and over. The next week this teen, who hadn't been in shul since his bar mitzvah, returned with his dad. That's the power of this work. It's a labor of love and one of the most important things I have done in my life.

Occasionally a parent asks me to remove his child's name from our list; I never do. My philosophy is that you can't give up on the kids even if some parents don't see the value in what we are doing. Once, a mom asked me to stop sending the packages to her son in London; she said he didn't want them. Her request went in one ear and out the other. Wouldn't you know, a few days before Passover, this mother called her son and learned he was making a Seder with his friends who were also away from home. "Oh, yeah," he told her, "Mrs. Mandelbaum sent this great package with a Haggadah and a funny bag of plagues. I'm bringing it along." That's why I never drop a kid's name from our list. You never know when the spark will ignite into a flame.

I really feel I'm contributing to the well-being of the Jewish people and maybe, just maybe, one day 30 years from now, these kids will tell their children about the plague bags or the way they celebrated Jewish holidays in college, or even make sure their synagogue has a college program.

Our synagogue received the Solomon Schechter Gold Medal Award for Excellence, not just once, but three times. Receiving the award has allowed us to reach out to other synagogues across the country. I have been asked to speak to congregations interested in duplicating our efforts. At least 80 congregations nationwide and in Canada have begun or enriched their own outreach programs to their college students through the guidance the College Connection Committee has been able to give.

I'm just one person, but I love kids and I had this dream of reaching out and touching as many as I could. My dream is coming true. Do the math. Say those 80 congregations each have 200 college students. That's 16,000 young adults who receive, in the guise of fun and zany care packages, meaningful reminders of their Jewish identity.

The college years are such a crucial time in a young adult's life. And it is a time when many young people become disconnected from their Jewish heritage. We have to be there. We want to be the ones giving them what they are seeking. As intermarriage rates continue to rise, I hope our packages help our kids feel close to being Jewish.

We call ourselves the College Connection and tell the kids we are sending them hugs from home. What we're really about is maintaining their links to the Jewish people. We're keeping the door open. When the time comes for them to go out on their own, they will embrace Jewish life for themselves and for future generations.

PART 6

Chanukah

As part of the eternal world-wide struggle for democracy, the struggle of the Maccabees is of eternal world-wide interest.

—*Louis Brandeis*

CHANUKAH COMMEMORATES THE Jewish victory over Syrian emperor Antiochus and his army. In 167 BCE, Antiochus decreed the practice of Judaism to be an offense punishable by death. The Temple was desecrated, and the Syrians went so far as to sacrifice pigs in the Temple. A Jew named Mattathias and his five sons began a revolt not only against Antiochus, but against the Jews who were quite willing to take on the ways of the majority population and jettison Jewish practice. Three years later, the Maccabees, as the Jewish fighters were known, and their followers, were victorious and the Temple was once again in Jewish hands.

Chanukah is celebrated for eight days. According to Jewish tradition, when the Temple was finally cleansed for rededication, there was but a single day's supply of ritually pure oil for the *ner tamid*, the everlasting light that hangs in every synagogue as a symbol of God's ever-presence. Miraculously, the oil lasted for eight days, the time needed to press and ritually purify additional oil for the ner tamid.

There is a second reason Chanukah is an eight-day holiday. The Maccabees were fighting during the eight-day fall harvest festival and thus were not able to offer thanks to God, as was customary. Once the Temple was dedicated, eight days were set aside by way of delivering belated prayers and ceremonies of thanksgiving.

The cornerstone of the Chanukah celebration is the lighting of the *menorah*, an eight-branched candelabra. There is a place for a ninth candle on every Chanukah menorah for the *shamash*, the "helper candle" used to light the other eight. Each night of Chanukah, an additional candle is lit.

Chanukah is not the time of year to start a diet, for the two foods most associated with the holiday are *latkes,* potato pancakes, and *sufganiot*, Israeli jelly donuts, both of which are fried in veritable lakes of oil. Chanukah *gelt*, chocolate coins wrapped in gold foil, abound as well.

Chanukah's other ritual object is the *dreidel*, a small four-sided top upon which are inscribed the letters *nun*, "gimel, *hey* and *shin*, commemorating the phrase "*Nes gadol haya sham*," or "a great miracle happened there." Dreidels in Israel are inscribed with a *pei* in place of the "Shin" to stand for the Hebrew word *po*, or here.

CHAPTER 24

Protestant B, Not

The Story of Mike Neulander

DOG TAGS. WHEN you get right down to it, the military's dog tag classification forced me to reclaim my Judaism. In the fall of 1990, things were heating up in Kuwait and Saudi Arabia. I'd been an army captain and a helicopter maintenance test pilot for a decade and received notice that I'd be transferred to the First Cavalry Division, which was on alert for the Gulf War. Consequently, I also caught wind of the Department of Defense's "dog tag dilemma" vis à vis Jewish personnel.

Then as now, Jews were forbidden by Saudi law to enter the country. But our Department of Defense flat out told the king of Saudi Arabia, "We have Jews in our military. They've trained with their units and they're going. Blink and look the other way." With Kuwait occupied and the Iraqis at his border, King Fahd did the practical thing and blinked. We shipped out, but there was still the issue of the dog tag classification.

Normally, the dog tags of Jewish servicemen are imprinted with the word "Jewish." But the Department of Defense, fearing that maintaining this customary marking for Jewish soldiers would put them at further risk should they be captured on Iraqi soil, substituted the classification "Protestant B" on the tags, "B" being a secret code for Jew. I didn't like the whole idea of reclassifying Jews as Protestant anything and decided to leave my dog tag alone. I figured if I were captured, it was in God's hands. Changing my tags was tantamount to denying my religion, and I couldn't swallow that. In September 1990 I went off to defend a country I was prohibited from entering. The "Jewish" classification on my dog tag remained, clear and unmistakable as the American star painted on the hood of every army truck.

A few days after my arrival, the Baptist battalion chaplain approached me. "I just got a secret message through channels," he said. "There's going to be a Jewish gathering. A holiday? Simkatoro or something like that. You want to go? It's at 1800 hours at Dhahran Airbase."

"Simkatoro" turned out to be *Simchat Torah*, a holiday that hadn't registered on my religious radar screen in eons. But it registered then and there. Services were held in absolute secrecy in a windowless room in a cinder-block building in Dhahran, Saudi Arabia. Rabbi Romer, the chaplain who helped keep us together during the war, led a swift and simple service. We couldn't risk singing or dancing, but the rabbi had managed to smuggle in a bottle of Manischewitz. Normally I can't stand the stuff, but that night the wine tasted of *Shabbos* and family and Seders long gone. My soul was warmed by the forbidden alcohol and by the memories swirling around me and my fellow soldiers. We were strangers to one another in a land stranger than any of us had ever experienced—but for that brief hour we were home.

Only Americans would have had the chutzpah to celebrate Simchat Torah under the noses of the Saudis. Irony and pride twisted themselves together inside of me like barbed wire. Celebrating my Judaism that evening made me even prouder to be an American; made me thankful once more for the freedoms we have in this country. I'd only been in Saudi Arabia a week, but I already had a keen understanding of how restrictive Saudi society was.

Soon after that service, things began coming to a head; the next time I was able to do anything remotely Jewish was Chanukah. Maybe it was coincidence, or maybe it was God's hand that placed a Jewish colonel in charge of our division's intelligence unit. Colonel Schneider's presence enabled him to get messages of Jewish gatherings to us immediately. Had a non-Jew been in that position, the information likely would have taken a back seat to a more pressing issue. Like war. But it didn't. When notice of the Chanukah party was decoded, we knew about it one, two, three.

The first thing we saw when we entered the tent was food, seemingly tons of it. Care packages from the States: cookies, latkes, sour cream and applesauce, and for some funny reason, cans and cans of gefilte fish. The wind was blowing dry across the tent, but inside there was this incredible feeling of celebration. As Rabbi Romer talked about the theme of Chanukah and the ragtag bunch of Maccabee soldiers fighting off Jewry's oppressors thousands of years ago, it wasn't hard to make the connection to what lay ahead of us. There in the middle of the desert inside an olive green army-issue tent pockmarked with holes, we felt like we were the Maccabees ourselves. If we had to go down, we were going to go down fighting.

We blessed the candles, acknowledging the King of the Universe who commanded us to kindle the Chanukah lights. We said the second prayer praising God for the miracles He performed, *Bayamim hahem baz'man hazeh*, "In those days and now." And since we were assembled on the first night of Chanukah, we also sang the third blessing, the *Shehecheyanu*, thanking God for keeping us in life and for enabling us to reach this season.

We knew war was imminent. All week we'd received reports of mass destruction, projections of the chemical weapons likely to be unleashed. Intelligence estimates put the first round of casualties at 12,500 soldiers. I heard those numbers and thought, "That's my entire division."

I sat back in my chair, my three cans of gefilte fish at my feet. I had tucked a trio of letters addressed to "Any Jewish Soldier" into my back pocket. There we were in the desert about to go to war, singing songs of praise to God who had saved my ancestors in battle. The feeling of unity was as pervasive as our apprehension, as real as the sand that found its way into everything from our socks to our toothbrushes.

I felt more Jewish there on that lonely Saudi plain, our tanks and guns at the ready, than I'd ever felt outfitted with *tallis*, prayer book and *yarmulke* in *shul*.

That Chanukah in the desert solidified for me the urge to reconnect with my Judaism. I felt religion welling up inside of me. Any soldier will tell you there are no atheists in a foxhole. I know a good deal of my feelings were tied to the looming war and my desire to get right with God before the unknown descended in the cloud of battle. It sounds corny, but as we downed the latkes and cookies and wiped the last of the applesauce from our plates, everyone grew quiet, keenly aware of the link with history, thinking of what we were about to do and what had been done by soldiers like us so long ago.

The trooper beside me stared ahead at nothing in particular, absent-mindedly fingering his dog tag.

"How'd you classify?" I asked, nodding to the tag. Silently he withdrew the metal rectangle and its beaded chain from beneath his shirt and held it out for me to read. Like mine, his read, "Jewish."

Somewhere in a military supply depot I'm sure there are boxes and boxes of dog tags, still in their wrappers, all marked "Protestant B."

PART 7

Tu B'Shevat

Trees ... have language, feeling and prayer of their own.

—*Baal Shem Kolitz*

TU B'SHEVAT, THE Jewish New Year for trees, falls on the 15th day of the month of Shevat. The Hebrew letters forming the word *tu* constitute the number 15. The holiday arrives between January and February, a time when the trees are beginning to blossom in Israel, although here in America, many are hard put to imagine spring will ever arrive!

It is a Tu B'Shevat custom to eat foods associated with Israel, particularly the seven kinds of fruits and grains listed in Deuteronomy. Though not a major holiday by any stretch of the calendar, it is growing increasingly popular to celebrate with a Tu B'Shevat Seder, a ritual meal reminiscent of the Passover Seder. Four cups of wine, containing different proportions of red to white, are served along with dates, figs, pomegranates, apples, carob chips, olives and various seeds and nuts, all of which help Seder participants identify with the land of Israel.

CHAPTER 25

A Tree Grows in the Vatican

The Story of Mike Nitzani

IT TOOK ME 25 trees to get to the Vatican, but I got there. A decade ago, the Jewish National Fund (JNF) asked me to give them a few years, representing them and their director in Italy. It was an opportunity to further the JNF's mission and also return to the roots of my grandmother's family, who made their way to Italy before the Inquisition and the expulsion of the Jews from Spain. On my grandfather's side, we trace the family's presence in Italy back 50 generations. None of us had been back since my grandfather had moved the Genazzani family out from under Mussolini to Israel.

Trees permeate Jewish life. Our expulsion from the Garden of Eden is linked to the tree of knowledge. Moses experienced God from the midst of a burning bush. We call our Torah a tree of life. In the Bible it is forbidden to destroy fruit trees growing even on one's enemies' lands. Our holiday *Tu B'Shevat* is known as "the new year of the trees" and is celebrated in Israel each year by tree plantings all over the countryside.

When I arrived in Rome, I lived in a neighborhood of the city called Trastevere. It is the oldest neighborhood in Rome apart from the Emperor's City, and it borders the Vatican state. Riding to and from work each day on my moped, I would pass by the Vatican and recall the centuries of enmity and anti-Semitism stretching back 2,000 years.

On one of my rides I had an inspiration. Call it a message from above, if you like. Why not find a way to use trees to make a connection with the Vatican? Something along the lines of literally extending an olive branch. The Vatican had not yet recognized Israel; there were no diplomatic relations between it and my country. I decided in a moment that during my stay in Rome I would do my best to make an approach between the two states.

It was a time of great potential. Rabin had made peace with Jordan, an event that was spurred by the peace crafted between Egypt and Israel. I thought, Israel is moving toward peace with the Palestinians, and that is a 100-year conflict. Here we have a 2,000-year-old conflict that needs resolving. With the strength of the JNF behind me, I decided I had a chance. Like the story of Johnny Appleseed you have in America, I would begin to plant olive trees in Italy. But not just any olive trees. Olive trees from Israel.

Olive trees are significant to both the Italians and the Israelis. In Italy, these trees form their biggest export: the olives, as well as the oil pressed from them. The olive tree has a strength that no other tree has. It can handle any kind of climate, resisting subzero temperatures and great heat. When I was a soldier, I could always find shelter in the shade of the olive trees by the roads I patrolled. For me and many, many Israelis, the olive tree is a symbol of ever-present relief.

I started in Milan by contacting Cardinale Martini. He was very warm to the idea, and not long after, we held a ceremony attended by the chief rabbi of Milan, Cardinal Martini himself and a number of Catholics, Christians and Greek Orthodox. A choir made up of people from all churches was positioned on the steps of the church in central Milan. They sang "*Haveinu Shalom Aleichem*" as we presented one olive tree at the Duomo. It was a very powerful moment to see something blossom from a passing thought on a scooter commute into reality. I had taken my first step toward my ultimate goal of planting a tree in the Vatican.

The Milan story was filmed by television crews, and soon we received a message in Rome from the mayor of Bologna. "We have the grave of twelve Jews who were murdered by the Fascists in World War II. We want to do something to honor their memory. We want to plant a tree." When we arrived, the date of the massacre had been engraved on a large stone. We planted an olive tree beside it. In attendance were nearly 400 people, many of whom were nuns who had hidden Jews from some of the nearby villages. My peaceful military strategic plan was progressing.

There is still anti-Semitism in Italy, but there is no real danger to the country's Jews. And while it is not systemic hate, it is still the Vatican's country, and the influences are strong. The day after the tree-planting in Bologna, the site was vandalized and the tree was uprooted. The mayor called us immediately to arrange for a second planting that was attended by every member of the city council and all of Bologna's Jews. The mayor also made plans to open an exhibit in city hall of the history of Jewish life in Bologna. He was not going to let the act of one vandal sever the links we were making. Jews tend not to make a lot of noise in Italy. The olive trees were a way to make noise, but positive noise, in an ecological way.

Then we planted a tree in Sotto Il Monte, hometown of Pope John XXIII. In 1962, this pope convened Vatican Council II, which ultimately led to the writing of *Nostra Aetate*. The document, also called The Declaration on the Relation of the Church to Non-Christian Religions, is the Church's formal recognition that the Jews were not to blame for the crucifixion of Jesus Christ. In attendance was an ambassador from the state of the Vatican and the Israeli consul general of Milan. Having planted a tree in Pope John XXIII's hometown, I approached the

Vatican officials about planting a tree on the Vatican grounds, also in his honor. To my delight, they agreed.

The day of the Vatican planting was calm and beautiful. We chose to have a 30-year-old olive tree sent from Israel, symbolic of the fact that Nostra Aetate had been written 30 years before. The consul general of Israel was there, as was the former secretary for Pope John XXIII, who had died in 1965. The JNF had procured two halves of a millstone and had them engraved in gold with these words: "This olive tree from the hills of Jerusalem is planted in the name of harmony with nature and in peace between our two religions. Keren Kayemeth LeIsrael." It had become the ritual of Pope John Paul II, to sit in the shade of this beautiful olive tree when he finished signing peace treaties or wanted to honor a visiting dignitary.

One day, a call came from the Israeli ambassador. We had been invited to a private meeting with Pope John Paul II. At last. My peaceful military campaign had succeeded. What would have been more natural than to bring an olive tree with us as an offering of friendship? This pope was a wonderful man. He was completely at ease with us, like he was one of the guys. He had a great sense of humor and radiated such a sense of warmth and love.

The tree we took to our meeting is planted in a section of the pope's private residence gardens. I have been told that once, one of the Vatican gardeners moved the tree to a different location. The pope insisted that it be returned to its original place so that he could see it during the day while he was writing or in prayer. This olive tree from Israel was the only plant in his garden that the pope watered and tended to himself.

The tree was as important a symbol to him as it was to us. This pope had been pro-Jewish and had done what no other pope had done—he established diplomatic relations with the State of Israel. The olive trees in Italy are going to live a long time and hopefully will serve as reminders of the positive bonds that can be forged between Jews and Catholics not just in Italy, but everywhere. As it turns out, virtually all the donations received by the JNF from Catholic organizations come from Italy. These trees have represented us well over there.

Relations with our neighbors in Israel aren't so positive these days. The accords and hopes of a two decades ago vanish daily with each new attack. One of the first things the Palestinians did during one period of unrest was to set fire to groves of trees in the Golan. Acres and acres of trees burned, forcing us to use precious water that neither the Israelis nor the Palestinians can spare to quench the fires. How do we plant trees enough? If the fires do not stop, there will be no olive branches left to extend. I pray for the strength of leaders to realize this cannot go on. It is time for us to plant olive trees together.

PART 8

Bar and Bat Mitzvah

Torah is a closed book until it is read with an open heart.
Torah sanctifies life; it teaches us how to be human and holy.
Torah is given each day; each day we
can choose to reject or accept it.

—*Siddur Sim Shalom*

IN ITS STRICTEST sense, *bar mitzvah,* son of the commandments, and *bat mitzvah,* daughter of the commandments, is a state of being—not a big party, nor even a verb. One does not "get bar or bat mitzvahed."

One becomes a bar or bat mitzvah simply by reaching the age of 13, the age at which one is commanded to follow Jewish law. In more traditional communities, girls become bat mitzvah at 12.

While many associate the bar or bat mitzvah with lavish parties, reaching this age obligates the male to do two things: one, to put on *t'fillin*, two small leather boxes containing biblical verses commanding their wearing; and two, to be called to the Torah for an *aliyah*, to say the blessing over the Torah before and after it is read.

Today's 13-year-olds study for many years in advance of their bar or bat mitzvah service. They learn not only the blessing for the Torah but all the prayers that are part of the service. They learn how to read Hebrew, as well as chant *trope*, the musical cantillations assigned to the Torah readings. Many also elect to study and chant the *Haftarah* portion, the commentary on the weekly Torah portion drawn from Prophets. The bar or bat mitzvah is also expected to deliver a *d'var Torah*, a short commentary on the Torah portion and perhaps Haftarah text.

The concept of a bat mitzvah ceremony is a relatively modern innovation. The first such celebration was that of Judith Kaplan, daughter of Rabbi Mordechai Kaplan, the founder of Judaism's Reconstructionist movement, on March 18, 1922. Reaching this age of religious maturity enables one to be counted in a *minyan*, a prayer quorum of 10 adults. Orthodox and more traditional Conservative communities count only adult males for a minyan. Reform Judaism does not require a set number of adults, male or female, for public prayer.

CHAPTER 26

Standing up to the Fires of Hate

The Story of Phil, Jan and Max Littman

"I HAVE BAD news," my mother-in-law said to us as Jan and I returned from an early-morning walk. "Your synagogue has been torched. The rabbi left his cell phone number. Call him right away."

Our son Max's bar mitzvah was to be held the next morning. Friends and family, 160 of them, were either already at the hotel or arriving within the next few hours to celebrate this milestone in our lives. You would think we'd be overcome with tears, but there wasn't time, no time even to go into shock. We had to immediately start thinking about notifying our guests, caterer and florist. But we had no idea what to tell them. Where, when and especially how were complete unknowns.

I called the rabbi. "I have Max's Torah," he said before saying anything else. In that one kind sentence, our rabbi communicated to us that our family's *simcha*, Max's milestone, was foremost in his mind and would go on as planned. "We are working on a change of venue right now," he continued.

Within half an hour we learned that the Sacramento Convention Center would be made available to us to hold services and the celebration afterward. By 11 o'clock we were meeting with their representatives. They rolled out the red carpet for us and temporarily voided their contract with their own caterer so that ours could come in. They gave us two beautiful rooms that were more than enough to hold our services and the celebration that would follow. Our *chavurah* began calling our guests to inform them of the change in plans. That accomplished, next on the list was Max's final rehearsal.

When Lou Anapolsky, our temple president, got news of the attack, he and his wife, Marlene, rushed to the building and found the firefighters in the last stages of extinguishing the fires in the temple library/administration building. At that point everyone thought the fire was contained in that part of the building. Lou received permission to enter the chapel at the other end of the building and remove the Torah from the chapel ark. Torah scroll safely in the trunk of his car, he watched as the firefighters wound the last of the hoses into their truck. Suddenly, the shrieking of a second alarm split the predawn air.

Racing to the sanctuary, Lou tried to enter to save the Torah scrolls but was pushed back by a wall of thick black smoke. The entire space was lit by the dull orange glow of fire. "Fire in the sanctuary!" he shouted to the firefighters, who immediately began unrolling the hoses they had just stowed in their truck. Once he explained to the fire chief the importance of the Torahs and the need to protect them, if at all possible, from smoke and water damage, all he could do was wait until he was given permission to enter the sanctuary.

The piano at the front of the room was black and charred. The reading table on the *bimah* was partially burned, as were the red velvet bimah chairs. The prayer books, Plaut Torah commentaries and wooden pews were drenched with accelerant. But the Torahs were safe. For some miraculous reason, the fire on the bimah had changed course and traveled away from the ark and the trio of Torah scrolls within. Thanks to Lou's quick thinking, the firefighters were able to rescue all three.

It is surreal to think that with the calamity going on around us, we were still holding to our schedule. I don't think Max really understood the impact of everything that had happened and what it would mean for him over the next 24 hours. The cantor welcomed us into his home for the final rehearsal, and at that moment Jan and I were totally overcome. The enormity of what had happened was beginning to sink in. The scroll in the cantor's home was a survivor Torah; it was brought to the temple by a Holocaust survivor from a synagogue in Czechoslovakia, and you can still see the imprint of a Nazi boot on it.

When the cantor unrolled the Torah, the smell of smoke filled the room. Jan and I were moved to tears. And then Max began chanting. His voice was strong and sure. If ever a statement of invincibility could be made, that was it. At 3:30 a.m., that surviving Torah had been rescued from a burning sanctuary. Barely eight hours later, its words were coming to life.

Then, in the time it takes to say "*L'hadlik ner shel Shabbat*" (to kindle the lights of Shabbat), sunset arrived. We headed to the convention center theater for services. Because the two other synagogues had also been firebombed, the service was community-wide. Thousands of people, of different religions and races, had made it their business to worship with us that night. Not only were congregants from three synagogues there, but also our rabbi emeritus, who had flown in from Phoenix and various dignitaries from the city council. Also present were many Methodist ministers who were in Sacramento for a convention. They came as a show of strength and solidarity; one of the ministers presented the rabbi with a check for $2,500, which had been raised during the day.

Jan, her mom, and my mom rose to light the candles. "May God bless us with Shabbat joy. May God bless us with Shabbat holiness. May God bless us with Shabbat peace." The power of those words reverberated in every corner of the theater. God had blessed us with so much that day. No lives had been lost. In the face of irreparable damage, caring and immediate outreach had been the order of the day.

We had looked forward to this day on so many levels. Our son was about to take his place in a long chain of tradition. My brothers have married non-Jewish women and so, on my side, I am the strongest link in the chain. For Jan, Max's bar mitzvah was a statement to her mother that her unbreachable commitment to giving Jan and her brother a Jewish education had not been in vain. My mother-in-law was raised in a small Mississippi town that probably doesn't even exist anymore. Despite her own scattered Jewish education, she persevered in giving her children their Jewish heritage. Max's becoming a bar mitzvah was another tribute to her dedication.

Our son had had no idea of the number of people who would be at the Friday night service. The numbers overwhelmed him. We knew Saturday would be more manageable. We and our rabbi were determined to preserve that sense of a family service. Saturday would be Max's day, the time for him to read his Torah and *Haftarah*, and deliver his talk.

But when we arrived at the convention center Saturday morning, Max totally lost his equilibrium. A dozen or so cameramen and news reporters were outside the building doing their thing—interviewing people, angling for shots. A half-dozen Sacramento police officers and a bomb-sniffing dog were present for security. There were chairs set up for 500 people. We delayed the service a bit to allow Max to regroup; then the rabbi asked the media guys to lie low. It was Max's time and we were moving forward.

Max did beautifully. You cry at any bar mitzvah. You certainly cry at your own child's. Considering what we had been through in the past 24 hours, our tears had special impact. Max looked so grown-up. He was relaxed, companionable even, with the rabbi. You could feel the warmth flowing between them. Max rose to the challenge of bar mitzvah—he mastered his texts and did all that parents hope their children do—and he did them under extraordinary circumstances.

Ascending the bimah to give our speeches to Max, we were overcome. Through my tears all I could see, in my mind's eye, were the ashes in the library, how they had sparkled in the sunlight as the wind blew them up through the rafters. The rabbi was wearing a *kittel*, a robe of mourning, instead of his *tallis*. It, along with the glass *yad* we were to present to Max, had been destroyed in the fire. Jan said to me later that the kittel was the perfect expression of so much that is Jewish life. We mourn and we celebrate, and sometimes we do both at once.

The weekend of Max's bar mitzvah, joy and grief danced on the head of a single pin. Max was the symbol that the hate mongers hadn't won. A few days later, over 3,000 people attended a unity rally. All races, religions and ages. Plain and simple, we were one. Sacramento, 1999, was not Berlin, 1938.

In addition to the unity rally, a memorial service was held in a park across the street from our synagogue. Days after the fire, people were still shoveling the ashes of the books into boxes to be buried in the cemetery. The air was still filled with the acrid smell of smoke. As we walked along, Max found a page from a book. It was singed around the edges and showed a picture of a boy and girl with their arms around each other, walking away from the camera. "It's a symbol, Mom," Max said as he picked it up. "They can burn our books, but they can't break our unity." Max keeps the picture in his room as a reminder.

The vandals reduced our synagogue's entire library—the video collection of Holocaust interviews, the children's section, everything—to a three-foot pile of ash. They burned prayer books and Torah commentaries, whole offices and precious artifacts. But as Max recognized, they didn't destroy our community. They failed to gut our faith. If anything, the neo-Nazis' terrorism only strengthened the very community targeted in their hate-filled cross hairs.

The day after the fires, a Sacramento newspaper printed the *chai* symbol as part of a full-page ad of support to the city's Jews. Readers were urged to cut the chais out and display them as signs of solidarity with the Jewish community. Six months after the firebombing, we still see newsprint chais taped to an occasional storefront door or peeking from the windows of a private home. Out of something so unfathomably evil, humanity's goodness blossomed. In the face of great tragedy, the people of our city came out by the thousands to show that hate has no home in Sacramento.

As Max grows into manhood, and then fatherhood, the story of his bar mitzvah might well become the stuff of legend. "Tell me, Daddy," my grandchild may say one day, "tell me about how they burned your synagogue on your bar mitzvah day." And what I hope Max tells my grandchildren is not only the story—the panic, the triumph, the fear and the joy—but the underlying message. Evil may never be eradicated, but as long as people have courage and stand up to hate, peace and goodness will triumph every time.

CHAPTER 27

Survival on the Back Forty

The Story of Margo Jakobs

GROWING UP IN Green Bay, Wisconsin, I wouldn't exactly say I was from the city, but we had enough of a Jewish community to sustain an active Conservative *shul.* My mother was fiercely proud of her Judaism. Oh, my God, was she proud to be a Jew! Some survivors left it all behind after the war, but not my mother. She raised all four of us to know who we were and to live our Judaism with pride and honor. She sent us to Camp Ramah every summer and crocheted each of her granddaughters a *tallis* when they became bat mitzvah. Mom overcame any obstacle that stood in the way of raising her Jewish daughters. "You do what you have to do, Margo," she told me all my life. "Hard as it is, you do what you have to do."

My husband, Dave, is one of those rare Jews who didn't grow up in a city. Of any size. After the war his father, a survivor as well, found his way to Sterling, Illinois and became a cattle dealer. Dave and his sisters and brother grew up on his parents' farm. Early in our courtship, he took me home to Sterling to meet them. I didn't know the difference between a steer and a cow, but the warmth and closeness of Dave's family bowled me over. I always thought you had to live in a city to have traditional Jewish values, but the Jakobseswere solidly Jewish—two days of Rosh HaShanah, not one; Passover Seders; *Shabbos* dinner every Friday night. Even Mrs. Jakobs's chopped liver and matzah ball soup had a familiar taste. If they could raise their sons to be serious Jews on a cattle farm, I reasoned, I stood a chance, too.

Little did I know what a challenge it would be. I wasn't prepared for the isolation from other Jews. I wasn't used to having to call up someone and say, "Let's bake *hamantaschen*" and have them ask, "Why?" I once told my sister that her Jewish life in the Milwaukee suburbs was like plowing a field with a John Deere tractor and mine was like furrowing the back 40 with a horse and hand plow.

Much as I loved Dave and his family, moving to the farm was an incredible culture shock. Sometimes I felt like Eva Gabor on *Green Acres*. Except Eva never had to mail-order Rosh HaShanah cards in June because the local CVS didn't stock them. She never had to worry about finding a bar mitzvah tutor.

I have had stretches where I begged Dave to leave Sterling and move to a place that had a larger Jewish community. But Dave wasn't leaving the farm, and if we had even tried to live in two places, it would have meant the beginning of the end of our marriage. I had no option, really, but to stay and find a way.

Anything we want to do that's Jewish, we have to do ourselves. If we want hamantaschen for *Purim*, we make and roll the dough out ourselves. We cut the dough into circles and smear them with poppy seed and apricot filling before we bake them. If we want our kids to hear Jewish melodies, we sing them ourselves. We don't drill them, but we make a conscious effort to remember who we are. Whenever I'd whine to my mom how hard it was, she'd shoot right back, "If it's hard, so it's hard. That doesn't mean you don't do what you have to do. Show me where life is easy and I will show you a fairy tale."

It fell to me to train my son Nik for his bar mitzvah when the person I was counting on to teach him moved away. Because of my background, I'm probably one of the more knowledgeable members of our community. I speak Hebrew and can chant Torah and *Haftarah*. There is a responsibility that comes with this knowledge.

I cannot sit back and refuse to help educate our community's children. From 25 families, we have 13 kids in grades one through seven, and I am one of their religious-school teachers. It's very much like what I imagine the *shtetls* in Europe used to be: intimate and gritty. In the air there's an It's-us-or-it's-nobody kind of self-reliance.

Nik and I started a year and a half before his bar mitzvah. It was hard at first, distinguishing my mom role from that of teacher. There were days that went incredibly easily and others where I literally had to stand over my son and say, "Nik, you have two months to go, you have to learn this paragraph!" Would it have been so different in a big city? Maybe not. Kids dawdle and procrastinate no matter where they grow up. Sometimes we were locked in such a struggle it felt like childbirth all over again. I had to work so hard to ready him for the day he would stand on his own two feet. Hard or not, I did what I had to do.

Nik's bar mitzvah was to be the community's first in three years. That's what I mean about living in a shtetl. One family's *simcha* belongs to the entire community in a way that doesn't happen in other places.

The other element that ratcheted up the emotions the morning of Nik's bar mitzvah was that I nearly missed it. At 2 a.m., a turn of food poisoning or flu wracked me with such bouts of vomiting and diarrhea that I had to be rushed to the hospital, where they started I.V.s to replace all my lost fluids. I made it to the temple with five minutes to spare—no makeup, no hairstyle. But I was there. I saw my son ascend the *bimah* and take his place in line as a child of Abraham, Isaac and Jacob. Show me where it's easy, and I'll show you a fairy tale.

Our tiny prairie temple was as filled to bursting as our hearts. My family came from all over: the six Jakobs families (one-third of Sterling's Jewish community!) were there, as were the rest of our temple members. There were a number of Christian friends and families as well. Everyone was sobbing. Tears flow at every bar mitzvah, and in small farm communities, the tears have extra meaning. Bar mitzvahs, even if they come only once in three years, are proof that we are not dying out. They are the validation of all our hard work and insistence on holding to a 6,000-year tradition.

Nik had us put an extra chair on the bimah, and, before leading the service, he placed a red rose on the chair seat to symbolize all the children who are denied their Jewish heritage because of religious persecution. My son's simple act of solidarity put the entire issue of Jewish isolation into perspective. Okay, so I can't buy Chanukah candles at the grocery store; so I make my own hamantaschen and help educate the community's children in a three-room schoolhouse. I am free to raise my kids as Jews. Whether he meant it to or not, that's what Nik's rose was telling me.

I was so proud to be Nik's mother. It had nothing to do with me and everything to do with what he did. I have never felt more pride in another person in my life. It did not matter that Nik was from a small, rural congregation in Sterling, Illinois. When you have to work so very hard to achieve something, the results are all the sweeter. You sow what you reap, and our harvest the morning of Nik's bar mitzvah was as bountiful as you could ever hope for.

The Yiddish expression *Shver tzu zein Yid,* "It's hard to be a Jew," didn't come from thin air. It's hard to be a Jew anywhere. Even though I envy the size of my sister's community and the availability of Jewish life where she lives, it has its downside, too. Her community can get preoccupied with making each bar or bat mitzvah distinct. They worry about themes and color choices and bar mitzvah boredom settling in after the 27th simcha. Jewish life on the farm has its definite upsides. In Sterling, Illinois, the theme is: Judaism. The colors? Israel's—blue and white. And as for bar mitzvah boredom, there is none.

After the ceremony, the Sisterhood served what looked like a month's worth of baking. My mom must have rolled out an acre of strudel dough for the rugelach she brought. For 35 years it's been Sterling tradition to embroider the name of each bar or bat mitzvah on a special tablecloth. Sure enough, Nik's name was there in navy blue floss, right next to his father's.

My mother died in the spring a year after Nik's bar mitzvah. Not having her for Alex and Bryce's bar mitzvahs is going to be so hard. There I go again with that word. If my mother taught me anything, it was to not let "hard" stand in my way. But she never taught me how to make her Rosh HaShanah *kreplach*. My three sisters and I all have the recipe, but none of us could bring ourselves to take up the reins, because to do so would have meant Mom was truly gone.

Three weeks before Rosh HaShanah, my friend Nicole called me up. "Give me your mother's recipe," she said. "I know you want to do this. I know you have to, so make the meat, bring it on over and we'll do it together." And we did. When I got to Nicole's, Jewish music was playing on the stereo. She had already started cutting the dough for the filling, but she had cut them into squares.

"I can't give my family squares!" I told her. "They have to be triangles. Grandma will come and say I screwed up the kreplach."

"Margo," Nicole interrupted me. "Isn't your grandma dead?" I started laughing and crying, and we made those damn kreplach. But we re-cut the dough into triangles in honor and in memory of my mother and her mother before her.

I know my mother would have been so proud of me. Nicole and I spooned meat onto the dough triangles, folding and pinching them together. I sobbed my way through each one. All afternoon I heard my mother's voice inside my head, saying, "There you go, see, it's not so hard. You can do it just fine. Now, go ahead, take up another piece of dough. You can do it." The family ate every last one.

If Nicole hadn't corralled me into making the kreplach, a strong sensory memory of my mother would have died away forever. Farm wives stick together because we have to. Our survival depends on it. Jewish farm wives simply have a double row to hoe. John Deere tractor or horse and hand plow—if it's important you just take up the reins and keep going.

CHAPTER 28

Out of Crisis

The Story of Nancy Kaplan

THE CHINESE PICTOGRAPH for the word "crisis" is composed of two separate symbols, one signifying "danger" and the other "opportunity." Over the years since my son was born with spina bifida, I've thought a lot about the logic of perceiving opportunity and danger at a time of crisis. Dan's birth was a shattering event that altered the entire landscape of my personal and professional expectations. But in an intriguing way, it also proved to be the catalyst for a profoundly positive reorientation of my life. I found myself able to move toward a goal that had lain dormant in my soul since childhood: forging a meaningful connection with my Jewish heritage. The crisis of my son's disability was also a supreme opportunity for change.

One night, three weeks before my due date, I woke up in the middle of a precipitous, fast-moving labor. We made it to the hospital less than an hour before our son, Daniel Saul Kaplan, was born. I heard his first cries and was on top of the world. Then I heard the doctor's muted pronouncement, "We've got a problem here." There was a fist-sized hole in the middle of Dan's back covered by a translucent membrane.

Because of his med-school training, my husband understood even before the doctor began explaining, that our son had spina bifida. Although not life-threatening, Dan's form of spina bifida would most likely entail major physical disabilities, including paralysis, incontinence and orthopedic problems. We saw Dan for the barest moment before the medical team whisked him across the street to Children's Hospital for the first of four neurosurgical repairs.

Dan's birth marked a pivotal shift in our lives. Everything changed. There was a "before" marked by great expectations for ourselves, our child and our future as a family. In addition to raising happy, healthy children, Mike and I would pursue professional careers—he as a doctor and I as a lawyer. And then there was "after," with all our expectations out the window, the future uncertain and all bets off.

I did work briefly as an attorney after Dan was born. My law firm was amazingly flexible and allowed me to work a three-fourths time schedule, then half-time. By the time Dan was 2½ years old, he needed the first in a series of orthopedic operations. Soon after his third birthday we received a diagnosis of "global mental retardation" and "developmental disability." There was no way to tell then where he would plateau in terms of cognitive skills. I realized I could not practice law effectively part-time. What's more, being an attorney was no longer compatible with my life and my personal goals. I retired from the practice of law and never looked back. One year later, our daughter Amy was born.

Prior to our move to Boston, we had been members of an informal *chavurah* congregation in Philadelphia. Before that, we had made no effort to connect as a couple with the Jewish community. In the wake of Dan's birth, I knew this was something I needed to do.

I had always yearned for a religious Jewish connection deeper than what my family was comfortable with. We belonged to a Conservative *shul* but rarely went. My parents blamed organized religion for much of the intolerance and hate they abhorred in the world. They believed fervently in principles of social justice as exemplified by the biblical prophets, but dismissed Jewish ritual observance as primitive and irrational. Consistent with this stance, my parents sent me to Sunday school but not Hebrew school. I was confirmed but did not have a bat mitzvah. I often wished that I could read Hebrew. Once I knocked on the door of our rabbi's office and asked him to teach me. He gave me a book and told me to go home and learn on my own. Needless to say, that didn't happen. In fact, I did not learn how to read Hebrew until I was in my mid-30s. That was one of the first tasks I set for myself after quitting my job at the law firm and embarking on my Jewish journey.

The first synagogue we joined in Brookline was the Conservative shul in our neighborhood, not necessarily because it jibed with what we wanted in religious life (at that point we didn't know what we wanted), but because Conservative was the milieu we'd both grown up in and we assumed that was that.

That Yom Kippur, Mike and I were assigned seats in the rear balcony section of the sanctuary. The prayer book was all in Hebrew; no one on the *bimah* announced page numbers. People were yakking and ignoring the service. Mike got disgusted and went home with a splitting headache. I wasn't willing to give up. I felt a desperate need to connect somewhere, somehow. I walked out onto the street, turned the corner and headed down the block to a Byzantine-domed building. A tall flight of steps led up to a beautiful set of sanctuary doors. I had no idea what kind of synagogue it was, but it looked inviting.

"I have no ticket," I said to the first person I saw as I entered the foyer. "I'm new in town (that was more or less true) and I really need somewhere to attend services." It was early afternoon, and the bulk of the crowd had already left. There were many empty seats in the sanctuary. The usher who welcomed me turned out to be the executive director of the congregation, Temple *Ohabei* Shalom (Lovers of Peace). I settled in and got my first exposure to the *machzor* of the Reform movement, *Gates of Repentance*. I was delighted to see that it contained non-archaic English as well as Hebrew. It was comprehensible. It was poetic. The sermon was wonderful. I was in heaven.

Ohabei Shalom became my first, true, spiritual home and my gateway to a lifelong journey of Jewish self-discovery. We joined and rapidly found ourselves part of a multigenerational friendship circle. The rabbi was just a few years older than we were. He was new to the congregation and became our teacher and friend. His sermons and *d'vrei* Torah were brilliant, stimulating and intellectually thrilling. He taught mini-courses on fascinating subjects that were new and absolutely riveting to me. Dan and Amy felt at home there, and for the first time in my life I was part of a caring Jewish community.

For the first time in my life it didn't matter that my parents, siblings and extended family members were not on my Jewish wavelength. I had a rabbi and friends I could study with. When I sat in a class studying classical texts, I felt nourished and supported in my desire to learn. I was a member of a group with shared values. The fact that some of the people in that group were commentators who had been dead for centuries was irrelevant! I no longer felt isolated. I had always yearned for that sense of Jewish connection, belonging and community but had never experienced it before.

In 1988, Mike left academic medicine and joined a private practice in suburban Detroit. Eventually it dawned on us that we should think about having a bar mitzvah for Dan. With the encouragement of the rabbi at the Reform temple where Dan attended *Shabbat* school for special-needs students, we realized that this was doable and appropriate. It wouldn't be a typical bar mitzvah, but it would be meaningful for us and hopefully also for Dan. We hired a bar mitzvah tutor for Dan, a teacher in the special-needs program. Dan's mission was to learn the opening and closing Torah blessings and three verses from the Torah portion *Vayeira*. We transliterated the Hebrew words into words that Dan could read phonetically and printed them in large type on laminated cards.

My parents and in-laws seemed nonplussed when we told them about our decision to throw a bar mitzvah celebration for Dan. They were polite; they didn't argue with our decision, but they weren't enthusiastic, either. Maybe they were afraid it would be uncomfortable or embarrassing—a disaster of epic proportions. I know I had some concerns along those lines myself.

As it turned out, Dan's bar mitzvah surpassed all dreams and laid to rest all anxieties. Somehow, Dan seemed to know that he was the center of attention, and he reveled in it. At the key moment, sitting at a special wheelchair-height table on the bimah where the Torah scroll had been placed, he read from his laminated cards and repeated after the rabbi the words of the Torah blessings and his three verses from Vayeira. The sanctuary vibrated with the energy of Dan's achievement. So many people came up to us at the *Kiddush* to tell us how much the experience had meant to them. All the friends we had made since moving to Detroit were there. Family members from Philadelphia and Washington and friends from Boston flew in to be with us and celebrate Dan.

The following day, my mother hugged me goodbye before returning home to Philadelphia and whispered, "Now I understand why you decided to do this." Although she was alluding to our decision to have the bar mitzvah, I felt that her words had a broader meaning as well. It was the closest she ever came to acknowledging the validity of my choice to follow a Jewish religious path in life. We had proved a point by insisting on a meaningful, Jewish rite of passage for our son.

A year after Dan's bar mitzvah, I got my first paid job in the field of adult Jewish education, which broadened my awareness of the many different Jewish approaches to lifelong learning and gave me the opportunity to meet and work with rabbis from all parts of the Detroit Jewish community. Eventually, my family and I joined a Conservative synagogue, where I was encouraged to learn and do more as a Jew. Our daughter, a student at the local Schecter day school, became bat mitzvah at our Conservative shul in 1994. From temple to shul, my whole Jewish vocabulary had changed from the day I first walked into Ohabei Shalom that Yom Kippur afternoon!

Five years ago, with the help of two Conservative rabbis with whom I shared an interest in community-based adult Jewish study, I organized a project to "bring the learning to the learner" and pool resources for meaningful lifelong Jewish learning in the Detroit Jewish community. As of today, the project is co-sponsored by nine Conservative movement institutions, including the five local Conservative synagogues and the local Conservative day school. We've offered study groups in book stores, coffee shops, kosher restaurants, private homes, workplaces, the Jewish Community Center (JCC) and other "religiously neutral" venues. We send out weekly emails to hundreds of adult learners on our data base describing upcoming classes; we maintain an active Web site and lend out audiocassette tapes at no charge to those who can't make it to classes.

The project is now in its third year of a seed grant from our local Federation. I served as volunteer project coordinator for the first two years, and for the past three years I've received a nominal salary. The work has been stimulating and fulfilling, but now I'm thinking of what other new nonprofit activities I might want to explore.

Today, when I look at Dan, I marvel at all he has accomplished and realize that had it not been for him, I wouldn't have taken the enormous spiritual leaps that have enriched my life and enabled me to fulfill my dream of working pro bono (or, as the Jewish learner in me would say, *l'tovah*) to help make the world a better place.

We were both in places unimaginable during those first critical weeks of his life. I gave birth to Dan. In his own unexpected way, Dan gave birth to me, to the Jewish learner I always wanted to be. Truly, opportunity was born out of crisis.

CHAPTER 29

From Generation to Generation

The Story of Naomi Pinchuk

"WOULD YOU LIKE me to buy you a *tallis*?" I ask my daughter. Her bat mitzvah is barely two months away. She has prepared with characteristic dedication, and yet I am awed at her ability to master all that she set out to do. My daughter's eyes are soft and brown, and though her hair is a tomboy tangle of chestnut curls, I see the woman she will soon become.

"Yes," she replies. "Very much."

"Would you like me to take you, or would you like Daddy to?"

"No, Mom. I want you to take me." Her smile pierces my heart and forges a new link between us—two daughters of Sarah, Rebecca, Rachel and Leah, born of different eras on the threshold of this next phase of Jewish life. And I think: "Wow, I've accomplished what I unconsciously set out to do when I had daughters. In one generation, here's a complete transformation from my being, a sidelined Jew, to having made Judaism my firstborn's central experience. From a childhood of Sabbaths wrapped in my father's prayer shawl, braiding, unbraiding and rebraiding the fringes to stave off boredom, to raising a daughter capable of chanting entire Torah and *Haftarah* portions and eager to buy a prayer shawl, too. It didn't occur to Judith not to wear one, just as it never would have occurred to me to even think of wearing a tallis, much less actually praying with one around my shoulders."

And so we go to the Judaica shop run by a rabbi's wife from her house. In 30 square feet, Alicia has any- and everything a Jewish home might need—from small cloisonné *Shabbos* matchboxes to ornate menorahs wrought in Jerusalem stone and brass. The tallisim hang in individual plastic bags on a rack in a corner of the room.

Judith tries them all on—traditional white ones with familiar blue stripes, reekingly female pink silk ones, funky woven ones and intricate batiked ones.

I am amazed at how comfortable Judith is putting them on and taking them off as if she's trying on skirts and shoes at Loehmann's. Finally she chooses one in the most female way possible. Judith's tallis is soft white wool striped with navy and maroon. It matches her dress perfectly.

I wonder what my father would have thought to see the granddaughter he never knew shop for a tallis. Would he have been pleased? Offended that so much religiosity was going on when there were other options? Would he have preferred we raise our girls in the secular Yiddish-based Workmen's Circle or would he have thought it cool that we lived in a society where women had the option of being counted? I know he would never have been offended that women were entering men's domain.

My father wore a tallis because that's what the men did in the *shul* we belonged to. In Wichita, Kansas, there weren't many options. There was the Reform temple, but it was American and there were no immigrants my father could relate to there. Had there been Workmen's Circle, he likely would have gone there. But for him, the shul was the only game in town. That's where he felt comfortable. The ritual didn't mean a damn thing to him. He didn't consider himself religious or spiritual in any way. He went to shul as a 10th-man kind of thing, to be there for the boys.

He had his little *treif* knife that he used to cut his ham with in the garage. But ritual? It meant bupkiss. Nothing. That much I understood.

Being a Jewish girl-child in Wichita, Kansas, was to be doubly marginal. I grew up knowing I was Jewish and connecting with the feeling that it was important to be Jewish, but I always felt I had to justify it or explain it. I wasn't embarrassed to be Jewish, but I was keenly aware of not being part of the whole. It must be the feeling that people who are gay experience when they come to terms with it and then struggle with being socially comfortable. It is a strange conflict for me: on the one hand, I know who I am, but maybe the difference is I never felt safe as a Jew. Can you be born in a displaced persons (DP) camp to Holocaust survivors and ever feel completely safe being a Jew?

My daughters, on the other hand, feel safe; they are part of the whole. They take it for granted that the entire range of Jewish expression is there for them to grasp. I had never thought to be resentful as a child that the men got all the action. Girls were allowed to lead *Kiddush* and hold the *Havdalah* candle. Looking back, it seems so paltry, but it never occurred to me to protest or demand or even expect more.

When I married, my husband felt strongly about joining a Reconstructionist synagogue. It was totally egalitarian, and since there was no rabbi, every member had to participate. No longer relegated to the status of passive onlooker, I had to learn how to lead an entire service. It was hard in the beginning, but I did it. It wasn't until I attended Congregation T'chiyah that it occurred to me that worship could be anything but what I had grown up with.

Then a friend said she was going to learn to chant Torah and wanted a buddy. Was I interested? "Hell, yeah," I told her, even though it never would have occurred to me on my own to learn. I found that I loved it. It was a challenge to learn the tropes and make them sound like they are supposed to. I had watched men chant since I was a child and I derived great satisfaction entering a space of competency I always assumed was reserved for the guys.

My husband gave me a tallis to wear the morning of the adult bat mitzvah service, but I never felt comfortable in it. I didn't grow up with that as part of my experience and it just didn't feel familiar. I didn't touch it again until, at his and Judith's insistence, I wore it for her bat mitzvah service. Judith, however, wore her tallis every time she prayed. It was an integral part of her worship experience. When she went to a non-egalitarian synagogue soon after her bat mitzvah, she asked me if she should wear it. She was scared some of the older men would be angry with her or tell her to take it off, that it didn't belong around her shoulders. "Why should you care?" I asked her. "If you want to wear it, wear it." And so she did. I was proud of how brave she was. When we walked in, she put on her tallis, said the appropriate prayer and sat down. Some of the old men smiled and nodded at her. It was a very affirming experience for her, not at all what she had feared.

When it was my second daughter's turn, not only did Beth want a tallis, but *t'fillin*, too. That blew me away. It wasn't part of my father's experience, and certainly not her father's, but she said she saw the boys wear them at day school and if she was going to wear a tallis, she was going to wear t'fillin. It was all part of the package. And so back we went to Alicia's for tallis and t'fillin, and bless her, she didn't bat an eye. We left with two green velvet bags—one for the multi-hued prayer shawl that is as vibrant as Bethie is and one for the two leather boxes my daughter would soon learn to strap to her upper arm and forehead.

The female rabbi at school taught Beth how to wrap them, and the first time I saw her I was amazed. I thought it was wonderful. There was my own daughter, a competent woman, wrapping these patriarchal leather straps around her arm. And we're not talking about flabby arms here; we're talking young, strong arms; muscular, solid arms wrapped seven times with thin black leather. T'fillin usually evokes images of pale, weak *yeshivah* boys, but on my daughter the t'fillin looked substantial and damn near macho.

Bethie was making a statement of spiritual confidence and competency that women of my generation just don't have. To watch my daughters undertake something unavailable to me and integrate it into their religious identities is very exciting for me. They breathe it. I still have to think it. If I ask the question, *Do I believe in God?* it shakes up how I think of myself as a Jew. But Bethie can ask that question and still feel solidly, safely Jewish. She can and has led *Shacharit* services at sunrise in the Grand Canyon whether she believes in God or not. She can just be a Jew. It's who she is. It's who Judith is. And, damn the conflicts, it's who I am, too.

CHAPTER 30

Beyond Music

The Story of Sara Zivian Zwickl

I'VE ALWAYS BELIEVED my voice was a gift from God, and I've devoted a good part of my life to training it, culturing it and sharing the gift of my voice with others through performing. Whether I'm singing liturgical music or secular compositions, it's always been the thread that connects me. Singing is my way of entering God's presence.

When a friend's daughter honored me with an *aliyah* at her bat mitzvah service, I was taken by complete surprise at the overwhelming feelings I had standing before the Torah and chanting the blessings. The only other time I'd been called for an aliyah was the *Shabbat* before my husband and I were married, and while I remember that moment for all it portended—marriage, family, the promise of our own Jewish home—I didn't feel linked to God the way I did that August morning on Judith's special day.

Before the Torah reading, another friend and I sang a duet to Judith using the 16th-century prayer "*Y'did Nefesh*" as the accompaniment to a moving English text. The song serves as a petition for God's blessing upon the bat mitzvah and ultimately requests God's protection of her soul. The melody is hauntingly beautiful, and singing the duet to a young woman I love as a daughter was a moving prelude to my aliyah.

I still don't quite understand what came over me. Perhaps it was the fact that I was participating in the service in a way traditionally denied to women. Perhaps it was that, combined with the setting. Our friends had arranged for an outdoor ceremony beside a beautiful lake, and all morning our prayers had been echoed by the ducks swimming in the water beyond our seats. Red-winged blackbirds, perched on slender cattails, seemed to daven in time with our chanting.

As I stood before the lectern where Judith was to chant from the Torah, someone placed a tallis around me. The gesture electrified me, made the moment all the more sacred. I'd always experienced my voice as my connection to God. I was accustomed to that pathway, used to the feelings of closeness to God singing brings me. And while having a tallis wrapped around my own shoulders was unfamiliar, it was something that I had seen men do my whole life. The gesture says, "Now you are ready to be in God's presence." On an unconscious level I understood it for what it was, even though I'd never been the "shawl-ee." I'd never entered God's presence like that, and it was a shock to have a swirl of silk bring me to God in a way my voice never had.

I remember the satiny tallis on my bare forearm, the heat of the day and the love I felt for my friend's daughter. When I began to chant *"Bar'chu et Adonai ham'vorach,"* the first words of the Torah blessing, my eyes filled with tears. My voice, which I could always trust, wobbled. And I felt a connection to God the likes of which I'd never felt before.

It's as if, that morning, a different door opened and I experienced God in a way that people, males anyway, have for centuries. I didn't rush out and buy a tallis of my own, but I do carry the memory of that aliyah with me whenever I daven. Threaded into my own path to God is the memory of Judith's morning, of being shawled in the joy of celebrating a remarkable young woman and realizing my voice is but one way for me to reach God.

CHAPTER 31

Bat Mitzvah Symphony

The Story of Jane Kahn

AS TRANSFORMATIVE EXPERIENCES go, chanting my bat mitzvah portion last year ranks right up there with saying my I dos, giving birth, surviving the death of my mother, watching my children leave for college and beyond. There is nothing like it on earth. Because I am a musician, raising this inspiration of two years of religious study to the level of music completed a circle for me. The origin of the Hebrew word *shalom* comes from the word *shalem*, meaning "complete." I didn't feel particularly peaceful before, during or after my bat mitzvah ceremony—my heart was racing, my soul was soaring, and I was scared and filled with chaos. Curiously, though, I felt complete as a Jew in a way I had never felt before. Some Jews are born into families whose Jewish identity is fixed and more or less directed. The vast rest of us, if we get anything at all, get strength in one area, discomfort or outright antipathy in others. We get a Jewish identity but few ways of expressing it. A taste of knowledge, but perhaps not enough.

I can only liken it to the difference between a solo sonata and a symphony. A solo sonata is brought to life by a single instrument. Sonatic Jews, if you will, have families who capably and comfortably transmit Jewish heritage—prayers, Hebrew, *mitzvot*, synagogue life. The rest of us, and I include myself in this category, are symphonic Jews—our Jewish identity is composed over time from a vast medley of people, experiences and influences.

I twinned my bat mitzvah with my mother. It mattered little that she had been dead for eight years and had been lost in the haze of Alzheimer's disease for seven years before that. I was in midlife when I took that *yad* in hand and chanted Torah before 700 people in my congregation for the first time. My mother was inside of me, beside me. I felt her presence in every word and prayer. In becoming a bat mitzvah, I fulfilled a dream my mother had always had for herself and for me—Jewish knowledge.

Today you would call my parents humanistic Jews—back then they were strongly secular. My father, adamantly opposed to organized religion, didn't believe in God. My mother longed for a religious education and sent me instead. She was never comfortable reciting *Shabbos* blessings or performing any other Jewish ritual. She would light candles occasionally, leaving the prayer recitation to me. I sensed early on how awkward she felt and quit pressing her to make our Friday family dinners match the pictures in *Hillel's Happy Holidays*—the daddy with a *kippah*, the mother's hands covering her face in front of glowing candles. It wasn't their kind of Judaism.

But when it came to *g'milut chasadim*, performing acts of lovingkindness, my parents had no equal. They might not have known the phrase *tikkun olam*, but they knew what it meant to repair the world. In 1938, when my parents were 23 and 29, newly married and supporting their own parents, a desperate letter arrived from a father and grown daughter who were fleeing Vienna. Our last name and their last name were the same—Frank. They had obtained a page from the Baltimore phone book and had written to each Frank family pleading that someone have the courage to claim them as relatives so that they could get a visa into the United States.

My parents signed the necessary affidavit claiming that they were our family and accepted responsibility for Rudi and Eleanor Frank's support if needed (it never was). A two-year process to get them out of Europe ensued; my parents tracked their movements as they furtively slipped from one country to the next. From the day Rudi and his daughter arrived at the train station in Baltimore and for the next 37 years, my parents treated Rudi as if he were their own father. They cared for him in his old age and they buried him as children do. With great devotion, they cared for his elderly Viennese friends who had also managed to escape.

I asked my mother many times why they went so far for strangers, why our family was the only one of all the Franks in Baltimore to help. "Why?" my mother said. "We're Jews. You save a life, you save the world." These were parents who rarely went to synagogue but taught me one of Judaism's most crucial tenets. Like a bride who wears something old and something new on her wedding day, on the morning of my bat mitzvah I wore a small opal necklace Eleanor had once sent my mother.

During the *hakafah*—the marching of the Torah through the synagogue before and after the Torah reading—Ariella, one of my piano students, left where she had been sitting with her mother and ran to the back of the *shul* to wait for me. When I saw her I ran out of the line and threw my arms around her. Hugging that sweet 10-year-old, with her dancing eyes and beautiful smile, I felt as if I was embracing all of my piano students who have inspired me over the years. They are not just my students, they are my friends. Their love of Judaism has come across in our lessons and their love of learning has been an inspiration to me to pursue Jewish study.

Part of what motivated my switch to a Conservative synagogue and my enrollment in my bat mitzvah class was that I had come to know the congregation by attending my students' bar and bat mitzvah ceremonies. I felt spiritually moved by their services in a way I was never able to feel elsewhere. I am where I am Jewishly because of them. I embraced Ariella one last time before joining my friends as we carried the Torah to the *bimah* to be read.

We were a motley group, women representing a wide range of ages and experiences. During our course of study, some of us had lost parents; one had given birth. All of us gained strength from Ethel, who at 87 years of age modeled what we could make of our elder years. Ethel taught us that you can question a rabbi—graciously challenge him, even. She was the mother we could go to for wisdom and companionship. She called us her "girls." Her presence in our group enabled us to be there for her, to extend the boundaries of our Jewish lives to honor her in our community. That's what Jewish community is about, after all—giving, sharing, exchanging care and encouragement. As I ascended the bimah, Ethel gave me a wink of encouragement. The time to chant had come.

The human voice is history's first instrument. In order to sing, you need breath. All music breathes. That's the core of it. And as far as I'm concerned, that's what being a Jew is, too. God is about breath. God is the breath of our lives. And so, the first thing you do before you chant is to take a deep breath, to bring God into you. Hold that God-breath there for a moment—in fear, in exhilaration, in awe—and then you chant. The first time I did that at practice and realized the visceral connection for me between breath, God and music. I became a Jew—complete and integrated. In Hebrew, shalem.

Before I took my place at the lectern, the classmate who had just finished chanting squeezed my hand and whispered, "This was really fun! Don't be nervous." With her encouragement in my ears, I was determined to chant with all the energy I could bring to bear. *Do it like Elaine*, I told myself. *Do it like Elaine*.

If my mother and father's Judaism was the drumbeat of my life as a Jew, and my students the chorus, Elaine and Barry Gittlen have been the conductors. When I was a new mother, living in our first small apartment and bereft because my best buddy and duet partner had just moved away, God smiled and sent me Elaine. Not only did she become my next duet partner, she and her husband, Barry, became our Jewish guides. My husband and I still thank them for showing us how to make Shabbat in our own home, 25 years later; for inviting us for Seders, Rosh HaShanah and Chanukah; for guiding us in our children's Jewish education. Barry has taught me *Tanach*. Over the years, Elaine never showed astonishment at my lack of knowledge—she was simply there with gentle encouragement, whenever I called upon her. Her vibrancy and love of Judaism are palpable, and "doing it like Elaine" meant chanting my Torah portion with every ounce of energy and love for Judaism I had. And so I did.

Euphoria doesn't begin to capture how I felt when I reached the final trope, the "*sof passuk*" notes that signify the ending of a reading. (My husband said afterward that my voice had been so strong because there were two people chanting the portion—my mother and me!) When I was done, I looked at my family in the front row before me and saw again what I had seen in their eyes when they hugged me during the hakafah—they related to what I had done, they understood how bound to Judaism I felt and, most importantly, they were coming along with me.

Two-thirds of the way through my studies, my children commented to me how much more relaxed I seemed. After my first practice Torah chanting on the bimah, I began attending *Shabbat* services regularly. I stopped doing chores or any job-related work after Shabbat services. Instead, I read, listened to music and spent time with my husband. The kids noticed how serene my Jewish studies had made me. My daughter, who lives in Alabama, began writing to me for books to study, candlesticks and candles to bless, a mezuzah for her door. After my bat mitzvah she began lighting Shabbat candles weekly, baking her own challah, and driving an hour and a half to the closest synagogue for services.

When I began the program, my husband asked that I not insist that he come to services with me and that any decision to *kasher* the kitchen would be a mutual one. After my bat mitzvah, he casually suggested on our 30th anniversary that I might like to buy our meats at the kosher butcher. *Treif* was already out; we had stopped eating seafood at home. My son and husband now wear kippot at the Shabbat table and we draw out our Friday evening dinners, filling the expanse of time with songs and Jewish-oriented discussion. I see in their eyes pride and love, of course. But more than that, I see their expanding Jewish lives. What I have done for myself has wrought meaningful changes in my family. My husband now attends a weekly class at the synagogue with me, and when my son returned to college, he began attending Hillel services and social events with more regularity.

Becoming bat mitzvah, a daughter of the commandments, was not an end unto itself. Instead, it is the most powerful of beginnings. That I am a bat mitzvah means a lifetime of Jewish study. It means an infinite spiral of Jewish opportunities—to chant Torah, to receive *aliyot*, to share a new dimension of experience with my family.

The phrase *l'dor vador* pervades Jewish tradition. It means "from generation to generation" and alludes to the fact that Jewish heritage—ritual, language, ethics, and learning—is passed down through the millennia. For me, l'dor vador is the Jewish way of saying the symphony plays on.

CHAPTER 32

And Miriam Led the Women

The Story of Miriam Chaya

FOR 60 YEARS I walked around with a name I never liked. The name my parents had given me at birth didn't fit me. From my earliest memories as a child, whenever I heard my given name spoken aloud, I assumed that people were speaking to someone other than me. I would look around to see to whom they were talking. I didn't know what my true name was; I only knew that the name Harriet did not fit the person I wanted to be. It was too formal and inhibited me. Because of that name, I went through life with more caution than I needed, carefully weighing decisions before acting; and lacking spontaneity. As my 60th birthday approached, I decided to embark upon a spiritual journey that would eventually culminate in my taking a new name.

I enrolled in a Jewish spiritual leadership training program where I studied *Kabbalah* and Jewish mysticism. As I delved into my studies, I found myself drawn to ritual and began to understand the important role it plays in Judaism. Ritual touches the very heart of our Jewish experience, bringing deeper meaning to the rites of passage that structure our lives. There are rituals for circumcision; coming-of-age rituals for 13-year-olds; rituals for marriage and dying. All of these come with their own scripts and pageantry. As I was nearing 60, recently divorced after 32 years of marriage and taking stock of my future, I realized that Jewish tradition had nothing to ritualize my stage of life. There was neither script nor ceremony for reaching an age of wisdom.

In making the transition from my midlife to my elder years, I knew it would be necessary for me to shed some of the trappings from my earlier life. Ritual played an important part in this transition. When I sold the house my former husband and I had lived in for 28 years, I created a ritual for saying goodbye to that house and that life. When I moved into my new house, I invited friends to join me as we marked this rite of passage by creating a *Chanukat HaBayit*, a dedication for a new home. We put up a mezuzah on my front door and everyone gave me a blessing.

The Chanukat HaBayit ritualized the change in my physical life—I had a new place to live—but I was still looking for a ritual that would celebrate my new spiritual awakening. Judaism was becoming more and more important to me, and I wanted to have a ceremony to acknowledge my new commitment. Because I did not know of any other ceremony, I decided to have an adult bat mitzvah for my 60th birthday. I studied Hebrew so that I could chant from the Torah in honor of the occasion.

Immersed in my studies, I began to realize that the bat mitzvah ceremony did not fit my circumstances. It is a rite of passage for a young person making the transition from childhood to adulthood. I was leaving middle age and entering into my elder years. I wanted a ceremony that acknowledged my six decades of my life experience. I wanted a ritual to celebrate my aging and my wisdom.

When the rabbi showed me *Va'etchanan*, the Torah portion that was read when I was born, I couldn't believe my eyes. Tears ran down my face as I read the *Shema* aloud: "*Shema Yisrael, Adonai Eloheinu, Adonai Echad*—Hear, O Israel: the Lord is our God, the Lord is One." As I looked at the Hebrew text, I saw that "*Ayin*," the final letter of the word shema, and "*Dalet*," the final letter of the word *echad*, were larger than the other letters. The rabbi told me that the two letters spelled *eyd*, which means "witness." As I looked at the Shema I knew that I needed witnesses to my rite of passage and my name-changing ceremony.

About this time, I discovered a celebration-of-wisdom ceremony created by biblical scholar Savina Teubal when she turned 60. With the help of her rabbis, friends and leaders in her community, she had created a ritual which included community participation, a naming ceremony, Jewish study, a healing ceremony, blessings, acknowledging mortality, creating a legacy and a covenant or commitment. I was thrilled. This was exactly what I had been looking for. In the *Simchat Hochmah* ceremony, I could celebrate my aging and formally take a new name.

When I was born, I was given the Hebrew name Chaya Mira. *Chaya* means "life," and Mira is the diminutive of Miriam. As a child, I loved hearing stories of Miriam, the biblical leader of women—a prophetess, a seer and the sister of Moses. I imagined myself taking up a timbrel and leading the women in song on the far shore of the Sea of Reeds. I wanted to be Miriam. That is why I decided to formally take the name Miriam. I wanted to celebrate life, so I kept the name Chaya.

The night before my Simchat Hochmah ceremony, I decided to go to the *mikvah* to purify myself for my transformation. The months of study, planning and preparation had also been a time of letting go, releasing things from my past that I no longer needed. I wanted to immerse myself in the mikvah's waters to say goodbye to Harriet and to welcome Miriam Chaya.

As I entered the mikvah, I could feel something holding me back from fully immersing myself. Each time I tried to dip my body in the water, I felt like another being was present. When I heard a voice whispering in my ear, I could not deny the fact that Harriet was speaking to me. "Do not abandon me," she said. "We have known each other for 60 years. I am your history. I need you and you need me. Together we can be stronger. Let me come with you." As I listened to her voice, I knew what I needed to do. I held out my arms to embrace my past. Together, Harriet and I dipped beneath the surface of the water three times as we moved into the future.

The next day was my Simchat Hochmah ceremony. As I stood on the *bimah*, I looked out at the 200 people who had come to witness my life transition. I could feel Harriet's presence beside me. When the rabbi called me by my new name, I took a deep breath and felt a profound shift in my heart as I relaxed into my new name. When it was time to read the Shema and chant from the Torah, I felt Harriet's strength enter my body. Together we chanted in a loud, clear voice. When we finished, there was a hush in the sanctuary and I could feel God's presence. I waited a long moment, and then, standing tall and looking out at all of my witnesses, I declared, "From this day forward, I will be known as Miriam, the leader of women."

When the service was over, all of my friends and family ran up to the bimah to congratulate me. With tears in their eyes, they clutched my hand and begged me to teach them how they could create a celebration-of-wisdom ceremony.

The days following my Simchat Hochmah, I was ecstatic. The phone was ringing off the hook with more people requesting me to teach them how to create this kind of ceremony. I hadn't realized before how important this experience could be to other women. Their enthusiastic response showed me that I had to write a book or make a film about my experience in order to reach a wider audience.

My good friend, Judith Montell, an Academy Award-nominated documentary filmmaker, had filmed part of my Simchat Hochmah ceremony. I asked her if she was interested in making a film with me. When she said, "Yes," I thought I would jump through the ceiling with joy. Since I was a little girl I had wanted to be a filmmaker, and because I had had created a Simchat Hochmah ceremony, I now had my chance to see my dream come true.

Little did I dream that three years later on my 63rd birthday our film, *Timbrels and Torahs, Celebrating Women's Wisdom,* would be having its world premiere at the San Francisco Jewish Film Festival or that a thousand people would come to see it. Little did I imagine that the film would be shown at Jewish film festivals in Detroit, Buffalo, Boston, Washington, D.C., Miami, San Diego and Hartford, Connecticut; also in Allentown, Pennsylvania and Vancouver, British Columbia; or that the Berlin Women's Film Festival in Germany would invite Judy and me to show our film and talk to women in Berlin about celebrating aging.

The promise I made on the bimah when I took the name of Miriam is coming true each and every day. *Timbrels and Torahs* is the fulfillment of the covenant I made at my Simchat Hochmah ceremony. I have become a leader of women. I have created something of value to give to the Jewish community as my legacy. This documentary is my timbrel. Like Miriam before me, I take it up and I dance. *Hinei.* Take note of this: Our elder years can be a time of great creativity and promise. *Hineini.* I am here.

PART 9

Purim

If you keep silent in this crisis, relief and deliverance will come to the Jews from another quarter, while you and your father's house will perish. And who knows, perhaps you have attained royal position for just such a crisis.

—*Megillat Esther*

ON THE 14TH of the month of Adar, hilarity reigns as the holiday of Purim is celebrated. One is commanded to drink enough liquor so that it becomes impossible to distinguish between the phrases "cursed be Haman" and "blessed be Mordechai." In Hebrew these words become a tongue twister, so it doesn't take much. Children (and uninhibited adults) dress in costume; *hamantaschen,* triangular cookies dabbed with poppy seed, prune, apricot, or chocolate fillings, are enjoyed by the dozens. Friends and family give one another food baskets called *mishloach manot*, filling them with all sorts of goodies—hamantaschen, fruits, candy and the like. Joy and abandon reign. Giving to charity is also an important part of Purim.

The story of Purim is told in the *Megillah*, the Book of Esther. Esther, a Jewish maiden chosen by King Ahasuerus of Persia to be his queen, learns of a plot devised by the king's viceroy, Haman, to kill all of Persia's Jews. Esther's uncle, Mordechai, initially urges her to conceal her identity. However, once she becomes queen and has the opportunity to save her people,

Mordechai instructs Esther to tell the king the truth about her heritage. The new queen is reluctant to do so but ultimately reveals to the king not only her identity but the fact that his own viceroy plans to do away with her people. Haman is hanged on the gallows erected for Mordechai, who, earlier in the story, had incensed Haman by refusing to bow down to him.

Each time the name Haman is chanted during the public reading of the Megillah, cacophony erupts. Noisemakers called *groggers* are shaken to drown out the evil one's name. Many communities perform Purim *spiels*, plays that reenact the story of Purim.

CHAPTER 33

Making the World Safe for Pastry

The Story of Valerie Peckler

THE *PURIM* STORY is the first story of the Bible that deals in a modern ambiguity—disaster is averted, things work out in the end, but God is not explicitly in the text. There are no showy miracles in the Book of Esther—no splitting seas, no walls crumbling before the sound of a trumpet. What you have instead is a series of coincidences and ironic twists and turns. An obscure Jewish girl becomes queen and is thus in the right place at the right time to save her people. The king's evil viceroy plots against the Jews and in the end is himself punished with death. Esther's uncle foils a plot to murder the king. On a sleepless night, the king is reminded of this good deed, richly rewarding Mordechai while humbling Haman.

Things work out in the Book of Esther because people take risks. Did God put Esther in the palace and Mordechai within earshot of the plotters? Did He hoist Haman on his own petard? It's up to the individual reader to decide. What is unambiguous is that the element of human intervention averted disaster.

Esther, eponymous heroine of the Purim story, is as human as they come. She is one of many maidens brought to the king's court for consideration to become his queen. Initially, Mordechai advises her to conceal her Jewish identity. When the Jews are threatened with annihilation, Mordechai urges Esther to tell the king the truth. Esther has to be willing to risk her life to save the Jewish people, her people.

Esther faces a struggle many Jews today face. How "out" do we want to be vis à vis our Judaism? Do we speak up when a co-worker tells a Jew joke, or do we remain quiet so as not to make waves? Do we take opportunities to educate people about Judaism, or let the opportunities pass? As I have become more observant, the Esther issue is certainly present. People who don't know me well think I just happen to like hats. Others who know me better understand that the berets and baseball caps are my way of fulfilling the requirement for married women to cover their hair.

Regardless of what I do, people will identify me as a Jew, so why not enjoy all the riches that are mine because I am Jewish? Especially in the post-Holocaust era, a lot of people are edgy on some deep, unspoken level; they feel threatened or embarrassed to be open about their Jewish identity. You have to go through the fear and deal with it. We are a minority, and a lot of horrible things have happened to us throughout the centuries. Being visible means being vulnerable. I look at it this way: even the most assimilated Jews in Nazi Germany were murdered, so I might as well enjoy my heritage and celebrate my inheritance.

Different people do things differently. We Jews are different and so we do things differently. But that doesn't mean our way is wrong, second class, or better. It stands on its own merits. It is beautiful, enlivening and filled with wisdom.

In the Book of Esther, Haman said to the king, "There is a certain people scattered and dispersed among the other people in all the provinces of your realm whose laws are different from those of any other people. … it is not in your Majesty's interest to tolerate them." Haman painted these differences as a horrible thing. Some Jews react to their difference with a squirmy feeling of discomfort. Sometimes that discomfort is the result of ignorance.

I look at the difference my Judaism creates as an opportunity for joy and learning. I approach being Jewish in what has been called a counter phobic manner. We Jews have a lot of good stuff going on. Why not share it? I dispel anti-Semitic myths by being myself. I enjoy being kind and generous. I do so openly and joyfully. When others perceive these qualities, they will know that this kind and generous person is also a Jew. If they have been raised with the image of the stingy Jew, they will have living proof that it is a slanderous lie.

I consider Purim a wonderful part of my religious inheritance because it combines two of my favorite things about being Jewish—entertaining and food. We are commanded to share gifts of food—*mishloach manot*—with friends and family. When the kids were young, we would make up a huge mishloach manot basket to put in the teachers' lounge. In the fall for Rosh HaShanah, I brought in honey cakes to wish everyone a sweet New Year. Bringing *hamantaschen* was another aspect of sharing who we were. Putting the sweets in the teachers' lounge (as opposed to distributing individual baskets to each teacher) impacted a large number of people and created a forum for positive discussion and sharing.

My family lives within two calendar systems. Since Purim comes when no other commercial holidays are being marketed, it really got a lot of attention. People like to be remembered, and this was a great way to do something nice for my kids' teachers and teach them something about their students' heritage. After a few years, the teachers would start asking me in February when the basket of those "really good apricot, prune, and poppy seed cookies" was coming. We weren't teaching religion; we were simply sharing something we loved about our Jewish life.

One year I got a call from one of my kids' teachers who is Jewish. She had shared part of the Purim basket with her class, and a student's mother became incensed when she heard about it. The mother was enraged that Mrs. L was "teaching religion" in the school. I'm a good cook, but I've never had one of my desserts compared to a religious experience. The biggest irony, of course, is that God's name isn't even in the Book of Esther. This is a story about a people on the verge of annihilation whose destruction was averted by the courage of one young woman.

Mrs. L was brought before the superintendent. The teacher's Irish Catholic lawyer instructed the superintendent on the law of the land. She was able to keep her job. The issue finally blew over, but I thought, "If they can't handle Purim hamantaschen, what are they going to do with Ramadan?" God has become the last obscenity. I don't have a problem with nativity scenes. For me, the problem comes when people try to say that anything to do with Jesus is American and not religious, and anything do to with Judaism is religious and therefore subversive.

The fallout from the hamantaschen incident inspired me not only to bring candy and hamantaschen to work on Purim, but to dress up, as well. Why shouldn't I? My co-workers come dressed as Snow White and the Seven Dwarfs on Halloween.

It's terrible to feel so vulnerable that something as innocent as a cookie is perceived as a threat. We need to change people's perceptions and enable them to feel free enough to enjoy their own culture and want to share it with others. I share who I am with an open hand and heart. I leave aside the fear. I love my tradition; it's who I am. Judaism provides color, depth and community in my life. It connects me in time to a living ancient tradition.

And I never miss an opportunity to make the world safe for pastry.

PART 10

Passover

Passover affirms the great truth that liberty is the inalienable right of every human being.

—M. Joseph, Judaism as Creed and Life

PESACH, PASSOVER, FOLLOWS Purim by a month and a day and commemorates the liberation of the People of Israel from Egyptian slavery. Outside of the High Holidays, Passover is likely the most widely observed holiday of the Jewish calendar. Celebrated for eight days (seven in Israel and by Reform Jews), Passover begins with a ritual meal called a *Seder*, an hours-long celebration filled with food, discussion and singing that enables Jews to fulfill the commandment to retell the story of our going out from Egypt.

The most distinguishing feature of Passover is *matzah*, a flat cracker that substitutes for bread during the holiday. When the People of Israel fled Egypt, there was no time to allow their dough to rise. The flattened cakes they ate come down to us as matzah. The laws of Passover dictate that prior to the beginning of the holiday, the home must be cleaned of all *chametz*, that is, any food that might have any leavening in it whatsoever. No bread, no noodles, no cereal or cookies. The night before the holiday begins, some families conduct a chametz search. By candlelight, children set out with a wooden spoon and feather to collect bits of chametz that their parents have set out around the house for them to find. These last bits of chametz are set aside to be burned the following morning. Those who observe the law in the strictest sense will have in their homes only those foods that have been certified kosher for Passover.

On the Seder table are other foods symbolic of the Passover story—saltwater simulates the tears of the Hebrew slaves; horseradish represents the bitterness of their lives. An egg symbolizes the cycle of life; *charoset*, a savory mixture of wine, cinnamon, apples and walnuts, symbolizes the mortar used in construction of the Egyptian cities. Greens, called *karpas*, symbolize spring; a shank bone, *zeroah*, symbolizes the sacrifice of the Pascal lamb. Four glasses of wine are drunk, at prescribed times during the meal.

To entertain the children during the long meal, a tradition developed to hide a small piece of matzah called the *afikoman* during the early part of the meal. Toward the close of the evening, all children present are invited to search for the afikomen and then ransom it back to the head of the household.

The Passover story is told in a book called a *Haggadah*. *Haggadot*, plural of Haggadah, may be simple or ornately illustrated. They have long been an art form in and of themselves; there are hundreds of Haggadot to choose from.

CHAPTER 34

Out of Bondage

The Story of Joanna Berger and Sholom and Esfira Ilyasov

WHEN YAKOV AND Bella Ilyasov walked into my English-as-a-second-language class that first morning, barely two weeks after fleeing the former Soviet Union, I had no idea that ultimately their family would teach me far more than I could ever have taught them. They had escaped bare-bones with their daughter and parents—a couple of changes of clothing, a few books, a classical record or two. But no dolls for their 6-year-old daughter, Emily; no photographs or family heirlooms to give elderly Sholom and Esfira a touchstone in this strange new place called Southfield, Michigan, USA. But for the difference in time, their situation was little different than that of my grandparents—Jewish émigrés hoping for a better life—a life free from fear and persecution.

"Let all who are hungry come and eat," the words of the *Haggadah* command us each year. With 10 days to go until the first Seder, I realized the opportunity to fulfill this sacred mitzvah was right before me. I was thrilled when Yakov accepted our invitation to come with his family to our Seder.

My husband and I wrote a modified Haggadah in simple English so Bella and Yakov could follow along. My mother would be there to help us translate readings and conversation into Yiddish for Sholom and Esfira. And Bella spoke enough English to translate for her daughter Emily, whose only language was Russian. In writing that special Haggadah, my husband and I knew we had to tell the story of deliverance in a less lengthy fashion; but even in its shortened form, our Haggadah made clear the incredible tale of escape from bondage, of redemption by God, of the chance for a new life.

My husband and I wrote and rewrote, cut and pasted our Haggadah; the words glowed with new relevance. As we copied and stapled, I wondered what customs, if any, the Ilyasovs would recognize. Would the food be to their liking? Would we feel awkward with one another, or would that abiding link that exists between Jews serve to unite us despite all the barriers?

We went through the entire Seder, telling the story of the Israelites' escape from Egyptian bondage. This was the first time ever that Yakov and Bella had heard of this cataclysmic experience. What connections were they making? And Sholom and Esfira—what bondage had they endured? Edginess seemed to envelop Sholom. All night he kept touching the blue satin *kippah* covering his wavy white hair, and more than once I caught him looking around behind him with a wariness that stayed with him all evening. And then, after the children had found the *afikoman*, after we had sung the last song and were unable to manage another crumb of macaroon, Sholom asked in Yiddish if he could speak. His tall presence filled our dining room. Cautiously he looked left and then right and hesitated once again, as if debating the wisdom of proceeding.

"You don't have to be afraid," I said to him. And then, touching his kippah once again, Sholom began and spoke for twenty minutes straight, the words flowing from him like water breaking through a crevice in the ice come springtime.

"It was very interesting to know I was going to Seder. The last time I was at Seder I was maybe five years old. It was at my grandfather Yankel's. We could never have one after that. It was 1925. Or maybe '26? When I was a child in Moscow, we were not allowed to go to synagogue. We were expelled from the *komsomol*, the youth organization. In Leningrad it was the same. And when I became adult, if I went to synagogue, I lost my job right away.

"For 70 years I acted with one eye open to make sure no one is watching. At my last Seder, when I was five, six, I got to look for the afikoman; it was under my grandfather Yankel's pillow. When we found it, all the children got a small gift. Just like you, we had a cup for Elijah. I opened the door, and when I came back it was empty; I think my grandfather drank it. I think he was knocking the table from underneath to make the wine spill over on my grandmother's tablecloth. The cloth was very, very white, and the candles glowed so brightly. But then we no longer had Seder.

"So each Passover we would walk by the synagogue. It was locked up and we couldn't go inside. But every year on Yom Kippur and Passover we would be in the habit of walking by just to see the *Magen David* on the wall.

"When we came here to America we went to the grocery store, to the A&P, and right on the store wall was a Magen David. And food! Food for Passover right there when you walk in! So freely was the Jewish kosher food on the shelves. That's when we knew we were safe in America. But still you look behind you. This kippah I have on my head … it is the first time I wear one since the Seder at my Grandpa Yankel's. When my grandmother died, I wore a hat because I was told Jews covered their heads. So I covered my head. But the only way to cover your head was with a fur hat. A winter hat. In June.

"You see, in Russia we knew we were Jews but we never had any conversations about it, about Jewish history or things like that. We were Jews, but we didn't know what it meant until we came here. I told my son he needed to marry a Jew; I wanted to bring my son up as a Jew. Being a Jew meant preparing my son to marry a Jewish woman without knowing what Jewish was. So he married a Jewish woman. But still he didn't know what it meant. Tonight he knows.

"And tonight I have this kippah on my head. I eat herring and matzah ball soup and see the silver cup for Elijah. But we never saw a Seder like this. In America this is freedom; there are no consequences for going to a Seder."

We were wrung out when Sholom finished and sat down. Tears flowed down our faces. I looked over at my granddaughters. They were still transfixed. It is one thing to reenact symbolically with *charoset*, bitter herbs and matzah, the Passover liberation. It is quite another to experience it through an émigré's whispered retelling. I was grateful my granddaughters were able to experience this so early in their young lives. Never will we dip parsley again and not think of Sholom's exodus, when, with an outstretched hand, God brought him and his family out of the Soviet Union.

It would have been enough had God brought the Ilyasovs out from Russia and not brought them to America. It would have been enough had God brought them to America and not to our Seder table. And it would have been enough had He brought them to our Seder table and not enabled us to hear Sholom Ilyasov's tale of bondage and liberation. It would have been enough. *Dayeinu*. Amen.

PART 11

Marriage and Divorce

Since creation, God has engaged in making matches, a task as difficult as dividing the Red Sea.

—Jose ben Halafta

Husbands must honor their wives more than themselves, and treat them with tender consideration.

—Eliezer Halevi

THE JEWISH WEDDING ceremony consists of two parts: the *kiddushin*, betrothal or sanctification, and the *nisuin*, or actual marriage, which seals the betrothal. In Talmudic times the betrothal, also called *erusin*, was a legally binding engagement ceremony performed a year before the wedding. During the ensuing 12 months, the bride prepared her trousseau and the groom readied himself to support his wife and future family.

Today erusin and nisuin occur at the wedding. The rabbi who officiates the ceremony recites the two blessings once recited at the erusin. The groom places a wedding ring on his bride's finger and says in Hebrew and then in English, "Be thou sanctified unto me with this ring according to the laws of Moses and Israel." Next, the rabbi reads aloud the contents of the *ketubah*, the wedding contract signed and witnessed immediately before the wedding ceremony. The ketubah stipulates not only the husband's financial obligations to his wife during the marriage and in the event of divorce or his death, but also his promise to satisfy his wife's physical desires. After reading the ketubah, the rabbi reads the *Sheva B'rachot*, the seven blessings that consecrate the wedding.

Two elements are associated with the Jewish wedding ceremony—the *chuppah,* wedding canopy, and the breaking of a glass. Many different meanings are ascribed to each. Some say that the chuppah symbolizes the tents in which the ancient Israelites lived. According to another teaching, the chuppah represents the roof of the bride and groom's future home, open on all sides to welcome their guests. Other scholars say the chuppah calls to mind the groom's home, to which the bride was taken for the consummation of their marriage.

The breaking of a glass signals the conclusion of the wedding ceremony. A glass is wrapped in a cloth and is stomped on by the groom. There are several purposes behind this custom. Some hope the noise will frighten away any evil spirits hovering around the new couple. A more common understanding of the ritual is that amidst the joy, one must still remember the destruction of the Temple in Jerusalem.

While Orthodox Judaism forbids same-sex commitment ceremonies, the Reform and Reconstructionist movements allow their rabbis to preside over such unions. The Conservative movement does not endorse officiation.

There is a single mention of divorce in Deuteronomy, instructing a man whose wife no longer pleases him, because she has done something "unseemly" or "obnoxious" (suggestive of immoral behavior) in his eyes, to write her a bill of divorcement and place it in her hands. This bill of divorcement is called a *get* and must be presented to the wife before two witnesses. While Judaism recognizes that not all marriages will be successful, only the husband is allowed to divorce his wife. Without the get, however, a Jewish woman cannot remarry, lest she be considered an adulteress. A woman in this dilemma is called *agunah*, or chained woman.

The Reform movement does not require a get, but the Conservative and Orthodox movements do. A Conservative *ketubah* may contain a clause, called the Lieberman clause, which states that both husband and wife agree to abide by the ruling of the *Beit Din*, the rabbinic court of law overseeing their divorce. If the husband refuses to give the get, it is considered a breach of contract; one remedy to this situation is the dissolution of the marriage.

CHAPTER 35

The 18th Ketubah

The Story of Laya Crust

WHEN I WAS a child I loved going to *shul*. The sanctuary was filled with such a nurturing feeling. I loved the meditative quality of the prayers and the feeling of being on an island untouched by time. I also loved the music of the prayers that filled the space around me with such beauty.

The melodies had a multisensory affect on me because, when I was a child, I experienced music as color. Poetry was soft blue deepening into violet. When the cantor sang "*Hallel*," the colors exploded into a riot of oranges and golds. Can you envision stained-glass music? That's how I experienced Hallel. I don't know any other way to describe it other than to say when I went to shul, I stepped inside a kaleidoscope. The lilting rhythm of the Hebrew prayers swirled themselves together into endless combinations of hue and tone. I experienced the poetry of the psalms as the colors of the sea. The patterns were strong and beautiful and meditative. When I got older, that gift disappeared. Designing *ketubot* is as close as I have come to that transcendent synthesis of liturgy and color.

Creating ketubot, Jewish wedding contracts, came at me like a bolt of lightning. New to Toronto, I had enrolled in a Hebrew calligraphy class, not because I was interested in the art form, but because I needed desperately to connect with other Jews. It was a very low-level class. We were taught how to hold the pen, how to make certain strokes. For the final assignment, our teacher gave us an abridged form of the text used in the wedding contract and told us to execute a ketubah.

Nothing more than a quick exercise, that assignment opened the gates to my future. I made one and then another and another. Before I knew it, quitting my part-time job and devoting myself to my art was a viable option. I didn't realize it then, but the two driving forces of my life–my Judaism and my art—crossed paths and held fast within the borders of that holy document.

The ketubah is really the world's first prenuptial agreement. It codifies the man's legal promise to his wife "I will ... give you food, clothing, and necessities and live with you as a husband according to universal custom." That phrase "live with you" is a euphemism for sexual relations. At a time of Jewish polygamy, the ketubah protected a first and presumably older wife from being spurned by a husband who had taken a younger bride. Jewish law recognizes a woman's physical needs and legally requires her husband to fulfill them. The ketubah also dictates a husband's obligations to his wife and their children should he divorce her or die.

There are many rules governing ketubah. Two in particular govern the document's visual and physical execution. First, it must be legible. Second, the text cannot be divided in the middle or have big spaces within, because that would allow for extra words to be inserted, thus altering the contract's meaning and stipulations. Heeding these rules of design, the artist is free to take artistic wing wherever she wants. She can venture as far into Jewish history as she can research; she can plumb the depths of Torah or take inspiration from Israel or her client's back yard.

When I graduated high school, I figured if I took enough art classes I could finally quench my lifelong compulsion to draw. I reasoned that I would take some classes, finally put art aside, and settle down into something logical and grown-up. I took a drawing class. Next, a year of drafting. Then etching and lithography. By the time I completed the second year of an interior-design class, I knew I'd never be able to get the obsession to create out of my system. It *was* my system.

Despite this dawning realization, I couldn't stand the rigid authority of degreed art programs. I took a series of printmaking classes but dropped out because I didn't want to deal with fulfilling administrative requirements. Magically, I found a little school in Toronto that seemed tailor-made for me. The Three Schools of Art had no deadlines, no roll call, no attendance sheets. You went when you wanted and took as many classes as you wanted to take, and you left when you wanted to leave. I took every single class that I could.

Following Three Schools, I took the Hebrew calligraphy class, and a year after that a friend gave my name to someone who was looking for a ketubah artist. I used an article by David Moss in *The New Jewish Catalog* as my bible. As I worked on that first wedding contract, I realized that ketubah took all the things I had learned and loved, and even the things I didn't love, and put them into the most perfect package. The mechanical drafting class, so difficult I felt like I was biting into a rock, surfaced in the tightness and repetition of the borders. The sets of lines I had loved from etching and lithography classes found their way into my design. And then there was the text. I love the sound of Hebrew. I love the feel of the words, the cadences within the phrases and the memory of the color of them.

Avoiding the traditional art-degree route has a silver lining. The eclectic mix of art, design, drafting, history and Jewish learning that I had pursued on my own is the perfect preparation for ketubah design. Because of my background, I view themes, text, technique and images as separate elements to be integrated into a unique composition. I deepen the meaning of the piece by weaving in elements of design, art and history from different parts of the world and even different periods of Jewish history.

My first ketubah commission was followed quickly by others. It wasn't until the 18th ketubah that I began to understand that this new endeavor is about more than making a beautiful commission for a couple. I'm proud of ketubot one through 17. They are good pieces, but they don't have the depth that came after. It's like they are weavings that lack the added dimension that would elevate them to tapestry status.

A couple came to me with an image from a 12th-century *machzor* from Worms, Germany. It showed a medieval German interpretation of Jerusalem—a city of tall, thin, turreted buildings, their spires punctuated with pointed windows. The colors clashed; the border was heavy with curlicues, another medieval German design element.

The couple wanted this illustration to be the basis of their ketubah. Jerusalem and Israel were important to them, and so they wanted the inscription "We will place Jerusalem above our chiefest joy" included somewhere within the design. They shared how important family was to them; we discussed the cycles of our lives and family trees. Then they left the illustration with me and departed.

The central design of this ketubah is an archway. Imagine a door crowned by a semicircular pane of glass. The legal text of the ketubah is within the "door," and filling the "glass" semicircle above is a single tree passing through all four seasons. Moving from west to east, I painted its branches in autumn leaves, then bare, then dotted with the new green of spring, and finally, on the right, the branch is in full leaf and heavy with fruit. Inscribed above this tree is the couple's quote, and above the entire archway I painted my interpretation of the machzor illustration. To Jerusalem's left is the deep indigo sky of night pierced by a crescent moon and stars. On the right is the yellow disk of a noonday sun. Taken together, sun and moon symbolize the passage of time, the polarity between man and woman.

Because the couple had stressed how important Israel was to them, I filled in the background of the page with the entire landscape of Israel. I started with the green hills of Mount

Hermon and painted my way through the Golan, down to the Aravah, the desert and Eilat. I inserted the flowers one finds in Wadi Kelt and the wheat fields and orchards and communities nestled into Israel's hillsides. A pool of water flowing at the bottom symbolizes *Aqaba*.

I needed something to pull all the elements together and thought back to what was going on artistically in 12th-century Europe. I found my inspiration in a Flemish tapestry. Framing the entire design is a very dense, leafy border woven through and through with flowers and berries. In the finished piece it looks as if that central archway is crowned by medieval Jerusalem and floating over the landscape of Israel like a fairy tale.

The medieval-arch ketubah, as I have come to call it, has opened my eyes to what can really be done: the opportunities to pore through Jewish history, art and texts and pull out what resonates with me and each couple's desires. I am not just artfully executing a Jewish contract but am creating something that has the potential of carrying holy energy into the new marriage.

I truly feel that God has given me a gift. When I do something like the medieval-arch ketubah, I go into a very deep and faraway place. When I finish something that gives me that wow feeling, that's when I know I'm using the tools that God has given me and using them in the way that God wants them to be used.

Knowing what God wants of me is a struggle. Not only am I an artist and a wife, but I'm the mother of six beautiful children. My husband and I are *Shomer Shabbos*. We keep kosher and attend an Orthodox *minyan*. For a woman who has trouble with authority, I am nevertheless Jewish to the depths of my soul. I believe the tenets deeply. I recognize how just, how fair the laws are. I could not live nor raise my children any other way.

But the way women are dismissed is wrong. And I don't believe that this is because of *halachah*, Jewish law. I place the responsibility for the exclusion of women not just upon the men, but upon the men and women who refuse to acknowledge the openness of Judaism's original rules. People get angry at Judaism, but they should channel their anger at the community and the ruling rabbinate that shrugs its shoulders and says, "Out of respect for learned rabbis in learned times the rules cannot be made as lenient as they once were."

My art allows me to rise above these boundaries. Through my art I can be whom I want to be. I can learn as much as I want to learn, and no man can touch what I do. No rule tells me, "No, you can't." I explore and create and educate myself and process whatever I need to process for my art. There are no strictures limiting my art.

I doubt that I will ever re-experience the colors of the Hallel. God gave me that gift for that time in my life. But God left me with something in its stead. He gave me the 18th ketubah. Not the 17th, not the 19th, but the 18th. That was the ketubah that deepened the life in my art. That was the ketubah that deepened what art could bring to my life.

CHAPTER 36

Two Weddings and a Chuppah

The Story of Rahel and Barak Pardo

OF ALL THE challenges I anticipated when my husband and I married, intermarriage wasn't one of them. Can you imagine, then, waking up after 12 years of being wed to your soul mate and realizing that, while you didn't start out in a mixed marriage, you were in one just the same? It was a devastating situation and one that I knew I had little power to change. My only option was to wait and trust that, in time, my husband would choose to convert to Judaism.

We came from mixed backgrounds. Our heritages are mixed and so were the messages we received about religion. While Barak was raised by non-practicing Christian parents, his father had a curious affinity for all things Jewish.

I attended Catholic schools and was often told by the neighborhood kids that I should pray for my mother, since she was a Jew and would one day go to hell for killing Jesus. The Jewish link in Barak's lineage was an ironclad secret until the day an aunt became drunk at a family gathering and blurted out the truth: Bill, Barak's father, was the product of his widowed

affair with a Jewish man. The aunt's outburst
plained Bill's taste for matzah and the like, but the
evelation sent him into a depression from which
vered. Bill died, and soon after, Barak's mother was
horrific car accident that left her unable to care for
Siblings were sent to live with relatives. Barak lived on his own in his early teens, finding community and emotional support from Baptists who ran an inner-city mission.

Until the sixth grade, I was "white bread" like everyone around me. My parents raised us to be Americans. I didn't even know what a Jew was. We were all raised lovingly with traits of loyalty, goodness and decency. Yet I knew nothing of Jewish ritual or the Jewish calendar.

When I was about 11, however, I became curious. I asked the school librarian for some books about Judaism and she gave me Sidney Taylor's *All of a Kind Family*. Reading the novels in that series showed me Jewish life as a happy, normal, everyday sort of existence—a far cry from the accusations of heresy that my classmates leveled at me for having a Jewish mother.

In high school we studied the *Tanach*, calling it the "Old Testament." The nuns' teachings troubled me. They couldn't tell me why Catholics didn't observe the Sabbath the way the Old Testament commanded. How could the New Testament supersede a holy document that had revealed God's edicts "for all time"? Each time we read the phrase "The Lord said to the Children of Israel," something deep inside came to attention. I felt that the words of the Jewish Bible were talking directly to me. None of my classmates felt this way. I had no idea of the current events in the modern state of Israel at the time. I just knew that any mention of Israel in my Bible classes ignited a desire to explore further.

My curiosity and my dilemma continued into college. The Jesuit priests had no more satisfying answers than any of my previous teachers. They gave me philosophy books on Catholicism in an effort to reorient my quest, but it all seemed wrong. If God commanded the Children of Israel to keep the

Sabbath and that Sabbath fell on Saturday, why was Sunday our day of rest? Ultimately, I graduated from a secular university, left the Catholic Church and sought out churches that kept a Saturday Sabbath.

I met Barak at a Bible-study class that I held in my apartment for seekers such as myself. My friend Sharon was convinced that her brother, by then an ordained Baptist minister, was a perfect match for me, but I insisted I wasn't interested. I didn't want to marry a Christian, because I was still puzzling out my own religious identity. I wasn't looking for a Jewish husband, either, because I was nowhere close to claiming Judaism for myself. Sharon brought her brother to my class anyway. The moment I met him I knew he was my *beshert*, even though I hadn't yet learned the word. Simply put, Barak felt like my missing half.

Early in our courtship, Barak told me how frustrated he was that his seminary teachers could never explain why they professed to believe the whole Bible but ignored the teachings of the Old Testament, the book the Jews call the Torah. They claimed to live the whole Bible but sidestepped the commandments about the Sabbath and the holy days. The more he talked, the more I knew that I had found someone to accompany me on my own spiritual journey. Some months later, we were married by a justice of the peace.

I knew Barak and I were soul mates even though we didn't know where our souls belonged. We were on a quest for truth. We wanted to understand our place in the world and wanted to find a religious framework in which to live. Sometimes I felt like we were the Children of Israel, wandering toward a promised land whose existence we couldn't imagine but had faith we would one day find.

Like that of the Children of Israel, ours was a circuitous route. Barak and I studied with Christians who rejected the Trinity and didn't eat ham. We attended conferences sponsored by a "messianic" group and even went to a meeting sponsored by Pentecostals. The claims of the Pentecostals were downright disturbing. One swore he had been healed and could see out of his glass eye; some people spoke in tongues; and others lined up to be exorcised. It seemed like an old-time medicine show, and we quickly left.

As coincidence would have it, the messianics led us right into the heart of Judaism. A group of Jews for Judaism were distributing pamphlets outside the messianic meetinghouse. We read their material on the spot and asked them question after question. Their answers made more sense than anything we had heard so far. Barak and I began to pursue Jewish study to the exclusion of all other religious study.

I soon realized that in all the Jewish communities we learned about, whether in Iraq or Bokhara or Poland, where there was an allegiance to the Torah, the Jewish communities survived. As soon as communities stopped adhering to the Torah, they vanished. How strong the Torah's laws must be, I thought, to preserve a people for so many centuries. Spurred by this newfound understanding, I began lighting candles and using the *siddur* for prayers. The words were poetry to my soul.

Despite our years of study and tentative steps toward Jewish practice, I had yet to think of myself as a Jewish woman. Rabbi Shlomo Carlebach changed all that. He was in the area for a concert, and Barak and I decided to go. We had heard such great things not only about his music but about the healing spirit that seemed to emanate from him wherever he went. As he headed for the stage, he made a detour and came to where I was sitting waiting for Barak.

"Do you need to talk with me?" he asked. His dark brown eyes held some sort of question in them.

"No," I stammered. "I don't think so."

"I'll give you my phone number," he said, offering me his card. "Call me when you have a question," he said and walked toward the stage, guitar in hand. The lights dimmed, and then Shlomo Carlebach began to sing the most beautiful music I had ever heard in my life. There is a whole side of Jewish music that intellectual inquiry can't begin to reach. Rabbi Carlebach's melodies gave me answers that years of study hadn't delivered.

They awoke in me connections to my people that I hadn't known existed.

At intermission, I made my way to the edge of the stage, where dozens of people were already reaching out to him. Rabbi Carlebach turned toward me, his eyes still holding the same unasked question.

"My mother is Jewish," I said. "And my father is Catholic."

"And what are you?" he asked.

His question stopped me cold. From way down deep, the answer came to me. "Well," I said, "I am a Jew." Saying those words filled me with radiance. The moment those words, "I am a Jew," left my mouth, I knew they were true. I had always been told, "Your mother is a Jew and that makes you one, too." But I had doubted that I, a one-time Catholic schoolgirl, could really identify as a Jew. In the briefest of moments, Shlomo Carlebach allowed me to do what years of Jewish study had not. My soul had found its place.

In the weeks following the concert, I realized with despair that, radiance aside, I was now an intermarried woman. Barak was still my soul mate, but by *Halachah*, Jewish law, I was Jewish and he was not. Many people said, "Forget Halachah. What matters are the causes you support, the lives that you lead, the love you have for each other." We both knew from our study, however, that for us there was no way around Halachah.

It was a painful three years loving my husband as I did and feeling the conflict of our different statuses in the Jewish world. I started keeping two sets of dishes and bought only kosher foods. It all felt so natural to me, but it didn't to Barak. It was a very painful time in our marriage, but I believed the day would come when he would be ready. I trusted that he was still my beshert, and I trusted that he would know when the time was right.

Once Barak did feel ready to pursue conversion, the next hurdle was finding someone willing to guide him. *Chabad* was only interested in working with Jews. The Reform rabbis we consulted told us that living a Jewish life was enough. Barak was doing that, and so they did not see the need for conversion. The many Orthodox rabbis we went to pushed us away. We didn't understand at the time that tradition required them to refuse our request three times. A Conservative rabbi agreed to work with us, but we knew that unless Barak converted with an Orthodox rabbi he might never be recognized in Israel as a Jew. Finally, we found a modern Orthodox rabbi willing to look beyond Barak's unusual background and oversee his conversion.

Instead of hurry up and wait, Barak's conversion was wait, wait, wait and then hurry up! Getting to the rabbi on a regular basis was difficult because we lived so far away. Barak had been studying for nearly two years when some very dear friends gave us an all-expenses-paid trip to Israel. Barak did not want to go to Israel as a gentile. He wanted to go as one of the Jewish people, but the rabbi wouldn't rush the conversion for the sake of the trip. A Chabad rabbi we spoke with understood our dilemma and agreed to get the ball rolling.

One week later, in the presence of three rabbis, Barak submitted to the *hatafat dam b'rit*, in which a pinprick draws a small drop of blood as substitute for the ritual circumcision. He immersed in the *mikvah*. He put on *t'fillin* for the first time. Then Barak headed to the rabbi's house for our wedding ceremony. In a four-hour whirlwind, my husband became Jew, bar mitzvah and *chatan* (groom), all in one glorious night.

Our second wedding ceremony, 15 years after the first, was held in upstate New York under the stars on a cold November evening. Snowflakes swirled around us and our dozens of guests. I felt like a bride all over again. I was as excited standing next to my beloved as I had been a decade and a half before. We had been soul mates for so long. A new life stretched before us, and at the same time I felt as if my husband and I were finally returning home side by side, finally in step with each another.

The trip to Israel that had hastened Barak's conversion became our honeymoon. Walking through Jerusalem's narrow stone streets, we felt as if we had been there together once before. As a child, I had been the odd, dark-haired duckling in a neighborhood of blond swans. So many Israelis looked like me—olive skin, black curly hair. Time and again I was taken for a *sabra*. In more ways than one I was no longer a traveler, but *bat Yisrael*, a daughter of Israel.

Barak and I have been married for 24 years and also for nine. Our love for each other is deeper than ever. We have weathered many storms together—illness, unemployment, difficult crises of identity. We have two wonderful foster children whom we are raising to adulthood. We live on Barak's salary from his computer consulting business and mine from my social-work practice. We till our own garden and chop our own wood for heat. It is hard, but we are a thrifty bunch. Our lives are so very rich in countless ways. Barak and I were brought together by an unremitting quest for spiritual shelter. It didn't take us 40 years to find, but if it had, we would have kept going. We are each other's promised land.

CHAPTER 37

My Beloved Is Mine and I Am His

The Story of Daniel Shapiro

THERE IS A tale from the *Baal Shem Tov* that makes me smile every time I think about it. The story resonates for me in a very personal way because it describes how Greg and I have felt about each other from the moment we met. The Baal Shem Tov tells us: "From every human being there rises a light that reaches straight to heaven. And when two souls destined to be together find each other, their streams of light flow together and a single brighter light goes forth from their united being."

When I began to come to terms with being gay, the hardest thing for me to reconcile was the assumption that my homosexuality would prevent me from ever having the kind of Jewish life that my parents and all our friends had—the kind of life I grew up with. It was a devastating thought. I was raised in a committed, loving and close Jewish family in Montreal. I attended day school until seventh grade and was active in my synagogue all through high school. But ultimately there came a time when I could no longer deny that I was gay—and I realized being gay did not preclude me from leading a fulfilling Jewish life.

Greg and I met on a blind date. As soon as he opened the door to my knock, we felt an instant connection to each other. We spent three hours over dinner talking, mentally ticking off all the similarities in our lives—our trips to Israel as teens, fluency in Hebrew (a plus on both of our lists), nurturing family relationships, lawyer fathers. We both love kids and had wanted to have them but dismissed it as ever becoming a reality. Talking with Greg, I began to wonder if having a family might actually be possible. Driving home from that first dinner, Greg said, "So tell me, what is it that you're looking for?" I was excited that he was asking, even though this was only our first date. His question made it clear that he wasn't looking for a short-term, casual fling any more than I was. "I am looking for the love of my life, a partner to spend my life with," I told him. I called my sister the next day and told her that I had found him.

In time, Greg and I bought a house together. Many people interpreted this move as our commitment to the relationship. But our commitment to each other wasn't based on some material purchase. True, the house was a substantial joint expenditure, but it was not a statement of lifelong devotion. For that we wanted a wedding—a Jewish wedding. We wanted to make not a political statement but a statement of our love for each other and our joy in having found each other. We began to search for a rabbi who would agree to perform the ceremony.

We didn't know what we wanted the ceremony to look like, but we knew we wanted it to be solidly based on traditional Jewish rituals. I imagine saying "traditional ceremony" and "two grooms" in the same breath sounds like an oxymoron. For us, a wedding celebration was the natural next step in our relationship, and since we both have strong Jewish identities, we knew from the start that the ceremony would be Jewish.

We met with five rabbis with whom we had interesting and insightful conversations about marriage. But somehow we did not feel the connection we were looking for. When we met Rabbi

Michelle Missaghieh, something clicked. She had such a sense of energy and excitement about working with us. Although she'd never performed a same-sex ceremony, she was eager to explore the possibilities. As the potential officiant at our wedding, she was more concerned that both of us were Jewish than that we were two gay men. Had one of us not been Jewish, she would have refused to officiate. I was glad that she held consistent standards for her congregants, straight or gay. As such, we knew our wish for a Jewish ceremony would be possible.

Rabbi Missaghieh met with us several times in advance of the ceremony to study the Orthodox rabbis' wedding manual. Greg and I wanted to understand the intentions of each prayer and ritual to better choose which would make sense for us to incorporate into our ceremony. We considered variations of the traditional wording of the vow for the exchanging of rings and thought about substituting the phrase "in the tradition of Moses" for "according to the laws of Moses." In the end, we decided to replace the reference to Mosaic law with a selection from the Second Book of Samuel in which David speaks of his love for Jonathan. Some gay activists read a homosexual union into their friendship. We have no way of knowing what the nature of their friendship was. Taken at face value, theirs is a story of incredible and abiding loyalty. That was enough for us. Instead of *chatan* and chatan, groom and groom, we chose the phrase *reim ha-ahuvim*, or loving partners, which in my opinion specified quite distinctly what Greg and I are to each other.

Greg and I also wanted to involve the children who would be at the wedding. Between our siblings' children and those of our friends, there would be nearly a dozen kids there. We decided that as part of the ceremony we would invite all the children to participate in a seed planting. We have cedar boxes edging the perimeter of our deck and decided to give the children little packets of grape seeds to plant. The fruit of the vine is a symbol of great gladness in Judaism, and we wanted the children to know that as the grapevines grew over the trellis that makes up our *sukkah*, we would always have a reminder of their special place in our lives.

The day of our wedding was California perfect—sunny, warm, the sky a cloudless blue canopy. Our actual *chuppah* was a surprise gift designed and made by some friends of ours. They had taken rose petals and olive leaves and scattered them loosely between two layers of sheer, silvery fabric that were then stitched together to form our wedding canopy. The four poles holding our chuppah had been coated in silvery glitter and then encircled with eucalyptus leaves. Visually and aromatically, it was quite something. Each of our siblings held one of the four poles. As Greg and I stood beneath the chuppah, we looked into each other's eyes. I could see my thoughts reflected in his face, that the thing we both assumed was the most unattainable dream we could have ever hoped for—committing to our soul's mate in a Jewish ceremony surrounded by friends and loved ones—was happening.

"With you I make this covenant for I love you as my soul. Journey with me in peace and the Holy One shall be with you and with me." Saying those words from the Second Book of Samuel together with Greg was the most powerful experience of my life. It fulfilled all my hopes and more. By finding Greg, the best parts of me were strengthened and made brighter. After the wedding, a friend came up and said that our ceremony had redefined her view of marriage. Again and again we heard from our guests that they could actually feel the energy of our love for each other beneath the chuppah. The Baal Shem Tov spoke the truth.

We know people came to our wedding with some uncertainty. It's hard not to have anxieties about things that are unfamiliar to us, that are new and outside the routines of our daily lives. Greg and I, by creating the ceremony we did, by loving each other as we do and sharing it with those we care most about, were able to open up true possibilities of understanding where none existed before. Our wedding elevated our relationship with every person there to a new level of closeness and understanding. The ceremony wasn't about making a gay statement; it was about love.

Greg is the partner of my soul. The divine energy surrounding our love is something that exists beyond ourselves. We are simply the vessels, fortunate to have found each other in this life.

CHAPTER 38

Living Waters

The Story of X

I DIDN'T SET out to be a trailblazer, but an abusive marriage can do that to you. Make you fight and push and insist on getting the one thing you know will make you whole again. Even if that thing is, by convention, off limits to you, you will not stop until it is yours. That's how intent I was to experience *mikvah*; I was determined to use its living waters to reclaim my soul.

My kids were two and four years old when, one day, my husband asked me for a divorce. Right out of the blue, as if he were asking me to please pass the salt. I was devastated, and although he quickly backed away from wanting to end the marriage, it was a turning point for me. I made sure I finished college; I got three business degrees. We went into therapy. While I worked to be a strong and healthy person in the relationship, my husband became more and more controlling. He began abusing drugs and alcohol.

Then he began abusing me. Not just emotionally and psychologically, but physically, too. One day he hit me one time too many and I vowed if he struck me again it was over. I didn't have long to wait. He started a daylong attack one morning after breakfast. He took a nap in the afternoon and I thought it was over. But when he woke up he began all over again. I called 911 and the operator kept me on the phone until the police came.

Leaving the marriage meant going from one nightmare to another. It's not easy getting out of a relationship like that, because the man fights to keep things as they are. I was slandered; my mental competency was called into question. At one point he convinced the courts to commit me to a mental institution. That was the lowest time of it all. My ex-husband was awarded the kids, and I couldn't sleep at night for fear of what he what he would do to them.

Not until he attacked my son did the courts believe my claims that he was a violent man. Sometimes it seems they just don't listen until there is a dead body. Just because there are no gashes requiring stitches or giant black-and-blue marks doesn't mean that damage isn't being done.

You know that song from *South Pacific* about washing a man right outta your hair? Well, I got to where I needed to wash my ex-husband from every pore of my body, every crevice of my spirit. And being a Jewish woman, mikvah seemed the logical place to go.

But first I had to convince my friend L. She is Orthodox, and I knew she would make sure everything about the procedure was exactly as it should be. Like a radio that won't play if one wire is not connected properly, mikvah depends on all the elements being just right. The phrase "God is in the details" applies big-time to mikvah. I knew that L would ensure that all the connections would be made.

Being Orthodox, however, L's only understanding of women and mikvah was its use by a bride, or by a woman ready to resume sexual relations with her husband. My idea was from out of left field, but it was the only vehicle I could imagine that would allow me to separate from all the garbage that was my marriage. It was the only way I knew to disengage Jewishly from all the negative, impure parts of my married life. I wanted to put it behind me. I wanted a future—not just an abusive past. It took a lot of talking before L understood that in the wake of all I had been through, mikvah was the perfect response. Finally, she said yes.

The day of my immersion, I did everything by the book. I showered; I removed all my makeup. Then I took off my nail polish and trimmed my fingernails and toenails. I brushed my hair to loosen any stray strands and then combed the hair between my legs. Yes, the preparations are that intimate. That is how finely the body is to be readied for the encounter with divine waters.

Once you come from the shower, you are not allowed to let anything of the earth touch your body. Since we didn't have disposable slippers, L made a trail of paper towels for me to step on from the shower to the entrance of the mikvah. I was getting closer and closer to my dream. Maimonides wrote that mikvah is not just about physical immersion but about feeling in your heart what you want to purify. I had thought about taking this step for so long. I had spent so much time thinking about what my life had been and how intent I was on changing it. I wanted to be holier; once and for all I wanted to be unblemished.

The mikvah itself looked like a huge Jacuzzi. The entire area was tiled with large, white ceramic squares; painted around the top in gold were the prayers I was to recite upon coming up from the water. The room was still and clean and filled with expectation.

Right before I entered the mikvah, L noticed the red string on my wrist. I had worn it for so long I'd forgotten all about it. When I was in Jerusalem, a rabbi at the Wall tied it around my wrist and said a prayer over me. I had come to think of the string as my special amulet. When things got crazy with my ex, I would look at it and remember the peace I felt in Jerusalem. In one quick motion, L yanked it from my wrist. The mikvah would be my protection from now on. I was ready.

The actual submersion was very difficult for me. I do not swim, and I have an enormous fear of putting my head underwater and holding my breath. When I went down for the first time, I was barely below the surface of the water before I came up sputtering and choking. I thought I was going to drown. You're supposed to submerge completely, splay your fingers so that every fold of your body is touched by water. I stood in the pool and gathered my wits to try again. The second time was no better. I just could not make myself go under. Everything was a fight. The marriage, the divorce and now the mikvah itself. But I was not going to leave without going through this.

A certain percentage of the mikvah water is supposed to be living waters, that is, rainwater or snow or water from a sea, lake or stream. I thought back to my reading. The purpose of having living waters is so that the woman immersing herself can be embraced by God. When you marry, you make a commitment before God. My marriage had been a dark and twisted reflection of what a true marriage should be. I wanted something back from God. I wanted God to give me back what was taken from me—my sense of self, my dreams of a whole family, comfort within my body. I wanted God to return to me the ability to enter a new relationship one day without all the scarring. I gathered my courage and went down a third time.

The third immersion worked. After I came up, I recited the blessings, and for the first time in years I felt that I truly did have a future and not just an abusive past. I barely have words for the feeling of liberation I experienced. My husband had hurt my body. He had attacked my spirit. Mikvah enabled me to reclaim body and spirit for myself. My body was mine again, no longer an object for my ex-husband to abuse or hurt. I reconnected with myself without any impurity surrounding me. I was electrified with the sense of renewal, as if the mikvah waters were the amniotic fluid of my second birth.

Mikvah's joy and elation have stayed with me. When I receive court papers or I have to deal with my ex-husband, I only have to think about the mikvah to gather strength from the memory. I have the strength to deal with anything that comes my way. The living waters of the mikvah liberated me from the death of my marriage. They released me from the dangerous grasp of an abusive husband. Thousands of women are killed each year by their partners. I very well could have been one of them. But the mikvah washed all that away from me. It restored me to myself. Now and forever. Blessed are you, Adonai our God, who commands immersion in the mikvah.

PART 12

Yom HaShoah and Yom HaAtzma'ut

We are in possession of the divine assurance that Israel is indestructible and imperishable, and will always continue to be a preeminent community.

—Maimonides

HISTORICAL EVENTS IN the last century have led to the creation of two new Jewish holidays—*Yom HaShoah*, Holocaust Memorial Day, which is the day set aside to remember the six million Jews murdered during the Holocaust; and *Yom HaAtzma'ut*, Israeli Independence Day, which commemorates the creation of the State of Israel on May 14, 1948. The Hebrew word chosen for the annihilation of six million of the Jewish people is *Shoah*, which means calamity. "Holocaust" has its root in the concept of sacrifice by conflagration. The rationale behind choosing calamity drives home the reality that Jews were not sacrificed but out-and-out murdered.

Both days occur during April/May—Yom HaShoah on the 27th of the month of Nissan, and Yom HaAtzma'ut roughly one week later, on the 5th of Iyar. There are no prescribed rituals for Yom HaShoah, although each year more and more communities hold memorial services and invite survivors to speak of their experiences. In Israel, at 11 a.m., sirens sound for two minutes. All activity stops as the entire country comes to a complete halt.

In Israel, Yom HaAtzma'ut is celebrated with exuberant parties and often military parades. In the United States, some communities sponsor solidarity marches and daylong events centered around Israeli culture.

CHAPTER 39

Ring of Fire

The Story of David Bergman

WHEN I WAS about eight years old I asked my rabbi, "What does God look like?" Sixty years later I still remember his answer.

"I cannot tell you what God looks like," the rabbi said, "but when you take your last breath, you will see God. You will see a ring of fire, and there you will see God, in the middle of it." As a child, I visualized God's ring of fire being about as big around as the wooden rain barrel we kept outside the doorway between the garden and the back entry to our home in Bockow, where I lived with my parents, grandparents, sister and brother, in the Carpathian mountains of Czechoslovakia.

I never questioned whether God really existed in a ring of fire. I visualized the ring of fire even though I couldn't visualize what God looked like within it. When you're that young, you obey your parents; you trust what they tell you. What they say is *emes*, the truth, and that's it.

Five years after that conversation with my rabbi, I was thrown into a ring of fire much larger than our rain barrel. The ring of fire encircled concentration camps and extermination camps. The ring of fire encompassed unspeakable cruelty, humiliation, the darkest and most brutal side of humanity imaginable. It was a ring of death. And just like my rabbi told me, God was right there in the middle of it. I am here to tell of it, and because I am, I cannot but think that God was there, too.

I have not been so much concerned with the question "Why did God allow the Holocaust to happen?" From what I have seen and experienced, I have to say that the urge to kill and the urge to be compassionate are a combination of inborn traits and external environments. God planted within us the capacity to be cruel or compassionate and the ability to choose the path we want to take.

The questions I have wrestled with all these years are: "Why me? Why did I survive?" After years of pondering this, I have concluded that God doesn't give us the privilege to know why. If you try to answer why, all you can come up with is speculation, a belief and a guess. God only allows us to see the results. Those results can be survival, Israel or our grandchildren; it's up to us to see God's results. What I am aware of is that the answer to the question "Why did I survive?" is a series of extended events—one result after another—that kept me alive. "Why did I survive?" is the relationship I forged with God within the Holocaust's ring of fire.

When the doors to the freight train opened in Auschwitz, my eyes were filled with scenes of beatings. Of shootings. Women, children and old men cut down by bullets and clubs. It seemed no one was to be spared. In a single moment, everything I had read and learned in *cheder*—following God's commandments, praying twice a day—all of it went blank, as if it never happened. In its place a new force of survival took control of my life. I wasn't even aware of it. I had no time to think. Survival was everything. I went from having a family to suddenly being thrown into hell; from somewhere deep within me, there came a strong desire to live.

In the midst of all the chaos I heard a voice telling me to get out of the children's line. It was a silent voice; the words were in my head like when you are hungry and you hear an internal voice saying, "It's time to eat." You don't hear it, but it's a silent signal. Well, this was the same type of voice signaling me that I was in danger. "Get out of the children's line," it said. And there, in the line, I had a conversation with this voice.

"How do I get out of the line?" I asked it.

"The guards are watching you now. But see how they are beating the children? See the adults trying to go to the children? When the guards are occupied with them, run quickly to the adult side."

I have no proof that there was a voice. At the moment, I wasn't even thinking that I was communicating with God. All I have are the results. I am here. Within two hours, those in the children's line were all dead.

And so I followed the voice's command, waiting for the guards to be distracted and then making my move to the adult line. When I did, I found my father. But don't think that being in the adult line meant I was safe. In the adult line it was look and point, look and point. The Nazi officer quickly appraised us and pointed us to life or death. With a flick of his hand he wielded a malevolent inversion of God's power. When it came to my turn the officer stopped. "What are you doing in this line?" he growled. "How old are you?" As I was about to admit my age, the force inside me suppressed my voice and prevented me from speaking up.

Standing beside me, my father sensed something was wrong and told the guard I was 14. I wanted to shout the truth; my father had never lied in his life, and there he was lying to a Nazi officer! I didn't know then that I was standing between life and death. The Nazi officer ordered my father and me into the work line. Shortly afterward, my voice returned.

We were seven days in Auschwitz when an officer entered our barracks and ordered me, my father and 15 others onto a freight train that would take us to a work camp. When the door was bolted shut and the train began to move, my father announced to everyone present, "Today my son is bar mitzvah." I had completely forgotten about it, but my becoming bar mitzvah meant so much to my father that he risked his life, hiding a small bottle of wine in his clothes. He passed around the bottle of wine. They all took a sip and made a toast to me in honor of my bar mitzvah.

Three hours later, we arrived in the work camp of Plaszov. We heard that only those who had a trade would survive. When they asked for tailors, my father stepped out of the line. When they asked for bricklayers, the voice returned to me once again, telling me to raise my hand. And so I did and was put to work as a bricklayer. I followed what the others did—mixing cement and placing the stones to build walls. Five, 10 times a day we walked from where they mined the stones to where we built the walls. After three months, my father and I were separated. I never saw him again.

By May 1944, the Russians were getting closer; the Nazis sent me from Plaszov to Gross Rosen, another extermination camp. By this time I knew my life depended on convincing the Nazis I was old enough to work. The voice returned to me. "Tell them you are 16. Look them straight in the eye; tell them you are 16 and do not break your focus for a moment." When you look someone in the eye, they have to look back. I must have convinced the Nazi officer that I was 16, because he let me go to the work line.

Was the voice of God helping me to survive? I know I didn't do it all on my own. I have the results. There I was, 13 years old, not knowing why I was there, why I was being exposed to such horrible things. But I didn't have the luxury to dwell on such thoughts. There was not time even to give thanks when each time my life was spared. This was survival. Do you want to live or do you want to die? If you want to live, focus on survival. I wanted to live, and that phrase "I want" became the hallmark of my survival, the connection to the voice that kept me out of death's grasp.

In Gross Rosen, and then again in Reichenbach, I had close call after close call. One day I was standing in roll call waiting to be sent to work. We had strict orders not to move, not to look in any direction. But when I heard a noise in the sky, I couldn't hold back. I looked up to see American bombers streaking through the sky. I gazed at the sky with envy, just wishing I was in one of those planes.

Suddenly, the Nazi officer saw that I had disobeyed a rule. "*Schweinhund*!" he bellowed. "Pig dog! Why are you disobeying me?" Club in his hand, ready to beat me to death, he waited for me to answer. And the voice that had guided me every step of this nightmare said, "Focus on his eyes and stay silent." You can imagine the restraint it took not to stammer some excuse, not to plead for mercy. The entire camp was looking in our direction.

"I've got news for you," he barked. "You'll never make it out of this camp alive!" Still I didn't answer, and the voice inside my head said, "You will be free again and you will see their mighty country destroyed." And all of a sudden the commandant turned around and walked away from me! No one had ever defied a Nazi officer and lived. But I had. I listened to the voice and I survived. But I knew I was living on borrowed time.

I was not Reichenbach's only underage captive. In an effort to flush out those of us who were under 16, the Nazi camp commandant promised extra food rations to any captive who turned us in. In this way, I and about 15 others were pulled from the work group to be shipped to an extermination camp. Facing death, I focused as hard as I could on the desire to live and be returned to a work group. *I want to live. I want to live!* I repeated again and again to myself. All of a sudden I began feeling pulsations, similar to electrical shocks, emanating through my mind like mysterious Morse code messages.

Then someone in a work detail suddenly fainted. Instead of choosing a captive from the line of replacements, the Nazi camp commandant went from one end of the camp to the other and stopped right in front of me and ordered, "*Heraus*!" "Out!" He could have taken any of the captives standing nearby. He could have chosen any one of the youths from the group I was standing in. But he didn't. He came at me with an angry voice. He seemed to be moving against his will, like someone was forcing him. And he ordered me back into the work group.

I have wrestled with this issue for decades. What made the Nazi commandant walk across the entire camp, stop right in front of me and send me in as a replacement for the man who fainted? Those youths I had been standing with were all gassed. I got back to work exhilarated, if exhilaration is possible in such a circumstance. My elation lasted only moments. I knew this Nazi camp commandant was obsessed with not allowing children my age to survive, and I wondered each morning if it would be my last.

From Reichenbach, I and 150 others were sent to Dachau. I escaped the crematoria by yet another miracle. During that seven-day journey, we received no food. Why feed those who can no longer work? I had passed out and, being taken for dead, was placed on a wooden stretcher bound for the crematoria. A worker saw my hand move and smuggled me into a barracks where he and other heroic captives shared their meager rations with me so that I could survive.

Two months later, I was liberated. I came to America and during the Korean War was drafted into the Air Force. I was sent to Germany, and just like the voice predicted, I saw with my own eyes World War II's destruction of that once-mighty and forever-horrible country.

Some people are given the gift of creating art or music. I was given the gift of survival, the ability to visualize what I wanted. When my feet were cut and bleeding, I saw them whole and healing. Never once did they become infected. Never once in 14 months of captivity did I have a cold or develop any of the diseases raging through the camps. Never once did I have a nosebleed, something that plagued me before and after the war.

In captivity I had the choice of striving for survival or giving up. God didn't come and tell me, "Give up or not." He left it up to me; he built into me a striving for survival. The voice is with me to this day. In the morning I am in pain from arthritis, but I want to walk. I want to be with my beautiful granddaughters. And so

I walk despite the pain, and, boom! the pain is gone. I chose to marry. I choose to enjoy my grandchildren. I choose to balance my terrible memories with things that give me pleasure.

After all these years, I have concluded that the "I want" element that sustained me is actually the soul and the spirit of our being. It is the pipeline connecting us to God. When I was in captivity and said to myself, *I want*, I was actually reaching out to God, asking God to give me whatever it would take to survive. And sure enough, God was always there for me when I reached out to Him. Within the ring of fire I drew not my last breath, but my next. Again and again and again.

CHAPTER 40

"I Kiss the Imprints of Your Fingers"

The Story of Samantha Ashley

IN HONOR OF my becoming bas mitzvah, my mother framed Great-Aunt Jennie and Great-Uncle Joseph's *ketubah* for me. It is all in Aramaic, of course, and the margins are decorated with birds, trees and animals in gold ink. The ketubah hangs above my bed, and every night before I go to sleep, I think of Jennie and Joseph, how in love they were and how sad it was that they never got to live "happily ever after." But I don't dwell on the sadness. Doing that would mean Hitler won.

Besides the ketubah and memories, all Great-Aunt Jennie had of her marriage to Joseph Perla were some photographs, a desperate telegram or two and letters—a whole box full of letters. One of my aunts found the letters during the week of Jennie's *shivah*. They were on the floor of her closet in a shoebox beneath some old sweaters.

No one ever talked about Aunt Jennie's marriage to Joseph. Growing up, my mom didn't even think it was a true story. She thought it was all made up, even though Aunt Jennie always kept a photo of Joseph on her dresser. Mom saw the photo often and still never even asked who Joseph was. By the time my grandmother, Jennie's baby sister, came along, Joseph's name and the fact that he had been my great-aunt's first and only husband were barely ever mentioned.

The basic story is that sometime in 1938, Great-Aunt Jennie and Joseph Perla met in Cleveland. She was visiting from Detroit, and he was visiting from Poland. Perhaps Joseph had a teaching assignment that brought him to America—we never found out. There must have been a strong spark between them, because Jennie returned to Poland with Joseph, met his family and married him there.

This was right before the war, and the U.S. government advised all American citizens living in Poland to return to America because the political situation in Europe was so unstable. Jennie returned to Detroit alone. Joseph wasn't an American citizen and, with the war coming, getting a visa was next to impossible. Jennie tried and tried to bring him over but failed. Eventually, Jennie got word that Joseph had been shot and killed in one of the mass deportations that took so many of Poland's Jews. But, in between their marriage and Joseph's death, the letters from the bottom of the closet tell the story of her husband.

Unraveling the mystery of Joseph took me from Aunt Jennie's house to a Yiddish professor at the University of Michigan, to Poland at the time of Hitler, and finally to the day of my bas mitzvah, when I shared all I had learned about my great-aunt's husband, Joseph Perla, with my friends and family. It was fate—my having begun to study Yiddish a few months before Jennie's death; needing a speech topic about a Jewish experience for my bas mitzvah at Workmen's Circle; and then finding Joseph's letters. It all fit together.

The first thing my mom and I did was to organize the letters—there are 150 of them—in chronological order. Since they are all either in Yiddish or Polish, that was the only thing we could do until we found someone to translate them for us.

My Yiddish teacher introduced us to a woman, a survivor, who was able to translate a few, but I think it brought back too many memories for her. She cried when she read the letters, and I also think she was uncomfortable because some are so personal. But my mom and I just had to know what was in them. Translating the letters was a quest we had to fulfill.

Finally, my mom found a man who teaches Yiddish at the University of Michigan—Holger Nath. Even Holger's story is incredible. He was born in Germany after the war. When he was a child, there was a trial in his town to determine if former Nazi officials who still lived in the town should be charged with war crimes. Most of the townspeople said, "Leave them alone." But Holger's mother wrote a letter to the newspaper stating that the men should be held accountable for their actions during the war. Holger's family (who aren't Jewish) were threatened by local people still involved in Nazi activities.

The experience got Holger interested in Jewish studies and the Yiddish language. He went to Oxford to study and from there to Columbia University in New York. When he found out the University of Michigan needed a Yiddish professor, he took the job. And that's where my mother found him. Luckily, Holger said he would help us.

The day we went to meet him in Ann Arbor was foggy beyond belief. Mom could barely see through the windshield; it was gloomy—spooky even—like everything was a black-and-white movie. We got lost a couple of times, and the tension in the car was pretty high. I think we would have turned around and given up if it hadn't been so important.

We finally found Holger's office, and when he took up the first letter and started translating, it was like the walls of his office disappeared. The story began telling itself. We were transported back in time to April 1, 1939, the date of Joseph's first letter to Jenny's parents, my great-grandparents:

> *Thank you for congratulating Jennie and Joseph on their marriage. Our luck will surely be your luck. Jennie is probably on the ship today. I wanted to keep her a few weeks, but the ship company advised her to leave immediately because the political situation is unclear. She left me with lots of loneliness*

and worry. Even so, I am very happy that I met, in my life, your dear Jennie. We have a bond forever. I smile at myself because in spite of my sadness I am happy.

Holger was a wonderful translator. He read the letters slowly and we took notes. We went through every letter, year by year. Holger did more than translate the letters. He paraphrased Joseph's words and gave us a sense of the emotions behind them.

April 1, 1939
I wrote this letter the day I took you to the train station. I wish we had a few more days together in Warsaw. I will stay in Warsaw and teach myself English so I won't be a complete " greena ."
Mid-April 1939
I got two letters from you from Paris. You write to me in Yiddish and Polish, and if it is not too hard for me, I will write to you in English letters. When you left you didn't take any documents. Who will believe you that I am your husband? Even Roosevelt will look at you strangely.
April 26, 1939
The consulate says they haven't received my papers. That is a lie. But I cannot prove it. So I am still working at the children's summer camp. I am very healthy and busy all day.

The more Holger read, the more alive Joseph and even Jenny became to us. Joseph had a sense of humor; he was kind; he was a strong writer. In one letter he wrote to Jenny, "I kiss your freckles." I began to see my aunt in a totally different light. I had always been close with her, but I never saw her as anything but an old woman. I realized how much I didn't know. In Holger's office, Aunt Jennie began to be more real to me in death than she was in life.

In one of his letters, Joseph tells Jennie about an evening he spent with his friends, talking about her. They were sitting in a barn talking about "Red," their pet name for Jennie. They traded stories about how American they thought she was.

When you study the Holocaust, all you ever get are horrible pictures of skeletons and piles of clothing. Or lists of facts and figures. Joseph's letters brought people to life for me. They weren't only victims; they had wonderful lives. They laughed; they had adventures; they went to school and worked. Of course, the sad part is it was all destroyed; but if we know more about them than the facts and figures of how they died, we can celebrate the wonderful parts of their lives. They cease being victims and instead become human beings once again. This is something I think Holocaust educators need to do better.

Holger noticed that as time went on and the situation got more desperate, Joseph's handwriting changed, became more frantic and the tone of the letters changed from optimism to despair.

August 20, 1939
I believe people will get through this. They are scared, but it is not serious.
August 26, 1939
I was going to wire you to send tickets for the ship, but unfortunately it is still not time ... the situation is stressful and getting more critical all the time.
May 10, 1940
I have received a letter from the American consulate that tells me that you have wired something to Genoa for passage. But I have not received a letter from the ship. Maybe you could intervene.
December 2, 1940
I have been working without a break to drown my sorrows.

There were times when we had to take a break. It was so sad. We knew how it would all end, but Joseph was still alive where we had left him in the letters. It was a very strange little bubble of time we were in. In an office in Ann Arbor, Michigan, in 1995 and spun back in time, too. By 1941 the desperation in Joseph's words is apparent.

April 25, 1941
I thank you for the 300 zlotys and your letter with Sylvia's child's photos. This encourages me and is a symbol that somewhere my dearest person is alive. I kiss the letter and

study it and I am already crazy. Jennie, my dearest you are my most important problem ... I only want you. Your breath, your smell, your nearness. If I can't have you, I can't have anything. ... To whom should I tell the secrets of my heart and soul? ... You left me alone that I should have to feel so much pain. You did too much injustice to me. How and when will I find you again, my dearest? ... Write, my dearest, write. I kiss the imprints of your fingers. Stay strong and healthy.
Always yours, Your Joseph.

I can understand why the woman we first went to was uncomfortable reading Joseph's letters, but I don't feel I am intruding. The joy of Joseph's love jumps off the page. Why should we remember his death and not his life? It's all part of who he was, this wonderful, loving man.

This is Joseph's last letter to Jennie:

November 16, 1941
I kiss you very much for your letters of September 20, September 30, and October 27. I love you more and more. I've written to you many times. Your letters encourage me and make it possible for both our lives to be better together in the future ... I would love to prove to you that I am okay. I work; I earn money, but that is not all I need ... When will we be together? When? What day? What date?
Good night, my good Jennie, good night.

By the time Holger finished that last letter, we were exhausted. Joseph's spirit was there with us, as if he had come through the fog to tell us his story himself. He had. It's one thing to be in a Holocaust museum and read those little information cards about the exhibits. It's quite another to live through what happened to one single person. The person who was my great-uncle. Joseph was smart and kind, and I am glad my aunt married him. I think if I had met him I would have liked him a lot. If I ever have a son, I will name him Joseph for sure.

At my bas mitzvah, Joseph came alive to everyone who was there. Through these letters, I was living witness that Hitler failed in his plan to destroy Joseph Perla. Doing this project meant that

I could give voice to one person's life. You can't destroy someone forever. You can kill them, but you can't kill what they stood for. What they gave the world stays. Joseph stays. If the letters taught me anything, it was that. Everyone who attended my bas mitzvah now remembers Joseph. And anyone who reads this will know that Joseph Perla died, but more importantly that Joseph Perla lived. This is what he wrote:

I am Joseph Perla. My father is Meir Perla. My mother is Leah Necha Perla. I was born on July 18, 1910, in Siedlce.

CHAPTER 41

Standing at Attention

The Story of Nancy Lipsey

IT TOOK THREE of us to carry the headstone off the bus and into the cemetery proper, mud sucking at our feet every step of the way. I realized that it had rained each of the seven days we had spent in Poland. The damp, gray skies fittingly underscored all we had witnessed and experienced.

In 1989, I was one of 4,000 American teens from all over the U.S. and Israel on a recently-developed excursion called the March of the Living. The march is a two-week trip held in the spring of each year. Scheduled to coincide with Yom *HaShoah*, Holocaust Memorial Day and Yom *HaAtzma'ut*, our trip was planned so that we would spend one week in Poland followed by a week in Israel.

The name of the trip was chosen in deliberate repudiation of the Nazi death marches that took the lives of two-thirds of Europe's Jewry during the World War. The march itself was to begin in Auschwitz and end in Birkenau, the former a work camp, the latter the final way station on a journey toward extinction. The Nazis, with customary inhumanity, forced thousands of starved and dying Jews to walk from one town to the other. Our purpose was to turn it around, to make that same march and leave Birkenau as so many hadn't—alive.

Four thousand of us, silent save for an occasional sniffle or sob, made the 30-minute walk. It was the middle of the day and the townspeople came out to watch. They didn't heckle us, but they stared at us like we were freaks. I suppose it was a bit strange, thousands of Jews converging upon their corner of the world to take a walk from town to town. But hadn't they seen it already? Likely some of them had anyway. It was impossible not to imagine what had transpired decades before. We could have been Jews from a roundup of nearby Kotzk, famous for the Hasidic Kotzker *Rebbe* who put the town on the map, as it were, a century and a half before.

Tales of the Kotzker Rebbe are anything but joyous and lighthearted. He is surrounded by whispers of darkness and anger. In his book *Souls on Fire*, Elie Wiesel writes of a Sabbath in 1839. The candles have been lit and the Rebbe's disciples await his blessing over the wine and bread. But no blessings are said. The Rebbe waits in a silence that begins to unnerve all present. Then, writes Wiesel, the Rebbe "throws back his head and—" No one knows what transpired. Wiesel tells us that according to scholars, the witnesses seemed to have taken a vow of silence.

More than a century and a half later and still no one knows. Wiesel offers three scenarios, the third of which is curiously prescient. "Having learned of the pogroms that were laying waste to the Jewish communities of Poland and Russia, the Rebbe reportedly flew into a rage, pounded the table with his fist and roared: 'I demand that justice be done! I demand that the supreme legislator obey his own laws!'" And then, according to supposition, the Rebbe fainted and was carried to his quarters upstairs, where he remained for 20 years until his death. Was the Rebbe calling for an accounting from God that, post-Holocaust, Jews still call for in vain?

In Kotzk we toured this tortured leader's home, now occupied by everyday Poles. Our guide pointed out the small opening in the center of the living-room ceiling, beneath which the Rebbe was said to have performed weddings. On winter nights when it was too cold to hold the ceremony out of doors, the wedding party and their celebrants crowded into the relative comfort of the Rebbe's home, yet still beneath the night sky.

It was our custom to go to the cemeteries of each town we visited. Nothing prepared us for Kotzk's. In others we had seen headstones, sometimes only a few, re-erected by loved ones, but in Kotzk there was nothing. Not a headstone in sight. It was as blank and yawning as the Rebbe's infamous *Shabbos* exhortation. We trod uneasily through the cemetery, disturbed to be walking on what were surely graves.

When we exited through the cemetery gates, people were standing around pointing at us and talking. Someone approached our guide. "Here, bring them to my house. I have something to show them." The guide translated the elderly man's garbled words. He was bent over; his coat was thin and shabby. You couldn't help but do the math and wonder where he was when the Jews of Kotzk were rounded up and deported in a single night. Where were his parents?

We followed the man into his yard, followed with our eyes the gnarled hand pointing to his porch. There, holding up the back stairs, were slabs of granite. We could make out scraps of Hebrew and realized that we were looking at headstones most likely taken from the vast waste of the Kotzk cemetery. How could they have done this, we asked, uprooted headstones from a cemetery and used them as building blocks?

Our guide explained that after the war the Poles assumed the Jews had all been eliminated off the face of the earth. And since there was a shortage of building supplies, well ... .

A second neighbor from across the street approached our group. "Come," he said, "follow me. I have one, too." And sure enough, propped under his stairs, leaning against a crumbling concrete wall, was another headstone. I don't know who in our group thought to buy it, but we took up a collection—50 or 60 dollars—and gave it to the man in exchange for the headstone. It was covered in mud, but you could make out Hebrew letters here and there. We paid the man and struggled with it to the bus, not knowing what we were going to do with a 100-pound piece of granite.

Then someone said we should return it to the cemetery. Our guide had the bus driver turn around, and in moments we were back at the cemetery gates. We paid the guard a second time and then huffed and puffed with our precious burden until we were well within the grounds. We didn't want to make it too easy to remove a second time.

As gently as we could, we leaned the headstone against a lone tree. Taking napkins and bottles of seltzer water from our lunch kits, we cleaned away decades of mud, hate and indifference as best as we could. "Yehoshua ben Dovid" was as much as we could make out, but that was enough. Whoever Joshua, son of David, was, his headstone was a prayer's length closer to being where it belonged.

The Hebrew word for headstone is *matzevah*, and it comes from the word *nitzaveh*, meaning "to stand at attention." Recovering the headstone, restoring it to its rightful locale if not its original place, was our way of standing at attention, as witnesses, mourners and even avengers.

By the time we got the headstone in place, we were covered in mud and the sky was rumbling once more. We wanted to mark the place, somehow make the statement that we had been here and record what we had done. Rummaging through my lunch kit, I found a wooden paddle. I had no idea why it was there, but I took a pen and wrote on one side of it how the headstone came to rest where it was. I wrote the date, signed my name, and stuck it in the ground beside Yehoshua ben Dovid's headstone. Then we said a quiet *Kaddish* and left.

As we trudged through the muck toward the bus, I felt good. We had done a mitzvah. Though one of the Kotzker Rebbe's main teachings was to disassociate one's mitzvot from one's self so as not to wallow in the ego, we couldn't help but feel gratified at the morning's turn of events.

There is a lot of *Kabbalistic* teaching that says a soul cannot get to heaven if it is not properly buried. Yehoshua ben Dovid had likely been buried properly, but without a headstone there was no way to remember him. Now there was.

From Kotzk we went straight to Auschwitz and the beginning of our march. As we filed off the bus in Auschwitz, I felt the souls of dead and dying Jews all around me. We were all thinking the same thing: that we would enter Birkenau and then leave it, not as smoke and ash but with bodies intact. I was somewhere in the middle of the marchers. There were 2,000 people ahead of me and 2,000 behind. The profound quiet was like nothing I'd ever experienced. The march ended in Birkenau before a pile of rubble—the remains of a crematorium bombed by the Allies. We had a ceremony and then were asked to take the paddles from our lunch kits, write the name of someone we knew who was lost during the Holocaust on them, and place them around the remains of the crematorium. Minute by minute, little slips of wood were transformed into makeshift headstones memorializing those who would never have real ones.

I was happy we had instinctively used my paddle for its intended purpose. We recited Kaddish once more, and I thought of Yehoshua ben Dovid. I had no idea who he was, what his place was in the town, whether he had been a disciple of the Kotzker Rebbe or had died in time to be spared the calamity that Hitler visited upon his town. Had his descendants perished and so never again said Kaddish for him? I was in tears like everyone else around me, but I was also quietly happy. One soul from Kotzk would now be remembered. I placed my lighted *yahrzeit* candle beside the rubble and returned to the bus.

CHAPTER 42

A Cohen by Any Other Name

The Story of Don (né Rogers) Cohen

YEARS AGO, PEOPLE would occasionally ask about my surname, "What kind of a Jewish name is Rogers?" In one way or another way, I explained that it was the kind of name a Jew uses when he needs to pass. That it was the kind of name my grandfather needed when he came to this country. There came a time in my life, however, when I needed the name Cohen. No one ever had to ask, "What kind of a Jewish name is Cohen?" It's as Jewish as *kreplach* and *Kol Nidrei*. Cohen is the kind of Jewish name a Jew sometimes has to give up to make his way in the world. It's the kind of Jewish name a grandson reclaims when the lives of his fellow Jews are in jeopardy.

"I'll give you a job," an attorney told my grandfather in 1922, "but I'm not hiring someone named Shalom Cohen." At 13, a greenhorn in need of a job, my grandfather became John Rogers on the spot and reported to work as a runner the next day.

When I told my grandfather that I was taking back the family name, he couldn't understand why I would do such a thing. Rogers had been his ticket into the workplace, his entrée into freedom and prosperity. As Rogers he had a life; as Cohen he had nothing. I understood where he was coming from. My grandfather's Jewish identity was fired in a different time and place; Rogers gave him a measure of deniability. For me, Rogers was an unnecessary scrim cloaking who I was in every part of my life but name.

My father had planted the seed of resuming the family name when I was quite young. "Your grandfather was born a Cohen," he occasionally reminded me over the years. "Maybe one day you'll take it back." His subtle hint stayed with me, but it was not until the hijacking of TWA Flight 847 that his suggestions coalesced into action.

The first thing the Hezbollah terrorists did upon taking over the TWA plane was to perform a selection. Going passenger to passenger, they confiscated wallets and purses looking for Jewish Community Center (JCC) or synagogue membership cards, or passport stamps revealing a past trip to Israel. They looked for *chai* and *Magen David* necklaces. They read driver's licenses and checkbooks, seeking Jewish names, doing anything they could to cull the Jewish travelers from the others.

I don't know what I would have done in that situation. We Jews have a commandment to live, to pursue life. Would I have hidden under the safety of Don Rogers? I am not second-guessing anyone who lived through that nightmare, whether they said proudly, "I am Jewish," or whether they stowed a JCC membership card beneath their seat. I just know that from my helpless safety in San Antonio, I needed to do something to express my solidarity, to make the statement "I am a Jew." The time had come to change my name.

As coincidence would have it, I appeared before one of the few Jewish judges in San Antonio. When she asked me the reason for the name change this far into adulthood, I explained the origin of the family name and the impact the TWA hijacking had had on me. I told her that taking back Cohen was my protest statement. "I wish you the best of luck," she said. "Go ahead and do it." She smiled and signed the paper, and it was done. I left the courtroom to be forever after known as Don Cohen.

It was stirring for me to be able to say, "This is my protest against the terrorists of the day." On a metaphysical level, Cohen is a very powerful Jewish name. It connects me to Jewish history directly back to the priesthood. I had always had first *aliyot*, but the first time I was called to the Torah after changing my name, I felt a deeper connection to the blessing I was about to recite. I was truer to who I was, truer to whom God had chosen me to be.

The second reason I changed my name had nothing to do with the Hezbollah hijacking but with an author by the name of Charles Silberman. In the early '80s he wrote a book whose thesis was that Jews had made it in America and that they no longer needed to hide their Jewishness. I think he went a little overboard with his theory, but the basic idea resonated with me. I wanted to test his theory and know that I was accepted for exactly who I was. It was important to me to know whether or not I could make it as a Jew in this country. If I couldn't, I reasoned, then this wasn't the country for me.

When I look back on my name change, I realize it was a statement of commitment to American democracy. And while I feel very comfortable living here in America, I still view being a Jewish American as being on the margin of society. Groups on the margins help keep America true to its democratic ideals. We Jews in America have a unique responsibility and opportunity to push in different ways to make sure democracy is applied to us and everybody else. That's how I viewed my job when I was regional director of the Anti-Defamation League (ADL). When I insist on equality and respect as an American Jew, I am doing it in the best tradition of what our laws, our Constitution and our Bill of Rights are supposed to be. They are the bedrock of what this country is all about.

I can't say that I fought with more zeal as Don Cohen, that I took on riskier issues or challenged the hate groups harder. I didn't. The reality is that I worked just as hard. The name finally caught up with the Jew.

CHAPTER 43

Getting Fit

The Story of Ellie Gersten

I WAS IN Israel like a zillion other Jews flooding into the country in the weeks preceding and following the blitz of the Six-Day War. At 21 and idealistic as all hell, I was going to live out the dream they fed us in the Diaspora. I found my way to Kibbutz Endor near Afula in the north. There was a song we used to sing as teenagers called "The Dreamer." It went something like this: "What did we do when we needed a town? We hammered and we nailed till the sun went down." That was going to be me. Picking apples from dawn till noon and studying Hebrew in *ulpan* till the sun went down.

I lasted three weeks. Picking apples wasn't for me, but there was no way I was returning to the States, either. Israel was in my blood and I wasn't ready to let it go. I hitched a ride to Jerusalem without a plan in my head and talked my way into a one-year study program at Hebrew University. Bible, Jewish sociology, history, psychology, Hebrew—it was a very special thing. Jerusalem was amazing. Was it Herzl who said we'll know we have a Jewish state when both the criminals and the police are Jewish? That's what electrified me about Jerusalem. Everyone was Jewish—the bus drivers, the mailmen, the cops—even the prostitutes.

An Orthodox student in my program befriended me and asked if I'd like to learn more about Jewish tradition. I was like a milkweed seed, content to go whichever way the day's wind was blowing. She took me to a session given by a rabbi and his wife. After one of the sessions, my new friend asked me if I believed in God. I shrugged an assent. "Then why don't you follow God's laws?" she asked. For some reason, that's all she needed to say. It all clicked. I quickly became religious. The whole nine yards: modest dress, keeping the laws of the Sabbath and of *kashrut*. I jumped in with both feet. I felt like Super Jew—ready to take what I was learning any- and everywhere.

The laws of kashrut bring a sense of holiness to the act of eating and dictate which foods are permissible to eat and which are not. I learned a lot in a short amount of time and was determined to follow the laws as closely as I could. Dairy products, or *milchig*, and meat products, or *fleischig*, may not be cooked together nor eaten together at the same meal. Only fowl such as duck, turkey or chicken may be eaten. Only fish with fins and scales are permissible. Shrimp, scallops, crab and the like are *treif*, as are all pork products. Eggs, fish, vegetables and fruits are classified as *pareve*, or neutral. They may be eaten with either meat or milk.

The laws of kashrut also extend to how an animal is slaughtered for human consumption. The Torah prohibits consuming an animal's blood, because blood is life's own source. Therefore, not only must all blood be drained from the ritually slaughtered animal, but the meat must then be salted to remove even the smallest traces of blood.

Neilla, another friend who kept kosher, heard about a trip to the Sinai organized by the university and signed us up. She said she'd take care of all the details, sleeping bags, towels and the like, as well as the necessary items to enable us to follow the dietary laws—double sets of plates, cups, eating utensils and cooking pots. All I had to do was show up.

The night before the trip, Neilla remembered that she had a major test the next day and bowed out. I had already paid my money and was really intrigued by the whole idea of Sinai. A weeklong trip in an open-air truck with wooden slats and no back? Why not? The milkweed seed was ready to drift again.

All I remembered from the prep instructions was to come dressed in layers, the idea being you'd layer up in t-shirts and sweats in the morning when it was cool and then take off what you needed to as the sun rose. What did I know from Israeli layering? Where I grew up, you layer up with heavy stuff in October and then don't take it off till spring shows up in June. I was cold. I was hot. I was miserable. And meanwhile I was hungry and had not the first fork, spoon or pot; milchig or fleischig.

So I scrounged. I didn't have a thing, and yet I never went without. Every meal someone would give me something—an extra plate or fork or cup. I had never been in a state of such absolute need and such instantaneous giving. It was like receiving manna from heaven—people on all sides helping me, giving me what I needed simply because I asked.

Keeping kosher gave me such a strong sense of community. It's funny because the party line has it that keeping kosher builds strong Jewish ties because you can eat only with other kosher-keepers. On that trip, I was the only one keeping kosher. Yet everyone, Israeli and foreign student alike, came up with doubles of everything for me. There was no ridicule, no snide comments or teasing. I'd go up to people and say, "I didn't plan for this trip. Can you spare a—" and they would hand me whatever I needed. For all I knew they thought kashrut was a silly relic from 17th-century Poland, but they helped me just the same. Burning with a novice's commitment, I felt I was doing what was right, and it brought me community and generosity every which way I turned.

After nearly a week of hikes and rides through the desert, sleeping under magnificent skies, in monasteries tucked into the mountains, and on concrete floors of captured Egyptian barracks, a half-dozen of us pooled our money and rented a hotel room in Eilat for the night. Six of us slept crosswise on the double bed. You don't know what a *mechayah* (relief) a hot shower is until you are covered eyebrows to toe hair in five days' worth of desert grime.

We woke up ravenous and of course had barely a shekel left over to buy breakfast. We were standing around trying to decide how we were going to eat, maybe scrounge some leftovers from the bus boys' trays, when a UPI reporter approached us and asked if we needed help. "We want to eat," we told her. And just like that, she bought each of us breakfast. She wouldn't give us her name or even her address so we could mail her money back in the States. "Don't pay me back," she said. "But when you are in a situation where you can help someone, do it." Ever since then, I help people whenever and wherever I can. You can't do anything in life on an empty stomach.

By '75 I'd stopped keeping kosher. I was married by then and my husband wanted no part of it. In the end it wasn't worth the fight. I still don't mix milk and meat and don't eat treif, but my kosher days are long gone.

Looking back, I realize that the whole adventure into kashrut wasn't so much about separation as about togetherness. Keeping kosher brought me dead center into the Jewish community, right into the heart of Jewish generosity. It taught me a lesson beyond waiting six hours between roast beef and ice cream. Like that movie that came out a while ago, *Pay It Forward*, keeping kosher showed me the beneficence of the world, modeled for me the commandment to give generously to total strangers. The word kosher has nothing to do with food, anyway. The literal translation is fit. It is fitting to give to those in need.

CHAPTER 44

Building a Relationship Stone by Stone

The Story of Dr. Lawrence Schwartz

TO BE HONEST, I don't like the scraps of paper in the Wall. I never have. I've never put a prayer in, either. Not when I was 16 and visiting for the first time, not when I returned for two weeks at 25, not when I led teen tours during a yearlong sojourn. When I look at all those scraps of paper scribbled with prayers and petitions, it makes the Wall seem like a wishing well. And the Wall is nothing like that to me. My relationship with the *Kotel* is so much more complex; it is a relationship that will last a lifetime.

The first time I saw the Wall, it seemed a lot smaller than my teachers had built it up to be during all my years of Hebrew school. It wasn't nearly as impressive as I had expected. I didn't walk into the plaza and see the Wall glowing with dawn or sunset. It didn't loom over me with importance or speak to me of martyrs or heroes. I thought to myself, *You mean that's it? It's only a piece of the whole thing anyway.*

I had been looking forward to this trip to Israel, but actually, at that point in my life, you could have put me on a bus to Topeka and if I knew that I'd be away from my parents for six weeks and have my Camp Ramah friends with me to party, I'd have been just as happy.

As I approached the Wall, I tried to feel some kind of emotion; I knew it was a momentous structure, infusing Jewish historic memory for centuries, but it made no more of an impression on me than would have a trickle of sand on my palm. People were crying, deep in thought, swaying in prayer. I put my head on my forearm and leaned against the Wall the way you see people do, trying to feel something other than a vacuum, but there was nothing there for me.

The Ramah trip was your classic teen tour. We spent three weeks in Jerusalem, had all the discussions you're supposed to have—religious versus secular, Arab versus Israeli. We spent a week hiking in the Negev and another two in the north living like *chalutzim*, pioneers. The details that I remember most center on going to the pubs with my friends and goofing around the dorms with them. The trip formed my Jewish identity, but I just didn't realize it at the time.

On the way to the airport, some of the kids were already crying, sad to leave what they had experienced as a wonderful place, a fabulous trip. "We have a few extra minutes," our counselor said as we neared the taxi ranks near the Wall. "We have time to make one last stop at the Kotel. But only for 15 minutes. No more." It was evening, the first time I had seen the Wall at that time of day. It had that glow you hear about; the play of colors from the setting sun tinted the stones, making it stand out, loom larger than I'd remembered from previous visits.

I watched people approach the Wall, pray, stuff their paper scraps in the crevices. My best friend, Ronnie, was crying and I wondered why I wasn't. I just stood there noticing everyone else. I wasn't feeling anything but confusion. I was upset that I wasn't crying the way Ronnie was; that I couldn't find it in me to pray; that I had no use for paper petitions to God. I felt the way I had during my every visit to what is supposed to be Judaism's holiest site—distant, unconnected.

And then, as I was walking away, I started to cry. I don't know what brought it on, but the tears just started flowing from my eyes. I headed toward the bus, and as I passed one of the guards at the checkpoint, he looked into my eyes and said in that accented English Israelis have, "Don't worry. It will be here the next time." And I stopped crying just like that. He smiled at me; I don't even think I looked back, but on the bus I began to think about that brief encounter. How a soldier not much older than I, had known exactly what I was thinking. That I did want to come back. That I knew I would one day.

That was the moment my Jewish identity was driven home to me with a clarity I've never since experienced. The soldier and I were kids whose lives were about to take such different paths. I was getting ready to go to college and party, and he was in the army, about to face an uprising that would last for many years. His experience and mine would be so different, but for that one moment, he knew what I was thinking simply because I was a Jew and he was a Jew and we were at the Kotel, and that was that. Still and all, the next time didn't come for nine years.

The winter of my fourth year of med school, I realized how much I really hated it. I withdrew all my intern applications from hospitals and took advantage of an opportunity for two weeks of travel in Israel. The experience was to be used as a springboard to write programming for a Ramah summer program. I had stayed in the Ramah movement, moving from camper to counselor. A lot about the Judaism that Ramah represented had become very important to me, and ultimately it became important for me to teach it to kids.

The Israel we saw during those two weeks was not what the Israel tourists see. We studied science, technology, the peace process and the environment. We went to industrial plants, not the Arab markets in the Old City; to sites from the wars, not Masada. I saw Israel in a completely different light: a country in its own right, a nation trying to advance as any nation would. I returned to the States to finish up my fourth year of med school and then determined that before my medical career went any further, I wanted my year in Israel. In Jerusalem, close to the center of the city. Close to the Wall.

I wouldn't always visit on Shabbat, but I began visiting the Wall more often. Just to go and be there in that atmosphere. I wouldn't necessarily pray, and I still wasn't interested in pushing a paper prayer into ancient cracks, but I began to visit the Wall as one would a close friend—picking up the conversation the way you can with someone you've known for a long time—without any awkwardness or preamble.

And then Prime Minister Rabin was killed. Up till that point I had kept quiet about political discussions. I spent a lot of time listening and getting a feel of the place. I was having dinner in a restaurant with a friend when we heard the news. My friend and I went to Kikar Tzion. We were surrounded by Israelis arguing about whose fault it was. Soldiers were constructing makeshift memorials. I awoke at 5:00 the next morning to make the walk to the Knesset, where Rabin's body was lying in state. The air was cool and crisp and scented everywhere with the smell of burning wax. The soldiers looked blurry-eyed with exhaustion. I heard later that one million people filed past Rabin's bier in the 20 hours before his burial. From then on, I was a part of Israel; I had completely bonded. It was my country.

A few months later I was asked to lead a tour group of teens visiting for a semester. It was a miserably cold, damp February morning. I walked the kids through the city and had them tucked in behind an alcove so that they were near the Kotel but couldn't see it. Then I gave them a reading I had found. It consisted of eight paragraphs telling the story of the Kotel from the Wall's own perspective. I can only paraphrase it now, but the gist of it was this: *I am a stone in the Wall, 3,000 years old and the center of Judaism; I am a stone in the Wall, a brick of desecration, a stone of destruction, of occupation, of liberation, of restoration.* The last reading was one that would have been mine a decade before: *I am not a stone in the Wall. I am just a kid, and I don't know what it means to me. Just let me be; quit overwhelming me and let me feel what I want to feel.*

What I feel for the Wall 15 years later is not a glow-in-the-dark kind of love or passion sparked with lightning bolts. There is nothing gushy about my feelings for the Kotel. Instead, it's something strong and close. You can go to Hawaii, love it, and have a great time, but it's not real. When I go to Israel, it's real. I pay bills, ride the bus; it's normal living, with all the frustrations and achievements that life brings.

I could talk to you about Israel for as long as you'd like to listen, I love it so much. I would make *aliyah* tomorrow, but my family is here. My friends. So my life is punctuated by next times.

I'm dating a girl now; we've become close and quite serious in a surprisingly short amount of time. There's no gushiness with her, either; no spinning cartwheels the way things had been with other girls before. But all the same, something just feels right. I know that when we part she will be there next time. I'm familiar with that feeling. It is deep and true. I trust it. I have felt it before.

CHAPTER 45

Mother Tongue

The Story of Eve Roshevsky

"*ADONI, TASIR ET hadegel mipni! Lo y'chola lir'ot!* Mister, move your flag from my face! I can't see!" Jerusalem, 1968. *Yom HaAtzma'ut*—Israeli Independence Day. And not just any Independence Day, but the first one since Israel won the Six-Day War. The crowds are berserk with joy. Everyone's shouting and singing. I want to see the tanks, get a glimpse of the soldiers in their cute little shorts. And so, with mounting irritation, "Buddy," I say, "get that flag outta my face. *Achshav*. Now!" And he does.

And then it hit me like a *p'tzatzah*, an onomatopoetic Israeli bomb. I had brusquely and impolitely without any American pleases or thank yous, told an Israeli, in Hebrew no less, to quit waving his flag in front of my face. And miraculously, he did what I told him to do. The Israeli listened to me, 23-year-old me from Elmont, New York, who had spent the year working in kibbutz fields and factories and exhausting her brain with daily *ulpan* classes. For all he knew I was just another bossy Israeli, and for that moment, I was. I was Israeli. I was Jew. I was Jerusalemite. And I loved it. The crowd was roaring; the tanks were chugging up Ben Yehuda Street in an endless olive-drab parade. God was there with all of us in our shorts and sunburned noses, with our flags and the dopey *kovahs* we wore everywhere to keep the sun off our heads. The entire world glowed with personal and national triumph.

My grandmother thought my parents had sent me to Israel to find a nice Jewish boy. I don't know, maybe that was their plan. I was drifting, enrolled at a local community college where I was doing well but wasn't terribly enthusiastic about anything. My parents felt it was time for a change. Mother went to Israel to "check it out" before sending me. She returned home absolutely turned on by the place. She found a volunteer program—*Sherut L'am*, or "Service for the People"—that would teach me Hebrew and give me a volunteer job and a place to live, and she sent me on my way.

I ended up at Kibbutz Gan Shmuel for my first three months in Israel. Located between Tel Aviv and Haifa, near Hadera, it is a long-established kibbutz and as such was home to a number of orchards, fields and factories, including an olive-processing and canning plant. To this day I cannot eat an olive with any enjoyment; I've had more than enough for one lifetime. But despite that culinary aversion, working in the olive factory was one of the best jobs I had during my year in Israel.

We were charged with separating the clumps of dirt from the olives as they came down a chute. Grab the dirt and throw it, grab the dirt and throw it. Fill the giant cans of olives full of brine with the kind of rubber hose we used to water the lawn in Elmont. Minute after minute, hour after hour, the routine never varied—except for an exhilarating break to move boxes around the warehouse with a forklift! Factory work was mechanical, and to an observer it probably looked boring as hell. But to this day I like doing repetitive things. When you do something so mechanical, you almost become part of the machine yourself, and there is something very hypnotic about it. The mindlessness of the work gave rise to an explosion of new thoughts and insights. I grew to like factory work—whether I was sorting olives or capping bottle after bottle of grapefruit juice as they shuttled down the conveyor belt—because of the mental freedom that kind of labor gave me.

The kibbutz was steeped in socialist philosophy—the more menial the work, the more respected the worker. This was a far cry from everything I had absorbed in capitalist-driven America. There was a Holocaust survivor whose sole job was washing the kibbutz silverware. Day in and day out, he was the one who scrubbed the leftover food from our utensils, and he was revered for the work he did. He was no less important than anyone else. We were all working for one another's benefit, and the commitment to the work bonded us together in a special way.

I had come to Israel rather unconscious of my Jewish identity. We lived in your typical suburban lower-middle-class, postwar tract-house community. Everyone we knew was Jewish; many kept kosher as we did. I had no sense of otherness or needing to be aware of my Judaism. Israel changed all that, expanding my sense of what it means to be a Jew, of history and the idea of a Jewish destiny distinct from *kashrut* and Sabbath services. I was stunned to experience another life out there that Jews were living. For the first time in my life, I realized that Israel was my country, that I had a place there.

Growing up, I was a good Hebrew student, had become a bat mitzvah and contributed to Temple B'nai Israel by singing in the junior and senior choirs. They even gave me a scholarship to study the organ, and I substituted for the organist from time to time. Yet I discovered in Israel that I had been practicing Judaism without really living it.

In Israel it all came together. The mind-numbing tasks in the canning factories and pushing my gray matter to the breaking point in ulpan had been *avodah*, work, in the most literal sense of the word. Laboring in Israel, and at an unprecedented time in Jewish history, no less, was tremendously affecting.

Watching the captured Russian tanks lumber through the streets of the Holy City, celebrating with thousands of Israelis the return of our shared heritage, I knew that if there were a God, this was exactly where God would be. And so when I told the Israeli to move his flag, I wasn't just standing ground with my own two feet. I was speaking as *mishpocha*, Jew to Jew, both of us rooted firmly in the *adama*, the earth, of our homeland.

PART 13

Shavuot

All souls stood at Sinai, each accepting its share in the Torah.

—*Alshek. q Ragoler, Maalot HaTorah*

WHILE THERE IS no Biblical link between the *Shavuot* holiday and the giving of the Torah on Mount Sinai, the Talmud does draw a connection between the two. The rabbis calculated the dates of the agricultural festival of Shavuot and the time of the Revelation and deemed them to be one and the same. This link enabled the rabbis to bring new relevance to an agricultural holiday at a time when many Jews were living in urban areas.

Shavuot, literally "Festival of Weeks," is so named because it occurs seven weeks and one day after the beginning of Passover. Shavout is also called *Chag Habikurim*, Festival of the First Fruits, and Chag *HaKatzir*, Harvest Festival. These names reflect the holiday's origin as the time marking the end of the spring wheat harvest. The 50 days between the second day of Passover and Shavuot are called the counting of the *omer*, omer being a unit of measure. In Temple times, on the second day of Passover, the priests would offer up for sacrifice an omer of wheat, to mark the start of the seven-week wheat-growing season.

Many communities hold a *Tikkun Leil* Shavuot, an all-night study session that enables those present to prepare spiritually for the morning's service, when the Ten Commandments are read. During the recitation of the Ten Commandments, the congregation stands, thus symbolically receiving them, as our ancestors did at Sinai.

The Book of Ruth is included in the Shavuot morning service for several reasons. Ruth's loyalty to her mother-in-law, Naomi, was such that she converted to Judaism. By consequence of that conversion and her subsequent marriage to Boaz (their courtship is said to have taken place during Shavuot), Ruth became the ancestor of King David, who, according to the Talmud, was born and died on Shavuot.

CHAPTER 46

Will the Real Anti-Semites Please Stand Up?

The Story of David Rosen

I WAS COMPLETELY covered in spit. On my hair and my *kippah*, down my shirt, the backs of my hands. As the cops marched us out in single file, the thought came to me that this is what it must have been like to be a Jew, deported from Warsaw or Lodz, or even out of Babylonia. You come to pray, to do what you have learned your whole life to do, and you are not allowed to do it. And as terrifying as it was, what made it worse, what made it unbearable, was that I was in Israel and that the people spitting on us, attacking us with stones and curses, were fellow Jews.

I had come to Israel to study for a semester. Public high school had ceased to be a challenge; I hated the social scene and knew I wanted more out of life than rote classes and clubs. I had gone to a Jewish day school through eighth grade, and while I enjoyed my weekly supplementary Hebrew classes, I wanted to learn more. So in February of my junior year, with my parents' OK, I left for Ramah's *Tichon,* high school, program in Jerusalem.

Tichon filled the void I'd felt since I started high school. We were a small group of 28 from all over the U.S. and Canada, and

I was thrilled to be back learning in a *chevra*, a small group, and exploring everything Jerusalem had to offer. My day-school background was great preparation, and I began to excel once again in my studies, secular as well as Judaic. I became good friends with Andy Sacks, one of the young Conservative rabbis who lived in Jerusalem and who taught some of our classes. The night before *Shavuot*, Andy called and said he had planned an egalitarian *minyan* in the *Kotel* plaza, and would we like to come? It sounded wonderful. Shavuot celebrates God's giving of the Torah to the children of Israel. The tradition is to walk to the Kotel and pray, dance and celebrate with as much joy as you can. We had no idea then that our manner of celebration would cause such venomous rioting.

So, 11 of us walked through the streets of Jerusalem at 4 a.m. When we got to the Kotel, it was packed. There was no chance of getting close to the Wall; it was so crowded with people. I found Andy and we started praying *shacharit*, the morning service. There were 20 of us at the beginning, and by the end we had grown to about 60 men and women all praying together; the feeling of community was incredible. We were just a small group, one of dozens and dozens that by then had swelled to encompass hundreds, even thousands of Jews. All of us focused on our prayers and on our amazing good fortune to be where we were that morning.

Then the trouble started. The *haredis*, the ultra-Orthodox black hats, had finished their prayers and were walking around. They saw our group of men and women praying together and they weren't happy. When they saw a woman reading from the Torah, all hell broke loose. "Nazis! Christians! Go home!" they shouted at us. Someone threw pebbles at us, and then a dirty diaper. We quickly rolled up the Torah scroll and covered it, trying to protect it from the zealots who claim their life's purpose is to live by the very parchment they had nearly desecrated with baby mess.

In a matter of moments, our small group of 60 was surrounded by swarms of ultra-Orthodox Jews. It wasn't just the teens, either. It was the men, the old ones with long gray beards, who looked at us with hatred in their eyes. Nothing can compare to your own people spitting on you, at the Kotel, Judaism's holiest site, calling you a Nazi. We looked diagonally toward the Kotel and saw a sea of black hats storming toward us. One minute we were praying and celebrating, and the next minute our lives were in danger. Literally. The cops finally came and marched us out in a single file. They surrounded our whole group and guided us through the crowd of old men, who continued to curse and scream at us. "Infidels! Go home, *treif*! Whores and sons of whores!" Our only response was to sing "*Oseh Shalom*," a prayer that asks God to let peace descend on us, all Israel and the world. What else could we do? We dispersed and left the plaza and again two haredis grabbed me; a soldier had to pull them off of me. There was no point in fighting back, which surprised my friends, because I usually came off as a tough guy. But that time was different. It was the kind of situation where the real tough guy was the one who can walk away and not fight back.

That day remains the worst and best day of my life as a Jew. It was so traumatic. I cried nearly the entire half-hour walk back to my dorm. I wrote in my journal and then called my parents. I knew once this hit the papers in the States they would be worried. And I needed to hear their voices. I was so confused, and yet surprisingly, I felt stronger, too. Never in my life had I been the target of any kind of anti-Semitism. No playground slurs, no "Jew boy" taunts. Nothing, until this. And I discovered I was able to weather anti-Semitism, from other Jews, no less. I have no regrets about going that morning. We belonged there every bit as much as the haredim.

I have to believe that God was looking down and knew it was wrong. Does God have emotions? I don't know, but if we are created in God's image, He couldn't have been happy with His people that morning. There had to be divine anger shimmering there above us.

I've come to realize that there is a lot of work that needs to be done. There has to be peace within the country before there can ever be peace with the Palestinians or with Syria. The issues between the secular Jews and the ultra-Orthodox are going to tear the country apart. Look at Jewish history. It's happened before. The haredi attitude toward the Reform and Conservative Jews in Israel will tear the Diaspora away from Israel. The only synagogues in Israel that get government funding are the ultra-Orthodox ones. It's a game that has to stop.

Is there room for all of us? There has to be. Remember how Abraham sat outside his tent, kept the flaps open on all sides, waiting for visitors? Well, we've got to keep the flaps open instead of pegging them closed with hatred and judgment. I don't agree with everything in the Reform movement, but the more Jews there are, the more ways there are to practice Judaism, the better. The Orthodox don't practice Judaism the way Abraham and Moses practiced it. Judaism is always changing. Who are we to say that Reform Judaism is wrong? Or Conservative? Or Reconstructionist? None of us knows. God isn't talking anymore. The communication is different today, and it's different for each person.

It's taken me a long time to get over the hate I had inside of me toward the Jews who attacked us that Shavuot morning. More hatred isn't the answer. I believe in what we were doing even though the haredim said it was wrong. I know they are terrified of us. Their ignorant assumption that they alone are "real" Jews is grounded in a fear that we are attacking what is vital to them. They are terrified by the 50 percent intermarriage rate here in the States. They are terrified of women reading the Torah. But what has Judaism always been if not about debates? Over the meaning of text, over appropriate action, over differing interpretations. Without the debates, Judaism will stall, and a stalled Judaism will die.

What we did that Shavuot morning was right. I know it. We acted within the context of centuries of debate over how to experience life as a Jew. I don't love getting spat on and having filthy diapers flung at me; the debate has to exist on a higher level than that. But spit or no spit, the debate has to continue. And if we have to be protected by riot police in leather gloves and plastic face helmets, then that is what we will do. The Torah has never belonged exclusively to this Jew or that Jew, but to *all* Jews. We're always so concerned with the "Who is a Jew?" question. I think we'd better start discussing who some of the anti-Semites really are.

CHAPTER 47

Single, and Together at Last

The Story of Kay Harris

EL AL SECURITY pegged me as a potential terrorist the minute I tried to board the Frankfurt-to-Tel Aviv leg of my trip to Israel. I seemed to fit their profile of a woman likely to be carrying a bomb. Me. A blonde, blue-eyed female, newly divorced, my kids left behind with their father in Michigan. I was photographed and then interrogated for what seemed like hours. Edgy guards combed through every bag I had, roughly unwrapped all the presents I'd brought for the friends I was visiting. Finally they allowed me onto the plane, but they eyed me suspiciously the entire flight. No one believed I was who I said I was—a Jewish woman going to visit friends in Israel. It was like converting all over again.

My conversion to Judaism was the most traumatic experience of my life. It wasn't warm. It wasn't lovely. It didn't feel welcoming. Even conversion's sealing moment—the *mikvah*—was less than I had anticipated. I was one of a group of bathing-suited women holding small cards printed with the appropriate prayers, dunking on cue in a synagogue swimming pool—once, twice, three times. I emerged from the water with disappointment lodged in the place I'd reserved for renaissance.

I converted for the one reason they tell you not to, because I had fallen in love with and was engaged to marry a Jewish man. A child of Holocaust survivors, no less. By the time my husband asked me for a divorce 17 years later, I had a kosher home, went to *shul* every Saturday and had daughters in a Jewish day school. Out of practicality, I knew I would keep a Jewish home for my daughters; I would not lose them for anything in the world. But the question haunted me: "I'm not married to a Jew any longer. I converted to marry him. How attached am I, really, to Judaism?"

When the *get* was final, I needed a change of scenery. I don't know why, but I decided to go to Israel. I'd never traveled anywhere alone and, up until then, Israel had always been connected to my husband and the visits we made to his family who lived there. But I had friends of my own I was eager to see in Tel Aviv and Jerusalem. If only the flight would land and I could prove that I was who I said I was—single mom, pleasure traveler and Jewish adult on a private mission.

My friend greeted me at the gate. He was glad to see me, but something in his manner was off. "I hope you don't mind coming with me," he said. "I have to make a stop before we go home."

"Sure. Where?"

"Well, I have to go to a funeral."

What could I say but, "OK."

The funeral turned out to be that of a boy who had studied in *yeshivah* with my friend's son. He had been stationed in Lebanon and was killed in an ambush. And now he was about to be laid to rest on Har Herzl. The cemetery was filled with young people crying and holding on to one another. In America, young people rarely bury each other; they go to funerals of old people. These young Israelis were burying one of their own. It was the first time for some, but not for others. For many, it would probably not be the last. The "mother" part of me wanted to reach out and comfort them one by one. There was nothing I could do but grieve with them.

The day was sunny and beautiful. The sky, clear and cloudless. I could hear the wheels of the caisson grinding on the gravel path, growing louder as it neared the grave. The mourners' keening spiked higher as each turn of the caisson's wheels brought the coffin closer. Then the plain wooden box was lowered into the earth and mourners began the sacred task of laying their loved one to rest. "*Yitbarakh v'yishtabach*"; the agonizing shoveling began; "*v'yit'pa'ar v'yit'romam*"; dirt thumped on bare wood. Then the sound grew muffled as the grave filled; "*v'im'ru amen.*" My ears were filled with the sounds of people shrieking.

It mattered little that I didn't know the 19-year-old soldier who had been killed. I mourned the boy as deeply as if he were my own. I mourned Israel's loss, and I mourned what this meant for the Jewish people. The funeral was the saddest thing I'd ever experienced in my entire life, even as it struck me how incredibly Jewish it was. Despite all my years connected to the survivor community, the funeral drove home to me the sadness of Jewish history in a way I'd never imagined.

We made it back to Jerusalem in time to eat a late dinner before nightfall and the start of *Shavuot*. Tired from the flight, I'd had little time to rest or process what I'd just experienced. It was my friends' custom to go to shul for study and then, at about 3 or 4 a.m., walk to the *Kotel* in time for sunrise. When we set out from their small neighborhood synagogue, it was so dark I had no idea where I was walking. I just followed those ahead of me. We arrived at the Wall as planned, just as the sun was rising. As the light grew, I saw masses and masses of people, all dressed in white, preparing to daven. It seemed like hundreds of thousands of people were there. Men praying together. Women praying together. Everyone was davening in different ways but focused on the same goal—devotion to God, transcendence of the mundane, acknowledging the significance of the holiday.

Opening up the *siddur* I'd brought, I realized I knew enough to follow the service in this huge crowd of people. I didn't have to ask anyone for page numbers or paragraphs. I didn't have to move ahead to a familiar prayer and listen for the group to catch up to me. Listening to the leader of our little section, I knew what was going on. I wasn't an outsider. I was davening with the group, within the group in this wonderful place as the sun brushed Jerusalem's ancient stones with the golden-pink of daybreak.

I continued to daven, and as the sun grew brighter, I felt it burning through years of insecurity, of self-doubt and anger. Once, upon meeting me, a cousin of my husband's thrust a prayer book into my hands and commanded, "Read!" His chutzpah and lack of respect infuriated me. I recalled how I always felt my husband and his family examined me, wondering if I were truly a convert. Rosy glow gave way to the candid light of day; I realized that throughout all the years of my marriage I had tried to reject my past and act as if the Christian part of my life didn't exist, as if there was something negative about the first 23 years of my life. The sun rose high in the sky. Before I knew it, the various prayer groups were breaking up and leaving the Kotel plaza in waves of white. We were nearly finished davening *Shacharit*, the morning service: "*Vatitein lanu Adonai Eloheinu b'ahavah chag hashavuot hazeh, z'man matan torateinu*. Lovingly, Lord our God, have you given us this festival of Shavuot, the season of the giving of our Torah." I closed the siddur. *My Torah*, I thought. *It belongs to me, too.*

My friend's wife came over to me. The exhaustion I felt was mirrored in her eyes. We exchanged no words but began walking back to her home for my first good sleep in Israel. Over the next few days, I realized how much my friends cared about me. Whatever doubts I had about myself, my friends didn't share them. I realized that I had kept questioning myself even though everyone around me had long ago accepted me.

From Jerusalem I went to Tel Aviv, and before I knew it, it was time to go home. I had unconsciously begun the trip thinking of it as the final test. That if I didn't enjoy it, if I returned feeling the same as I did when I was married, then I would have some hefty issues to confront. But the trip made me realize that the rabbis are right. Converting isn't a true decision if you make it for someone else. Don't do it for marriage. Do it for yourself. After that trip, I felt I'd really paid my dues. I returned home realizing that I am a blended person. I'll never be like a person who was born Jewish, and I don't have to be. I'm my own special kind of Jew. All the years I'd been married I was surrounded by survivors, and I'd felt I could never measure up. But that trip made me feel like a survivor in my own right.

The flight home went off without a hitch. No one interrogated me; no one stopped me or searched me. I fit a profile that earned me mere glances of boredom from security—tired but ecstatic traveler returning home to America, a piece of Israel cradled deep within her Jewish heart.

CHAPTER 48

My Nana Is Jewish

The Story of Erma Feigelstein

"MY NANA IS Jewish," said my 7-year-old granddaughter, trying to make conversation with a classmate's grandmother. We were having lunch at her school for Grandparents' Day. "My nana is Jewish," she repeated. Something in my soul wanted to scream, *SO ARE YOU, MY PRECIOUS NESHUMALAH, SO ARE YOU!* But I held my tongue. Not only because Jewish law and matrilineal descent didn't go with peanut butter sandwiches in a public school classroom, but because I had been warned by my daughter, married 13 years now to a Catholic, against confusing the children with how the Jewish world sees them. Not for the first time and not for the last, I zipped my lip.

Downing my pint-sized carton of orange juice, I nodded at the bewildered woman seated opposite us. In the silence, I remembered a physical therapist I had worked with after being injured in a car accident. "You know," he said when I told him I would have to miss a session or two because of the Jewish holidays, "my grandfather was Jewish. We used to go to his house for Seder and things." When Cara brought up the curiosity of her grandmother's Jewishness I thought, *She's going to be like the owner of the gym, her link to Judaism nothing but an aside in passing conversation.* I wanted to die.

Of all my children, I would have laid bets that Dawn would be the one to carry on the seeds of Judaism I had planted within her spirit. When we did the *chametz* search I would tell her, "You will do this with your daughter one day." When I lit candles each Friday night, I would place my hands on her sleek head and say, "You will light candles and kiss your daughter just like this one day." She was the child who tried the hardest to please.

And while we did everything we could to instill in all our children the belief that their future happiness depended on marrying within the Jewish community, we could understand why Dawn loves Roger. He is energetic, resourceful, talented and outgoing—and he adores my daughter. Roger is a *mensch*; he has a good and giving soul. Soon after their engagement, Roger told my husband how proud he was of his father, who had managed to send him and his four siblings to parochial school; he expressed the desire to do the same for his children one day. My husband's *kishkes* must have lurched, but he kept quiet.

The other shoe dropped weeks later when Dawn told me a friend of Roger's, a priest, had offered to perform their wedding ceremony. Dawn had no objections, and I could only respond that while it was their choice, I could not be present at such a ceremony. Nor would I try and find a rabbi to officiate—with or without a priest in attendance. A Jewish wedding celebrates the establishment of a Jewish home. To have a rabbi reading a script would be as meaningless as it would have been to have a priest recite blessings when my daughter wasn't prepared to be a Catholic or create a Catholic home.

All I asked of Dawn was that she make no promises to Roger that she wasn't certain she could keep. The daughter of a close friend had promised to raise her children in her husband's Catholic faith. When she held her firstborn, she was devastated to recall the pledge made in the excitement of becoming engaged. In the end, Dawn and Roger were married by a judge. Dawn made no promises to raise their children Catholic, which I thought was tragic for Roger, since Catholicism was so important to him.

Dawn wasn't indifferent to Judaism. She just preferred taking her chances on a totally secular marriage rather than fighting about which religion to follow. She never would have asked Roger to give up his faith, and she never thought for a moment that if she did, she would prevail.

For a few years they attended a Unitarian church, but it fulfilled neither of their needs, and when their children were young, they quit going. They celebrated *Pesach* and Chanukah in our home and had a Christmas tree and Easter baskets in theirs. They avoided mentioning Jesus, but Judaism remained little more than holiday dinners at Grandma's house.

The low point in all this came the day Dawn asked me not to recite the *Shabbos* blessings in Roger's presence. He had asked his family not to cross themselves in front of Dawn during Sunday dinner, and she wanted me to extend the same sensitivity to Roger when they came to us on Friday nights. I was appalled that they had asked Roger's mother to censor herself in her own home and was shattered that they would ask it of me in mine. That I recited the blessings in English out of consideration for Roger went totally unacknowledged. The issue soon became moot as their lives grew busy with karate, working late and other Friday-night activities.

Still they came for Seders, and once Roger brought a prayer a client had given him in support of the Soviet Jews. I sensed a flicker of interest in Roger, but my husband told me repeatedly, "Keep your mouth shut and mind your own business. Let them lead their own lives." You have to adjust your thinking when your kids hit adolescence. When they become adults, the whole relationship changes again. You have to think through what you believe so you can make the stand you might need to make. And you also have to know what compromises you're willing to make.

During the past year or so, Dawn would occasionally tell me that many of Roger's clients who know me had taken it upon themselves to urge him to visit one or another of the Reform congregations in our town. I'd also heard through the grapevine that Dawn and Roger had discussed the possibility of visiting a synagogue and even attending lectures aimed at intermarried couples. I tried not to get my hopes up, but this past summer Dawn started telling me that Roger was serious. His children needed to be brought up within a religion.

My daughter was diffident—unwilling even to encourage him. I don't know if she was being a brilliant tactician or it was just incredible dumb luck that he was taking tentative steps toward Judaism. Dawn had long ago given Roger her own take on Jewish life, trying to convince him that *shul*-going isn't crucial to being a good Jew, that a good deal of Judaism involved home celebrations. She was content with that approach and Roger tried to go along. But maybe his spiritual needs called for more ceremony than hers.

Too, Roger had grown very close to us over the years. It might have been different had they been married by his friend the priest; we would have all started out from a place of great alienation. But Roger saw how our whole family pitched in for one another and dropped their lives when crises arose. He saw how my daughters visited me every day when I was in the hospital after a car accident, how my other son-in-law came each evening with a meal from his restaurant and stayed with me while I ate. When their 2-week-old son needed emergency hospitalization, they left Cara with me on a moment's call, knowing my husband would leave work as soon as possible to pitch in. This total support system was a revelation to Roger.

Roger had begun to do some reading on his own as well. One book, *Joshua*, spoke to his soul and seemed to make a bridge for him. The premise of the book is this: Jesus returns to a small town in America as a simple carpenter and finds himself more comfortable in synagogue among Jews. The author wasn't trying to make Jews out of Christians but to revive the true Christianity. The more reading Roger did, the more he came to see that Judaism was so sufficiently inclusive that even someone who went to Catholic parochial school could recognize kernels of worship and moral structure and find them acceptable, if not for himself then for his children. Judaism was the father of his church, and I think that, recognizing that, he couldn't find fault with Judaism or with what we do.

In early September we journeyed out of state to celebrate a family bat mitzvah. The entire weekend was one of those rare spiritual high points that electrified all who were present. During the bat mitzvah ceremony, the rabbi suggested that we either read silently from the *Amidah* or say "whatever prayer your heart directs." I prayed my one, fervent, oft-repeated prayer that all of my grandchildren should be Jewish. It wasn't a petitional prayer. I wasn't asking God for anything. My prayer was the kind of plea I say when I have no power to change reality. My prayer was simply the outpouring of my heart's longing, an expression of my own personal need in a forum where it would do no harm and cause no offense.

We talked about the weekend during the entire drive home and I called Dawn when we got back to let her know we arrived safe and sound. "Mother," she said, "are you sitting down?" I gasped, awaiting bad news.

"No, no," she said, hearing the sharp intake of my breath. "Everything is okay. I just want you to know that we joined a synagogue this weekend. Roger forced me to join Temple Shalom. We signed the kids up for religious school, and they loved it. Roger and I stayed to attend the children's service with them. It was great. Roger loved it; the kids loved it; we all love it."

When I recaptured my voice, I asked Dawn to pass the phone to Roger. "Thank you, Roger," I said when he picked up. "I feel your father's hand in this. He was a man of faith, and I know that he would have supported your decision. I want to honor his memory. For the rest of my life I will remember his *yahrzeit*."

Since then, Roger has begun to learn all he can about Judaism. Two weeks after the kids' first morning at religious school, he affixed a mezuzah on the doorpost of his and Dawn's home. My daughter doesn't quite know what to make of her husband's enthusiasm for a thing she thought she could live without. He brings home books on the Torah and Jewish history and reads them every day.

They came for Rosh HaShanah and, before we sat down, I helped Roger light a yahrzeit candle and recite the blessing in memory of his father, who had died at this season 10 years earlier. Then he called my grandchildren around him and said, "I am going to start a new tradition in our family. Every time we light a memorial candle I am going to tell you a story about the person we are remembering."

Of course, I still have to hold my tongue. A bat mitzvah date has to be set for Cara, now 10. She needs to catch up with her religious-school classmates. What about the Christmas trees and Easter baskets the kids have grown up with? This is all so new and full of endless possibilities.

I don't think God looked down and granted my prayer at my great-niece's bat mitzvah. That's not part of my belief system. And I don't think it's because I was a good mother-in-law and held my tongue, although I realize the wisdom of having been urged, cajoled and ordered to shut up. Roger has been growing and maturing over the years. He recognizes that his children needed the moral structure that religion gives. But I never thought this would happen. I thought that it would be so easy to accept the majority's level of practice along with the majority's faith. Judaism hasn't won and Christianity hasn't lost. Rather, God—and religion's place in defining God—is the victor.

On the way home from that first morning of religious school, Cara asked her father if she was now a Jewish girl. "You are my Jewish princess," Roger told her, "and the boys are my Jewish princes." He wasn't tapping into that awful stereotype but was inviting Cara to see herself in a new light, to envision herself linked to her birthright and to her heritage. And, dearest to my heart, my son-in-law opened the door for my granddaughter to connect, neshuma to neshuma, soul to soul, with her nana.

CHAPTER 49

A Child Chooses Jewish Life

The Story of Walter Raubeson

"MOM SAYS YOU can't sleep over unless you go to religious school with me tomorrow," Ari told me. "I have to go, and it's too far to take me there and then take you home. It's not so bad. Want to come?"

Ari was my best friend in third grade. We both liked baseball cards and doing wheelies on our bikes at the far end of his street. My mom says we were probably brothers in another lifetime, we spend so much time together. Sunday school was an OK trade for a sleepover.

I had no idea what Ari's Sunday school would be like. He's Jewish; my parents and I are Christian, but they haven't gone to church in a long time. I didn't go to any kind of Sunday school, but I figured, why not? It's just one morning.

Ari's teacher is great. There's this neat feeling of closeness in the classroom. There's not tons of heavy religious stuff, but there are a lot of games and a lot of talking back and forth. You learn things without really realizing it.

"Hey, Ari. Can I come back?"

"I guess so. You really want to?"

"Yeah."

That was six years ago. Last year, I converted to Judaism the week before celebrating my bar mitzvah at Temple Israel in Hollywood, California, my friend Ari's temple. It doesn't seem like such a big deal to me, that I am Jewish and my family isn't, but I guess it is. I live a Reform Jewish life. We celebrate *Shabbat* each Friday night. I recite the blessings. I go to Passover Seders. I bring my friends over for a Chanukah dinner every year. In the fall, our family builds a *sukkah*.

My mom was worried about my going to Ari's temple at first. Not because she didn't want me learning about Judaism—my parents are real open and encouraging about whatever we kids want to explore—but she was concerned about my being accepted in the temple. When she met the teachers and the rabbi and all, she was assured and then she let me continue.

Third grade ended, and when I wanted to go back for fourth grade, the school principal wasn't sure what to do. The rule is kids can only go to religious school if their parents are members of the temple, but in my case, since my parents are Christian, that couldn't happen. But the principal understood how important it was to me to keep learning about Judaism, so I was allowed to stay.

In the fourth grade the kids begin their preparation for bar mitzvah, so I did, too. We picked my bar mitzvah date and Torah portion. My Torah portion was to be *Ki Tissa*, which deals with Moses' breaking of the Ten Commandments and the Children of Israel's beginning again. That story seemed to fit my life. Learning about Judaism felt like a rebirth for me, too.

I hadn't thought about officially converting until it came up just before my bar mitzvah. I had pretty much considered myself Jewish. I'd been learning for almost four years and celebrating Shabbat and all the holidays. But my rabbi told me the options of conversion, and I chose to make the experience complete by converting. So, two days before my bar mitzvah ceremony, I went to the *mikvah*.

The location of the mikvah reminded me of a synagogue in a way. There was a gift shop and all these different levels. My rabbi showed me into a little office. There were two doors. One was a bathroom where you showered and prepared; the other door led to the mikvah.

When I went through the door to the mikvah, I forgot about everything in the world. It was just me and the rabbi and God. I walked down the seven steps into the mikvah. Mixed into the mikvah water is melted ice from a natural stream. That's required.

When I was in the water up to my chest, the rabbi recited the blessings and told me to repeat them. I did and then curled my body into the water and let it cover me completely. It's hard to describe exactly how I felt. I walked out and felt different. I felt happy and responsible. I felt light on my feet like I was ready to take on the world.

Two days later I awoke to my bar mitzvah day. The night before, I was totally nervous, but the minute I got on the *bimah* I wasn't nervous at all. As I read my Torah portion, I wasn't aware of anything around me. I was totally engulfed in God and in theTorah and in the prayers. I had on my new *tallis* that Mom and I had picked out the day before. It's white and has beautiful silver letters embroidered around the neck band. I kept running my fingers through the fringes at the end of my tallis. The fringes are a reminder of God's commandments and our obligation to obey them. Now I was the one taking on the obligations.

Then, all of a sudden, I was done. I chanted the final blessings. My friend Ari came up and held the Torah while it was dressed. My parents were on the bimah with me. I looked over at them every once in a while and saw from the expressions on their faces how proud they were of me.

I believe in the teaching of the Torah. I live it as much as I can. My mom gave me a Torah commentary as a bar mitzvah gift, and I take it down and read it a lot. When I think about having kids (it's a long way off; I'm still just a teen) I know I won't force them to be Jewish, but I know I want them to have the option. It's funny to think how all of this happened, how I came to be Jewish.

A year after my bar mitzvah, my family moved to Portland, Oregon. I joined the temple there. We have plans for my friend Ari to visit from California for a long weekend. I can't wait to have the kids in my temple youth group meet him.

CHAPTER 50

I Belong Here

The Story of Geralda Miller

MY FATHER ONCE told me that when I was little, every fourth word out of my mouth was "Why?" The nuns didn't care for students who asked "Why?" They told me that my faith was supposed to be so strong that I should just believe and not ask any questions. I spent an awful lot of time as a grade-school detainee. I'm sure the nuns still have beautiful gardens because of all the weeding and planting I did as penance for what Rudyard Kipling would have called my "'satiable curtiosity."

But I couldn't help it. I didn't understand the Immaculate Conception. How did Mary conceive a baby out of thin air? Please explain this to me. And then there was the Jesus question. Jesus was born a Jew. How did he become a Christian? How does a man who is a Jew, who lived the life of a Jew—how in the world can millions of people deny that fact and think of him as something else? Something other than Jewish? The nuns didn't like those questions, either. Undoubtedly, I did not make a good Catholic.

When I was in my 20s, I moved to LA. My mother will tell you that's when my life ended, and in many ways she is right. In California I lost my faith. I lost my God. I wanted to forget about God and the whole shaming thing that is a part of Catholicism.

I was single and beginning to experiment with sex. But if you do, it's a sin. If you use birth control, it's a sin. Everything was a sin; you live, you breathe, it's a sin. So I had to put it all away, dump it in the trash bag and forget it. I went the other way, smoking a joint every day, getting my after-work buzz, drinking and partying every weekend. I partied with Nicole and I remember that white Bronco. I went out with him, too. I lived a fast California lifestyle.

I worked in retail fashion, itself a very superficial world. It's one of those worlds where you are wined and dined by salesmen who want you to spend your money on their clothes. I have tons of stories from those days. But there's no place for God in those stories. There's no room for faith in those stories.

After LA, I moved to Boston and then to Philly. In each city I found the same group. The drugs were the same; the parties were the same. Even the men weren't much different from city to city. When I got to Philly, I started an affair with a married man who was a pro ball player. There's no place for God in that kind of relationship, either.

It was in Philly that things began to change for me. I went to work as a buyer for a string of small retail stores owned by a Jewish family. They didn't decorate for Christmas; we got off all the Jewish holidays. I felt very much at home with them. Something about it felt good to me. They were constantly yelling and screaming at each other, blustering, "You don't know what you're talking about!", and then the next day they came to work and tomorrow was another day. It felt right. I felt like I fit in, and they felt it, too.

They invited me to my first Seder. I was familiar with the story of the Exodus because the nuns had told it to us. It hadn't been told as a this-is-the-father-of-our-people story but as a fable about a great man who liberated slaves into freedom. On one hand it wasn't my people, but since I'm black, it was, wait a minute, we're talking about black folk, too. We're talking about Egypt, about Africa. My connection with Moses and the Exodus and my empathy for the entire process of redemption was understanding slavery from the perspective of a black person wanting to be set free.

What was so incredible, so liberating about attending the Seder was the fact that I was face to face with people who were celebrating their heritage as slaves, celebrating their deliverance into freedom. In black families, slavery is never talked about, but not talking about something doesn't mean nothing gets passed down. What gets passed down in black families is shame, deep and crippling shame. I was in my 30s before I came to terms with my blackness.

Let me tell you something, you can't ignore your heritage. You can't ignore who you are. I can't ignore my kinky hair, my wide nose and my black face. It has taken me years to be proud of who I am. It's not something I was raised with. It's not in the family structure. I could never put my finger on the reason, but I had always felt disconnected from my black ancestral heritage. We were an Air Force family, and perhaps our identity was organized first and foremost around belonging to the service. In other words, we weren't black, we were Air Force.

The Seder showed me that for Jews, the connection to ancestry is still alive. It is an unbroken thread, an umbilical cord that still pulses with life. That's what attracted me to my Jewish co-workers. They wrote their heritage down. They pass on their history, proudly reenacting their enslavement once a year. It blew my mind. At a time when I was questioning my whole existence and the lifestyle I was living, Judaism began creeping into my life.

Despite my growing closeness with the families running the business, I began to outgrow the job. Still living in Philly, I took a job with J.C. Penney in New York City. Soon after the job switch, J.C. Penney invited me to Dallas for an interview. I went out for a look-see, found an apartment, and Saturday night I went and checked out the town. Four hours flat and I knew it was possible to move to Dallas the same way I had moved to Boston and to Philly. But for some reason, I knew I couldn't. I woke up after a night of partying and I hated myself. I will only say that the windows on the 27th floor of the Sheraton do not open, because I checked.

I returned to Philly and called a man I knew who rode the commuter train with me. He had once given me some pamphlets about addiction and alcoholism. "Stick them in a drawer for a rainy day," he said. I called him and said, "I need help." We met at noon and I went to my first AA meeting.

I moved to Dallas a sober and changing woman. I still couldn't look in the mirror. I hated what I saw in its reflection. No longer able to be the woman Geri Miller had been, I took back my birth name. One day my sponsor gave me a slip of paper. On it she had written these words: "I am Geralda Miller, a recovering alcoholic woman and a loving child of God."

I said to her, "I don't know who this person is." But I began to form the woman I wanted to be. I surrounded myself with women I admired and took little bits from each of them until I found who I really was. I was learning to love myself as an authentic black woman. Without the drugs and the partying. Without the drinking. Without the men. As I began to redefine who I was, I realized that Catholicism was no longer a part of who I was or who I was becoming.

I traveled to Rome on buying trips twice a year, and during one trip I set aside time to go to the Vatican to say goodbye. I knew it had to be official before I could get on with my life. It was a beautiful spring weekend; seeing all the priests and nuns walking through the plazas was like having my past laid out right in front of me. Through my sobriety, I had begun to meditate and define an understanding of my own God. The God of my own understanding was a loving God, a non-punishing God. I took my God and my angels and we walked into the Vatican. I sat in a meditation room and just prayed for the strength to say goodbye. Then I saw a cardinal; he was dressed in beautiful scarlet vestments.

"I have to talk to you a minute," I said. He took me into a room where there was a font. "I am here to say goodbye. I have found that the Catholic Church is not for me."

He looked at me for a moment, studying my face. "I wish you well in your endeavors," he said. And I left.

Freed from a faith I had no faith in, I decided that spirituality would have to be enough. I wanted to build a connection with God and began to pray and meditate daily. I'd sit and find God's beauty around me, in people and in everything life brought my way.

Eventually, life brought a trip to Ghana my way. From J.C. Penney I had struck out on my own, working with African manufacturers and designers to bring authentic designs to the United States. On one buying excursion to Ghana, I visited the castle in the city of Cape Coast. I walked for hours and hours through the castle dungeons, where hundreds of thousands and eventually millions of my black people were holed up shoulder to shoulder, cheek to elbow, living in their own waste and tears while awaiting shipment across the Atlantic. It is a horrific place, and the spirits are strong. Centuries later, my ancestors' agony, their sadness and despair, still hangs in the fetid air of the castle's dungeons.

At 2 a.m. I awoke in my hotel bed in tears. That's when it hit me that my family's shame and the shame of every black family began where our lives ended—in the castle. We lost every connection imaginable—mother to child, man to woman, proud people to their way of life, all of it—severed. Who I was as a proud black person ended the moment my ancestors were put on the ship. I lost my connection to myself, and I lost my connection to my people. Through my sobriety, I had been regaining my self. But how to capture that sense of belonging to a people whose link to their history is unbroken? Could Judaism be the answer for me?

When I got back to the States, I went to the JCC and took a class—God and something. I don't remember the exact course name, but I figured if it had God in the title I couldn't go wrong.

It was taught by a young rabbi, and every word he said took my breath away. Finally I had found a place that welcomed my questions, a place that answered my questions with more questions.

What impressed me was the sense of study. I couldn't wait to get to class each week. But even that class couldn't quench me. I told the rabbi I wanted to study more, that I was thinking about converting. I signed up for a 13-week intro to Judaism class, team-taught by two Conservative rabbis and one Reform rabbi. I learned some Hebrew, got familiar with the holiday cycles. I wanted more. The rabbi gave me 200 questions and said, "Answer them and we'll discuss them every week." I was ready to be dipped in the *mikvah*, but he said, "No, let's take our time with this."

I flew home to my mother over Christmas with my list of questions and my book by Rabbi Telushkin. I finished them in January and went back to the rabbi. "I'm ready," I said. "Please, please, please."

It was electrifying, becoming Jewish through the mitzvah of mikvah. In black history, water is an important element. There are many references to rivers and waters being symbols of freedom and cleansing in Langston Hughes' poetry. And even though the vast Atlantic Ocean represented a rupturing of my ancestry, folding myself into the waters of the mikvah allowed me to join with a new ancestry. I entered the mikvah waters the black daughter of nameless slaves and emerged the daughter of Sarah, Rebecca, Rachel and Leah. I was reborn.

Even before I converted, I had begun attending Shabbat services and Torah study classes at a temple in Dallas. People began recognizing me as a member of their community, until the day a woman approached me and asked whose maid I was. I was devastated. It was inconceivable to her that I was there to worship my God. "I belong here," I told her, burning inside. On Monday I called the rabbi to tell him he needed me in his congregation as much as I needed him. The members must learn that Judaism isn't synonymous with whiteness.

The Jewish community is not colorblind, and that makes it difficult for me. Having a Jewish family is so very important. I want to have children and bless them each Friday night; I want to pass on my Jewish heritage as much as I want to transmit my black heritage, but it's hard to find Jewish men who are capable of getting past my blackness. It's who I am. I walk out the door and down the street and what you see is blackness. I am very proud of this. And I take my Jewishness with me just as proudly. They both have a home in my heart and my soul.

Who will say *Kaddish* for me if I never marry and have children? This has hit me really hard lately. I called my sister one day. She witnessed my conversion to Judaism and it touched her deeply. "Make sure I am remembered," I tell her. "Be sure Kaddish is said for me. Promise me my name will not be forgotten."

I am Geralda Miller, a recovering alcoholic woman and a loving child of God.

PART 14

Tishah B'Av

Lonely sits the city, once great with people. She that was great among nations; is become like a widow.

—Lamentations 1: 1-5

Take us back, O Lord, to Yourself. And let us come back: Renew our days as of old.

—Lamentations 5: 23-25

THE LAST HOLIDAY of the Jewish calendar, *Tishah B'Av*, falls in late summer and is the most somber day in Jewish history. On this day, the 9th of Av, both Temples were said to have been destroyed—the first in 586 BCE and the second burned by the Romans in 70 CE. On this date in 1290, all the Jews of England were expelled from the country; and in 1492, King Ferdinand and Queen Isabella expelled Spain's Jews as well.

Tishah B'Av is a fast day. It is forbidden to drink any liquids, engage in sexual relations, bathe, wear leather shoes or put on makeup. These restrictions drive home the point that all of Israel is in mourning on this day.

During evening services, the Book of Eicha, Lamentations, is read. Written by the prophet Jeremiah in the wake of the destruction of the First Temple, the book chronicles innumerable horrors visited upon the Jewish people. It is customary to sit on the floor to hear it read, just as mourners sit on low chairs during the week of *shivah*.

CHAPTER 51

On the Knife-Edge of History

The Story of Harold Berry

FROM THE TIME I was six years old, my Hebrew teachers continually impressed upon my classmates and me how great Israelis were. By the time we were teenagers, we had grown weary of their claims of greatness. "If they're so great," my friends and I would mutter to one another at the back of the classroom, "why do they need our help so much?" Our sarcasm was rooted in adolescent cynicism and perhaps faint resentment at the large amounts of time our fathers spent in helping the Jewish homeland become a state.

Over the years, however, my teachers' refrain took root in my psyche. Coupled with the fact that my mother, father and grandparents raised me on the Zionist dream, I became unabashedly committed to the idea of the restoration of the Jewish people in Israel. The dream didn't become reality until I was in my early twenties, coincidentally the age my son was when he and I journeyed to Israel in the wake of the Six-Day War.

Our trip was a two-week whirlwind sponsored by our local Federation. By the end of those 14 days, we knew just how great the Israelis were. On the go from sunrise to sunset, we saw Israeli flags everywhere. We saw the carnage in the wake of the battle, the total ruination that drove home what the Israelis had actually done when confronted by a crisis of survival. I will never forget the spirit of life and relief that permeated the air. The state was suffused not with the glory of might but the glory of life-affirming survival. Everywhere we went, from the Sinai to El Arish, from the West Bank to the Galilee in the north, Israelis were gathering up captured tanks, loading them on flat railroad cars. It was a flash of history that many do not see. Unbeknownst to us, there was an event of even deeper historical significance yet to come.

Although we couldn't wait to wash away the grit of the road when we arrived in Jerusalem in late afternoon, I felt it was only right to go to the Wall first. We joined the throngs of people making their way to the plaza where the last remnant of the outer wall of the Second Temple still stood. Mind you, there wasn't this nice sanitized plaza and neat little checkpoint booths you see today. Instead of modern lighting, bare bulbs had been strung up catch-as-catch-can, nothing permanent or secure-looking about any of it. We tried to get close enough to touch the Wall, but it was impossible. We were just two hungry and tired specks in a mob of sweating, pushing people. We were so worn out that all we could do was turn around and head in the general direction of our hotel.

Then I caught the phrase "*Tishah B'Av*" in the blur of a passing Israeli's Hebrew and understood why there were so many people shoving to be close to the Wall. Tishah B'Av acknowledges the destruction of the First and Second Temples. As it happened, my son and I were present when, for the first time in nearly 2,000 years, the Wall was under Jewish sovereignty on the eve of this mournful holiday. We, sons and grandsons of passionate Zionists, were present on the very twilight when the Jews' holiest site was once again in Jewish hands.

On the way to our hotel, ready for a good shower and some dinner, I glanced into the doorway of a barbershop in the Arab quarter of the Old City. An Israeli soldier was slouched in a battered wooden chair, getting a shave. What an element of trust there had to be for an Israeli soldier to have laid his rifle by his dusty boots and exposed his throat to the blade of an Arab barber! It was the kind of moment when something cataclysmic could have happened and didn't. I didn't realize it at the time, but that knife and the scene framing it in the dusky alcove in the Old City epitomized the entire span of events of the next 40 years, as if in the aftermath of the Six-Day War, all of Israel's fate was on the knife edge of that blade.

To be in Israel at the time my son and I were there was to be in a country at a fluid time in its history. At that point, the Arabs were in complete shock over all that had happened. The Israelis' victory had not only stunned the Arabs but the Jews as well. Who the hell had expected the Israelis to win? Despite what our teachers had told us year after year, despite all the prayers and Bunyanesque rhetoric of ten-foot-tall Israelis, they were mightily outnumbered and outgunned. Yet in a desperate move of self-preservation, they had charged the door and the door had come right down. I think the Israelis were as astounded as the Arabs when the door collapsed. It was as if in those early days the Israelis were saying, "Well, what do we do now?"

Right after the war, the situation was liquid, like molten steel before it hardens. You would have hoped something could have been reshaped. The tragedy was the Arab reaction. I always had the feeling the Israelis would have gladly given back something had someone reached out in peace. There is historical precedent for the exchange of populations after war. The Arabs' reaction was, "No recognition. No peace." So the situation hardened, and Israel has since been faced with this decades-long occupation. People think life goes on. Well, it does, but not always as well as it could have. Once you lose an opportunity, that molten moment, it is gone for good. Such possibilities don't come around too often. And today, nearly four decades later, what Israel is left to work with is steel.

I often think back on that evening when my son and I were two mere specks in a crowd we later learned was 30,000 strong. It occurred to me the next morning that I had been present at something as historic as witnessing the signing of the Treaty of Versailles, as defining as being upon the grassy knoll on November 22, 1963. And because I was there, my *zayde* was there and so was my *bubbe* and my parents and all the teachers whose arrogance I now realize was an unfulfilled hope, that one day the world would see them as they saw themselves—victorious, independent and 10 feet tall.

PART 15

Death

When we are dead and people weep for us and grieve, let it be because we touched their lives with beauty and simplicity. Let it not be said that life was good to us, but, rather, that we were good to life.

—*Jacob Philip Rudin*

THE LAWS AND customs surrounding a Jewish death and the process of mourning are steeped in respect for the deceased and compassion for their bereaved. The concept of *kevod ha-meit*, honor and respect of the dead, ensures that the body of the deceased is treated with care and concern at all times. The tradition of *nichum avelim*, comforting the mourner, creates a structure that is psychologically healthy and enables the mourner to pass through many stages of grief.

There are three set time periods of mourning. The first, called *shivah*, seven, begins immediately following the burial and lasts for seven days. Shivah is observed for a father, mother, husband, wife, son, daughter, brother or sister. *Sh'loshim*, 30, is the next period and begins at the conclusion of shivah through the 30th day after burial. A third period of mourning, *avelut*, is observed for a parent and concludes 12 months from the day of death.

During these three periods, the mourner recites *Kaddish*, which is not a prayer for the dead but one declaring God's greatness. The Kaddish, recited in Aramaic, the ancient language of the common people, is a petition for redemption and salvation.

CHAPTER 52

How Goodly Are Thy Tents, O Jacob!

The Story of Judith Bardach

THE SURGEON DID all he could. There would be no more surgeries, nor would there be any true recovery. As my father slept under post-op sedation, I sang to him not knowing if he could hear me but wanting to reach him nonetheless: "*Mah tovu ohalecha Yaakov, mish'k'notecha, Yisrael.*" *How goodly are thy tents, O Jacob, protector of Israel.*

My father's name was Jacob, and thus the song always held special meaning for us. He was a Park Avenue doctor who had spent the first 14 years of his life in a Russian *shtetl*. His home had a dirt floor. His mother kept cows. His was the classic immigrant story of rags to riches unimaginable in Russia.

While my father slept, I sang to him with gratitude for providing my sisters, my mother and me with food and shelter. In song I thanked him for Sundays at the Bronx Botanical Gardens and summers by the shore, for being a guiding presence in the lives of my children. I sang to hold at bay the hellish reality that had descended upon us that summer.

Three months before, my 84-year-old father had diagnosed his own colon cancer and called out of retirement a younger relative of a med school classmate to operate. The operation was successful and the surgeon predicted a "few more good years" for Jack. Unfortunately, as he walked in a park to rebuild his strength, one of New York City's bicycle messengers, the kind who give new meaning to the phrase "hell on wheels," ran into him. The force of the blow was so great that it resulted in more surgery and the unleashing of the cancer.

My husband and I were opening a series of clothing stores in Buffalo, and I spent those humid summer weeks shuttling between home and Manhattan, where my father lived. I would wake at two, three in the morning, not knowing if I was in my own bed or in my father's apartment near the hospital. I would reach for my *siddur* and read on my father's behalf the psalms and supplications referred to as "Prayers in Sickness."

For myself I read, *And under His wings shalt thou take refuge ... thou shalt not be afraid of the terror by night ... I will be with him in trouble ... cause us, Lord, to lie down in peace, and raise us up, O our King, unto life*. Prayer gave me something to do when nothing else was left. Repeating these words of succor linked me to generations of Jews who had held bedside vigils for dying parents.

When my father was moved from the ICU to the recovery room, he was groggy but conscious. I held his frail hand in mine while we recited the *Shechecheyanu*. He had taken to saying the prayer whenever he visited with us—Seders, Thanksgiving dinner, summer barbecues. If he was with family, it was reason enough to utter this prayer of thanks.

"*Baruch atah Adonai, Eloheinu melech haolam, shehecheyanu, v'ki'manu, v'higi'anu laz'man hazeh.*" *Thank you, God, for sustaining me, for guarding me, and for enabling me to reach this moment.* Silently I added, *Thank you, God, for giving me my father one more day.*

For years Jack had preceded any discussion of the future with the phrase "If I die." Then he would instruct us on the handling of his estate, the details of his funeral. My father lifted weights well into his seventies; he practiced medicine up until the day before his cancer surgery. We nearly believed in "if." Watching him struggle for breath, tracing the lines of his skull so visible through the transparency of his skin, I realized the time was drawing ever nearer to replace if with when.

I hear it often happens that the family of a dying patient will take a five-minute break from their watch, only to have their loved one die while in their absence. So it was with Jack. My sister, my niece and I stepped away to the hospital's coffee shop downstairs. By the time we returned with our paper bags of day-old muffins and weak hospital coffee, my father had died.

And under His wings shalt thou take refuge. This time I prayed these words asking God to shelter Dad's soul as lovingly as he had sheltered me.

My father's coffin was beautifully crafted and classically carved—a reminder of Jack's appreciation of fine furniture, while honoring the concept of simplicity in the bareness of the wood. Nightfall brought *erev* Rosh HaShanah, and thus there was no formal *shivah* period. I ended the last day of one Jewish year and began the next by reciting *Kaddish* for my father.

When he was alive, my father and I were bound by many ties—daughter to father, rebellious child to disciplinarian, student to teacher, and eventually adult to adult. During my father's final days, that bond stretched anew, binding us ever more tightly. That summer, my father's last, we related to one another as Jew to Jew. *Amen v'amen.*

CHAPTER 53

Beyond Time and Death

The Story of Mintzi Bickel

TWILIGHT SUN FADED over Jerusalem, sheltering the city in gossamer pink light. *Shabbat* was coming. Jews streamed toward the Western Wall: black-coated fathers, sons trailing after them, a blur of white shirts and bouncing payess; tour groups chattering in bunches; a scattering of Orthodox women, many more I imagined were back home preparing a Sabbath meal. Then there was me.

I marveled that I was in Jerusalem at all. The trip was a spur-of-the-moment journey. Anwar Sadat had been assassinated just a week before; tension thrummed in the air. There were better times to go to Israel, loved ones said, trying to dissuade me. Indeed, there had been better times, but I had never gone. When a spot on a women's mission opened up unexpectedly, it was an opportunity I couldn't pass up.

I had always wanted to go to Israel, not just because Israel is our spiritual homeland. I wanted to discover for myself just what had captured my brother's heart. What in God's Torah had touched his soul so much that he dreamed of making *aliyah* as soon as he was able? What was it about the country that made him and his young wife want to raise their family there and not in America, close to home and everything familiar?

Each *Pesach* after the second Seder, I light a *yahrzeit* candle for my baby brother. He died of an undiagnosed brain bleed six months after his second child was born, the first having been stillborn. He never made it back to Israel. I joined the tour not only to see the sights but to find my brother, to draw closer to him in a way that lighting a lifetime of yahrzeit candles had never helped me do.

My siblings and I were brought up Orthodox, but don't let the label sway you. We rarely went to services, not even on the High Holidays. As the old joke goes, the synagogue we didn't attend was Orthodox. My mother kept a kosher home, our grandparents were observant, but my father was the black sheep of the family, and while we were raised with strong Jewish feelings, observance was not a part of the package.

Yet somehow my brother fell into an observant way of life. He became involved in *B'nei Akiva*, an Orthodox youth Zionist movement. After high school he took a year off to study in Israel. He lived on a kibbutz. He returned to attend my wedding and planned to go back permanently. But he met and married a lovely woman, started a family of his own, and was cut down before he could fulfill his life's dream.

I gazed at the backs of the davening men. They were so close to the Wall I wondered that they didn't bump their heads each time they bent at the waist in prayer. But for a tragic twist of fate, my brother could have been one of them.

It was warm; my jean skirt and long-sleeved shirt felt heavy on my body. I drew closer to the Wall, near enough to trace my finger across its smooth, worn stones. Its crevices were filled with prayers jotted on paper scraps. I looked over at the men's section. Their movements were hypnotic; their coats swayed rhythmically.

All of a sudden, I felt my brother right in the midst of the black coats, swaying in prayer. I felt the familiar childhood mixture of love and mock resentment that used to suffuse me when I was the butt of his teasing. In one electrifying moment, I felt the energy of all the Jewish people who had ever lived. Corny as it sounds, it was as if all the Jewish voices that had ever spoken were praying all around me.

Out of nowhere, a woman approached me, a total stranger. She looked straight into my eyes and whispered two words, "I understand." Tears streamed down both of our faces. We embraced and stayed like that for a moment. I knew we were feeling the very same thing, although we had no name for it. It was such an incredible sense of belonging. *I'm Jewish*, I thought. *I know who I am. I may not be as observant as some, but I belong. This is my people.*

Then, as quickly as she appeared, the woman released me and disappeared.

I didn't see her join any tour groups. She simply vanished, leaving me with a strong sense of the destiny and interminability of the Jewish people.

I knew then that in finding Israel, my brother had found himself, had anchored himself to something as wide and deep as time. I turned from the Wall and headed for the bus that would take us back to our hotel. Shabbat descended, light deepening to violet. My brother was with me. I looked back at the shuckling men; I thought of the mysterious woman who had embraced me and of the souls we both had felt. They all were my brother.

CHAPTER 54

She Is Pure

The Story of Kathryn Engber

THERE IS ALWAYS some kind of mystical connection when we close the door to the men outside, and I realize once again that we are more than just the sum of the individual women present. Our reader begins the blessings that will be recited throughout the entire process, and as I listen to her, I feel as I do each time we begin our preparations—that God is in the room, that God is in our hearts, guiding our hands, assuring that our touch is gentle, elevating our work out of the profane into the realm of the sacred.

"Master of the Universe! Have compassion for Joyce/Zer'el this daughter of Lily/Leah Chana, for this deceased, for she is a descendant of Abraham, Isaac and Jacob. May her soul and spirit rest with the righteous, for You are He who revives the dead and brings death to the living."

Not everyone perceives that they are capable of doing the sacred work of the *Chevra Kedisha*, the Jewish burial society, but when my rabbi asked me if I would consider learning these ancient procedures, I sensed that it was something I could do. I've always chosen things that are a bit outside the lines of tradition. I am a strong feminist; I've worked in what has historically been a male-dominated industry. Honoring the rabbi's request just seemed to fit with who I was. I became one of five women in the small Wisconsin city where we live who are on call to prepare our community's female dead for burial.

Although we five are from all walks of life, we are all mothers. This common thread frames our approach to our sacred responsibility—we have all done the intimate hands-on care of children. Preparing the deceased for burial brings us back to that time in our lives when we were involved in the intimate physical care of someone who couldn't care for herself, who couldn't thank us yet needed our ministrations all the same. I didn't know that is what I would draw on when I first went to Minneapolis to be trained, but I now realize that we all feel quite strongly the link between the care we gave our infants and the care we give the deceased, the *meit*. When you care for a newborn, you want each touch to be done with love; you want your child exposed to everything soft and gentle. That is also the sensation we want to come to the meit through our hands.

I am usually the first to go into the room; this is my role and I want to be sure that nothing will go awry. I make sure we have everything we will need—buckets and pitchers for water; *tachrichim*, the garments we will use to clothe the meit; strips of linen for washing; natural-fiber boards for *taharah*, the ritual purification; earth from Israel to place in the casket. Then, when we are all assembled, we take turns washing our hands—pouring water first on the right hand, then on the left, three times, until we are ready to begin.

> Blessed are You who pardons and forgives the sins and trespasses of the dead of Your people, Israel, upon petition. Therefore, may it be Your will, Lord our God and God of our fathers, to bring a circle of angels of mercy before the deceased, for she is Your maidservant, daughter of Your maidservant.

The mood in the room is solemn, of course, but it is also filled with love. We are keenly aware that the meit has a family in mourning and they may be worried about the treatment she is getting; we want it to be the best that it can be. We strive to maintain a high level of modesty for her as we begin our washing. First the entire head, then the neck, the right arm down, including the hand. We often talk as women do to children: "Now we are washing your left arm, now we are washing the upper part of your body, your back."

Our communication focuses on what is happening in the room, and often someone has a memory of the meit, or we remember something she particularly loved doing. We are a circle validating this woman's life, and we keep that in mind as we clean her and ready her for the ritual immersion.

The first time I worked with the Chevra Kedisha in Minneapolis I was scared, but I really wanted to perform the procedure for a woman I had cared about so much. I found that once you start the process, you put yourself aside and focus on what you are doing and there you go. You forget where you are and just move forward.

"And I will pour upon you pure water and you will be purified of all your defilements and from all of your abominations I will purify you."

The taharah that we perform is not done in the traditional sense—standing the meit upright and pouring the required 24 quarts of cold water over her. Instead we place her on several natural-fiber boards that lift her off the table. The boards' absorbency assure she will be surrounded by water. The water has to be poured from our buckets in a continuous stream over the body, and while we are pouring we recite, *"t'hora hee, t'hora hee, t'hora hee," she is pure, she is pure, she is pure.* We make sure the water touches every part of her body before we dry her and ready the tachrichim, the set of burial shrouds.

When we were first trained, there were quite a few deaths in our community all at once. We never want to perform another taharah, but we are prepared for the moment when we're needed.

I look at Judaism as living in tension between two endpoints. For every issue there are two extremes; you have to find the path between the extremes.

The hardest part of all comes after we've dressed the meit, after we've laced the bonnet over her hair and face and put on and tied the pants and the blouse, winding a band once around the waist and twisting its ends four times to represent "*Dalet*," the fourth letter of the Hebrew alphabet. We've placed the *kittel*, a robe-like garment, on the meit, wrapped a sash around the kittel, and tied it with three loops to form the letter "*Shin*." The meit herself represents the letter "*Yod*." In essence, the entire body spells out *shaddai*—Shin, Dalet, Yod—and thus is dedicated to God. We've recited, "*v'El Shaddai yitein lachem rachamim*," and *May God give you mercy*, and it is time to wrap the meit in the *sovev*—a sheet that I think of as swaddling—before tucking her into the casket. It is the very last thing we can do for her, and it is very hard to let go and close her in. It is a moment of great sadness for all of us. Sometimes, when the meit is a particularly good friend of one of us, this final act is shadowed by even greater emotion. As we close the casket, we ask forgiveness from the meit for any roughness or inadvertent mistakes we may have committed.

I don't find this distasteful at all. It is meaningful. It's wrong that American culture alienates us from death. You can't begin to understand death when it is so far removed from you. I think it is the genius of Judaism to have developed this ritual to such a degree that it is respectful of both life and death.

Being a part of the Chevra Kedisha has made me appreciate life so very much more. We all know that life can end at any time, but you can't live your life fearing death. You square up with death and return to living your life. But I tell you, when there's a *simcha*, a celebration, I really, really have a good time. In life you get X number of ceremonies. One is definitely a funeral, but there are simchas, too. And by gosh, I enjoy myself when they come around.

The next stage has to happen—that of handing the meit over to her family and setting the whole painful mourning process in motion. But we know we have laid her to rest in honor; at her most vulnerable time she was not with strangers, but with her own. It is comforting to me to know that when my time comes, I will be in the care of my friends; my children will know I was treated with respect and care during the final stage of my physical existence.

After the meit is taken from us, we wash a third and final time and hold hands in a circle for a few moments and think once again about this loving act we have just performed. We thank God and thank one another and talk about the emotions we have felt. Sometimes our hands offer consolation as well as the affirmation that we have just completed Judaism's highest mitzvah.

We stand in awe of having witnessed once more Judaism's logic and genius, realizing that those who were created in the image of God will now live on in memory. And then, with one last squeeze of our hands, we open the door and depart into that tension between life and death, going our separate ways, until the next time.

> For He will give His angels charge over you to watch you in all your paths ... no evil shall befall you nor shall any plague come near your tent. The Lord is a warrior, the Lord is His name. The Lord will fight for you and you shall hold your peace. Amen.

Glossary

READERS WILL NOTE some dual terms: bas mitzvah/bat mitzvah; b'ris/b'rit; Shabbos/Shabbat; tallis/tallit. The former is based on Eastern European/Yiddish pronunciation, the latter upon modern Hebrew.

- **afikoman**—the middle matzah on a Seder plate. At some point during the Passover evening meal (Seder), it is hidden and the children in attendance go on a "treasure hunt" to find it. Once it has been "ransomed" back to the adults, it is eaten as part of dessert.
- **aliyah** (plural, **aliyot**)—the act of being called to the Torah to say the blessing over the Torah before and after it is read.
- **am Yisrael chai**—the Jewish people will live.
- **aron hakodesh**—holy ark containing the Torah scrolls.
- **Ashkenazic**—Jews descended from medieval Jewish communities of the Rhineland in Germany and later Eastern Europe.

- **Avinu Malkenu** (Our Father, Our King)—Hebrew prayer of confession and supplication sung during the Rosh Hashana and Yom Kippur services.
- **Ba'al Shem Tov**—mystic Rabbi Yisroel ben Eliezer (Master of the Good Name) was an 18th century rabbi credited with the founding of Chassidic Judaism, whose philosophy embraces not only the study of Torah, but a joyous engagement with the spirit of God that is in all things.
- **bar/bat mitzvah**—literally, son/daughter of the commandments. This coming-of-age ceremony is held when a Jewish boy or girl reaches thirteen years of age. Orthodox girls celebrate at twelve.
- **Bar'chu**—prayer extolling God as the Supreme creator.
- **bimah**—platform in the front or center of the synagogue from which services are conducted.
- **b'ris /b'rit**—literally, covenant. This word has come to mean the ritual circumcision performed when an infant boy is eight days old, thus entering him into the covenant between God and Abraham.
- **bubbe**—Yiddish for grandmother.
- **Chabad**—a denomination of Judaism that grew out of the teachings of the Ba'al Shem Tov. A major focus of Chabad is to bring Jews back into the fold of Torah observant Judaism.
- **chai**—life.
- **chametz**—literally, vinegar. Those foods that are not kosher for Passover.
- **charoset**—mixture of wine, apples, nuts and cinnamon eaten at Passover. Its texture is symbolic of the mortar used by Hebrew slaves in their building for Pharaoh. Sephardic Jews make a charoset of figs, dates, wine and nuts.
- **chavurah**—based on the Hebrew root ch-v-r which means friend, a chavurah is a group of individuals who come together for Jewish study, worship and socializing.
- **chuppah**—wedding canopy.

- **erev**—literally, evening. Jewish holidays begin at sunset, so "erev Rosh HaShanah" is the night preceding the first day of the holiday. Erev has also come to mean the day before.
- **ezrat nashim**—women's section in an Orthodox synagogue.
- **gelt**—money (Yiddish).
- **get**—Jewish divorce document.
- **frum**—observant; (a follower) of the mitzvot.
- **g'milut chasadim**—acts of lovingkindness.
- **Haggadah** (plural, **Haggadot**)—book relating the Passover story.
- **hakafah**—the process of walking the Torah scroll(s) through the sanctuary.
- **Halachah**—Jewish law.
- **Kaballah**—Jewish mysticism.
- **Kaddish**—mourner's prayer written in Aramaic, said in memory of the deceased.
- **kasher**—to make kosher.
- **ketubah** (plural, **ketubot**)—Jewish wedding contract.
- **Kiddush**—ceremonial blessing recited over wine. The term is also used to refer to refreshments served following services.
- **kippah** (plural, **kippot**)—skullcap. Traditionally worn only by males, some females now also follow the practice of wearing a kippah during religious occasions. Some males also wear a kippah at all times as a sign of respect for God.
- **kishkes**—Yiddish for intestines, innards.
- **Kohen** (plural, **kohanim**)—of the priestly tribe.
- **kosher**—Although the initial meaning of this word signified the state of being fit or proper and concerned itself with ritual objects or witnesses, kosher food is food that meets certain dietary laws. Animals whose consumption is permitted (certain fowl, beef, lamb) must be ritually slaughtered. Forbidden animals include pigs, crustaceans, carrion-eaters.
- **Kol Nidrei**—service held on Yom Kippur eve.
- **Kotel**–Also called the Western Wall, or Wailing Wall, this structure in Old Jerusalem is all that remains of a wall that surrounded the Second Temple, destroyed in 70 CE.

- **kreplach**—stuffed noodle dumplings. Think Jewish ravioli; they are stuffed with chicken, meat or cheese.
- **Kutz**—the Reform movement's national leadership camp in Warwick, NY.
- **machataynister** (plural, **Machatunim**)—no real equivalent for this Yiddish word exists in English. It refers to the mother-in-law of one's child. The plural form refers to one's child's in-laws.
- **machzor**—High Holiday prayer book.
- **Magen David**—Star of David.
- **matzah**—unleavened bread eaten during the holiday of Passover.
- **mechitzah**—refers to the curtain or partial wall in the sanctuary of an Orthodox synagogue whose purpose it is to separate men and women during worship services.
- **Megillah**—Scroll of Esther.
- **mezuzah**—a piece of parchment on which are written verses from the Bible. It is rolled up and inserted into a case and attached to the door posts of Jewish homes.
- **mikvah**—ritual bath.
- **minhagim**—customs.
- **minyan**—Traditionally, it was necessary to have present 10 males above the age of 13 to recite certain prayers. If no minyan is present, those in attendance pray but omit the prayers requiring 10. Orthodox synagogues still require 10 males, as do some but not all Conservative synagogues. Reform temples do not require a minyan.
- **Mi Shebeirach**—prayer for healing.
- **mitzvah** (plural, **mitzvot**)—commandment; often translated as a good deed.
- **Passover**—week-long holiday commemorating/celebrating the Israelites' Exodus from Egpyt. Hebrew: **Pesach**.
- **rebbe**—rabbi.
- **Seder**—literally, order. The Seder is the Passover meal during which the story of the Exodus is told.

- **Sephardic**—from the Hebrew word for Spain, Sephardic Jews are those whose origins can be traced to Spain and Portugal.
- **Shabbat**—Sabbath.
- **Shabbat Matot**—Each Shabbat carries the name of the Torah portion that is read that morning. Therefore, on Shabbat Matot, the Torah portion Matot is read.
- **Shacharit**—morning service.
- **Shavuot**—holiday that celebrates the giving of the Torah upon Mount Sinai.
- **Sh'ma**—claiming the oneness of God, this is Judaism's most defining prayer.
- **shivah**—the seven-day mourning period.
- **shnorrer**—Yiddish, one who collects for charity; also has the more negative connotation of a moocher.
- **shofar**—ram's horn blown during Rosh HaShanah and Yom Kippur services.
- **Shomer Shabbat**—those Jews who observe the Shabbat laws, which prohibit, among other things, work.
- **shtetl**—Yiddish, a term that referred to small towns of Eastern Europe with a large communities of pious Jews. With the rise of Naziism and the Shoah (Holocaust), these communities were essentially destroyed.
- **shul**—synagogue.
- **siddur**—prayer book.
- **simcha**— this Hebrew word for happiness is also used to refer to a joyous celebration such as a wedding or a Bar/Bat Mitzvah.
- **Simchat Torah**—holiday that celebrates conclusion of the yearly cycle of reading the Torah.
- **sukkah**—literally, booth. This is a temporary shelter constructed during the harvest festival of Sukkot.
- **tallis** (plural, **tallitot**)—prayer shawl.
- **Tanach**—acronym for Torah (the Five Books of Moses), Neviim (Prophets) and Ketuvim (Holy Writings), all of which constitute the three parts of the Bible.

- **tefillin**—a set of small black leather boxes containing parchment scrolls inscribed with verses from the Torah. Observant Jews strap the teffilin to their head and one arm during weekday morning prayers.
- **tikkun olam**—repair of the world.
- **treif**—not kosher.
- **ulpan**—intensive study of the Hebrew language.
- **Workman's Circle (Arbeter Ring)**—Founded in 1900, this secular organization fosters Jewish identity and participation in Jewish life, particularly through Yiddish culture and education and the pursuit of social and economic justice.
- **Yahrzeit**—anniversary of a loved one's death. Observing yahrzeit includes attending services, reciting the Kaddish in the loved one's memory, lighting a yahrzeit candle, which burns for 24 hours. It is also custom for those observing yahrzeit to donate to a charity, lead a study session, or perform other acts of loving kindness in a loved one's memory.
- **yarmulke**—Yiddish for skullcap. See also: **kippah**.
- **yeshiva** (plural, **yeshivot**)—usually refers to Jewish schools whose curriculum is devoted to the study of Talmud. Traditionally Orthodox institutions, their students are males who have attained bar mitzvah age and beyond.
- **Yizkor**—"to remember" The Yizkor prayer is recited in memory of a loved one during services on Yom Kippur and the holidays of Passover, Shavuot, and Sukkot.
- **yontiff**—Yiddish for holiday.
- **zayde**—Yiddish for grandfather.

Bibliography

- Abramowitz, Yosef I., and Rabbi Susan Silverman. *Jewish Family & Life: Traditions, Holidays, and Values for Today's Parents and Children*. New York: Golden Books, 1997.
- Baron, Joseph L., editor. *A Treasury of Jewish Quotations*. New Jersey: Jason Aronson, Inc., 1985.
- Donin, Rabbi Hayim Halevy. *To Be a Jew*. New York: Basic Books, Inc., 1972.
- *JPS Hebrew-English Tanakh*. Philadelphia: The Jewish Publication Society, 1999.
- Kolatch, Alfred J. *The Jewish Book of Why*. New York: Jonathan David Publishers, Inc., 1981.
- Plaut, W. Gunther, editor. *The Torah, A Modern Commentary*. New York: Union of American Hebrew Congregations, 1981.
- ---. Translation by Chaim Stern with assistance of Philip D. Stern. *The Haftarah Commentary*. New York: UAHC Press, 1996.
- *Regulations and Procedure Including the Traditional Prayers and Translations for the Jewish Sacred Society*. Chicago, Illinois.
- Rosten, Leo. *The Joys of Yiddish*. New York: Washington Square Books, Simon & Schuster, 1968.
- Scherman, Rabbi Nosson. Contributing editors Rabbi Hersh Goldwurm, Rabbi Avie Gold and Rabbi Meir Zlotowitz. *The Chumash, The Stone Edition*. Brooklyn, New York: Mesorah Publications, Ltd., 2000.
- Stern, Chaim, editor. *Gates of Prayer*. New York: Central Conference of American Rabbis, 1975.
- Telushkin, Rabbi Joseph. *Jewish Literacy: The Most Important Things to Know About the Jewish Religion, Its People, and Its History*. New York: William Morrow and Company, Inc., 1991.

Notes on Interviewees

AFTER GRADUATING FROM the University of Wisconsin-Madison, **Samantha Ashley**, spent 10 weeks as an intern with the AFL-CIO's Solidarity Center in Dhaka, Bangladesh. She earned her Master's Degree in Health Care Policy and Management from the Heinz College of Public Policy at Carnegie Mellon University in Pittsburgh, PA. For the last two years she has been working at UMass Memorial Health Care in Worcester, Massachusetts and is currently working as a Senior Policy Analyst for the American Medical Association (AMA) in Chicago, IL. She married Thomas Katers in 2009 *Her story can be found in Chapter 40.*

Judith Bardach was born in New York City in 1934. She attended Hunter College and in 1954 married Robert Bardach. They have three children: David, Sheila, and Leah. Blessed in marriage to her teenage love, Mrs. Bardach is an enthusiastic worshipper/volunteer at Reconstructionist Temple Sinai in the Buffalo, New York area. Her two daughters, sons-in-law and four grandchildren live nearby. *Her story can be found in Chapter 52.*

Joanna Berger's volunteer work teaching English as a second language to recent immigrants from the former Soviet Union led to her completion of an M.A. in linguistics. She has directed her local JCC's ESL department and continues to teach English as a second language on a volunteer basis. Mrs. Berger is an affiliate of the National Council of Jewish Women, Hadassah, ORT, and the Sisterhood of Congregation Beth Shalom in Oak Park, Michigan. *Her story can be found in Chapter 34.*

At the age of twelve, **David Bergman**, his family, and all of the Jews from his hometown in Czechoslovakia were deported to Auschwitz. Of all the youth in his village, Bergman alone survived. He came to America in 1947, graduated from Cleveland Heights High School and supported himself through college. Mr. Bergman served in the Korean War in 1952 and in 1960 completed his degree in electrical engineering. Since 1967 he has devoted much time to sharing his experiences during the Nazi Holocaust. He and his wife divide their time between Michigan and Florida. *His story can be found in Chapter 39*

Batya Berlin is a retired psychotherapist and is very invested in her congregation. A leader of her temple's *shacharit* services for many years, she has studied at the Union of American Hebrew Congregations Kallot and the Silverman Institute study sessions. *Her story can be found in Chapter 11.*

Harold Berry was imbued by his parents and grandparents with the dream of Zion restored. He and his wife, Barbara, have imparted this vision to their two sons and daughter and their spouses. As a businessman, he has given of his time and means to Israel and the Jewish community and currently serves on the Board of the Hebrew University of Jerusalem. *His story can be found in Chapter 51.*

Mintzi Bickel was born and raised on New York's Lower East Side. Following school and a brief career in dance, she married Richard Darby, a medical student. In 1963 they moved to Phoenix, Arizona, where he practiced medicine and Mintzi sold real estate. They raised their two children, Bruce and Marni, in a Conservative household. She now resides in California with her present husband, Yale, a retired UCLA Professor of Medicine. They were married in 1993 in a Reconstructionist synagogue and share five children, ten grandchildren, and everlasting friendship and love. *Her story can be found in Chapter 53.*

Deena Sue (Heifetz) Borzak, a native of Madison, Wisconsin, now lives in Boca Raton, Florida, with her husband, Steve, and four daughters. She is grateful for the opportunity to put many miles on her minivan for carpools, sports, and orthodontist appointments and not for pediatric neurologists, orthopedic surgeons, and retinal specialists. She plays tennis moderately well and is an active volunteer at her girls' day schools. *Her story can be found in Chapter17.*

Miriam Chaya is an actress, writer, producer, director and documentary filmmaker. She has co-produced and co-directed (with Academy Award nominated Judith Montell) the popular film *Timbrels and Torahs, Celebrating Women's Wisdom*, which explores *Simchat Hochmah*, a new rite of passage ritual for Jewish women making the transition from midlife to their elder years. Miriam is currently performing a one-woman play that she wrote, called *Sentimental Journey*, about her own spiritual journey. Email: mirchaya@aol.com *Her story can be found in Chapter 32.*

As a child, **Laya Crust** fell in love with art and Jewish learning. As an adult she fused the two, combining the Hebrew word and Judaism with color and form. She has created paintings, books, illuminated manuscripts, *ketubot*, and presentation pieces. Laya lives in Toronto with her husband and six children and accepts commissions. She may be contacted at layacrust.com. *Her story can be found in Chapter 35.*

An avid amateur photographer, **Paul Darmon** maintains a family and cosmetic dental practice in Beverly Hills Michigan. He and his wife, Cheryl, have three children. They are members of Congregation Beth Ahm and live in Farmington Hills, Michigan. *His story can be found in Chapter 5.*

Hannah Dietz, a native of Copenhagen, Denmark, came to the United States in 1971 following her marriage to a U.S. citizen.

She and her husband, Ed, live in northern Michigan. She serves Congregation Beth El in Traverse City, Michigan, and Temple Israel of Dover, New Hampshire, as cantorial soloist. *Her story can be found in Chapter 6.*

Born in Philadelphia in 1919, **Jules Doneson** served with the 8th and 28th Infantry Divisions during World War II. In 1948 he volunteered in the Israeli Army, where he commanded an infantry company in the 7th brigade. In late 1948 he was named regional director of the Zionist organization of America. He is the author of *Deeds of Love: A History of the Jewish Foster Home and Orphan Asylum–America's First Jewish Orphanage*, published in 1996. Mr. Doneson died in 2006. *His story can be found in Chapter 18.*

Dr. David Elcott, author, lecturer, and organizational consultant, has brought his insights and analyses of Judaism and contemporary Jewish life to well over 100 communities across North America. Author of *A Sacred Journey: The Jewish Quest for a Perfect World*, he works with Jewish communal organizations and international corporations to retool their missions and vision in response to the new conditions of 21st-century life. David lives in Westchester County, New York, with his wife, Rabbi Shira Milgrom, and their four children. *His story can be found in Chapter 14.*

Kathryn Engber credits her wonderful husband, Steven, and their children Jake, Hannah, and Elise, along with the local Jewish community for their continuing support of her synagogue activities. In addition, she enjoys gardening of native prairie and woodland flowers, bird watching, and is active in faith-based environmentalism. *Her story can be found in Chapter 54.*

Marcia Ferstenfeld has been married to her husband, Larry, for 48 years and is mother to three daughters and grandmother to ten grandchildren. She is a clinical psychotherapist specializing in Imago relationship therapy, provides Clinical Training and, with her husband, presents Getting the Love You Want Weekend Workshops for couples and Connect Parents,Thriving Kids courses for parents. Her journal writing helped document the events that are portrayed in this piece. *Her story can be found in Chapter 3.*

Ellie Gersten teaches English as a second language in Phoenix, Arizona, where she lives with her family. She continues to nurture her Jewish roots through participation in Hadassah and National Council of Jewish Women. A self-described "Jewish Junkie," Ellie has a passion for her heritage. Her novel, *Hidden Star*, traces the lives of a hidden Jewish family who came to the New World from Spain in the wake of the Inquisition. She can be reached at elliewriter@aol.com. *Her story can be found in Chapter 43.*

Product of a Protestant family, **Kay Harris** converted to Judaism after college. Her two grown daughters are Conservative day-school graduates who are actively involved in Jewish life and studies. Kay married a fellow member of her *shul*, and together they enjoy Jewish observances and many secular activities. *Her story can be found in Chapter 47.*

Mark Isaacs is an architect and builder who specializes in innovative urban residential development. He holds a Masters in Architecture from MIT and was a Lady Davis Fellow at the Technion in Haifa, Israel. *His story can be found in Chapter 13.* .

Dr. Michael Isaacson, composer of more than 400 published works, conductor, and producer of more than 40 CDs and albums, pioneer of the NFTY American folk music style, Founding Music Director of the Israel Pops Orchestra and the Milken Archive of American Jewish Music, creator of the New York Museum of Jewish Heritage's permanent exhibit symphonic music, and recipient of the largest co-commission of synagogue music in history (To Recreate the World), has singularly defined and elevated American Jewish music in our time. His *Michael Isaacson Songbook Volumes I & II*, containing 100 of his Jewish works, is published by Transcontinental Music in New York City. *His story can be found in Chapter 10.*

Deanna Silver Jacobson (Glenview, Illinois) is married to Mark Jacobson, and together they are raising their three children, Joshua, Ari, and Rebecca, to rejoice in their Judaism. Deanna loves spending time with her family and friends, and hopes one day to repeat her incredible South Seas voyage with her family to share in the beautiful diversity of our world. *Her story can be found in Chapter 4.*

Born in Green Bay, Wisconsin, **Margo Glickman Jakobs** received much of her strong Jewish identity from her parents. She earned her degree in genetic counseling and human awareness from UW Madison. While working at Harbor/UCLA Medical Center for the Tay Sachs Disease Prevention Program, she was set up on a blind date (thank you, Dena Borzak) and moved to Sterling, Illinois, to marry the cattle farmer of her dreams. She lives there today with husband, David, and sons Nikolas, Alex, and Bryce. Margo is currently a high school SAP counselor. *Her story can be found in Chapter 27.*

In the years since her bat mitzvah, **Jane Kahn** has continued to devour adult Jewish education courses at her synagogue and local Hebrew university. Among her greatest joys are chanting Torah for her congregation and pursuing independent Jewish study "*L'dor vador*" has taken on a special meaning. *Her story can be found in Chapter 31.*

A native of Brooklyn, New York, **Judith Kaplan** is an aspiring set-designer who created her own major at Stern College for women in set/production design. An avid reader, Judith's hobbies include dancing, singing, painting, drawing, sculpting and playing the piano. *Her story can be found in Chapter 15.*

Nancy Kaplan has directed Eilu v'Eilu, the Adult Jewish Learning Project of the Michigan Conservative movement, since it began in the fall of 1996. Born in Philadelphia, she is a graduate of Brandeis University, class of '68, and has been an active member of and lay leader at various Reform and Conservative congregations in Boston (1977-88) and Detroit (1988-). She lives in West Bloomfield, Michigan, with her husband, Mike, an endocrinologist. They are the parents of Dan, 35, and Amy, 32. *Her story can be found in Chapter 28.*

Lisa Katzman, a dietitian by profession, works part-time in cancer clinical trials at Beaumont Hospital in Royal Oak, Michigan. The 37-year-old Canadian is a married mother of three. Shoes That Fit is a passion she hopes to pursue for many years to come. *Her story can be found in Chapter 20.*

Nancy Lipsey is a native of Memphis, Tennessee, where most of her family still lives. She has a B.A. in broadcast journalism from American University and a Masters of Nonprofit Organizations from Case Western Reserve University. Since graduation, Nancy has worked for Jewish communal organizations in Cleveland, Detroit and Atlanta. Nancy is also a Jewish educator and has taught in the Florence Melton Mini-School in Atlanta. *Her story can be found in Chapter 41.*

Philip Littman, a San Francisco Bay-area native, and Jan Opper, a Floridian born and raised, met in Sacramento at Rosh HaShanah services. Married in 1984, they were blessed with the birth of their son, Max David, in 1986. They currently live in Sacramento, California. *Their story can be found in Chapter 26.*

Alan May, an honors graduate of the University of Michigan law school, is a practicing attorney and a special assistant attorney general. Former chairman of the Michigan Civil Rights Commission, he is president of the Detroit region of the National Conference for Community and Justice (NCCJ). He also serves on NCCJ's Executive Board, Chair of Investments and National Vice Chair. Alan and his wife, Liz, are the parents of Stacy Klein and Julie May and the grandparents of Katie and Carly Klein. *His story can be found in Chapter 12.*

Although no longer chaired by **Susan Mandelbaum**, the College Connection is still very active at Temple Beth Shalom. She still hears from some students, now parents themselves, who received the packages in college. She and her husband, Howard, delight in spending time their three grandchildren and their continued connection with Temple Beth Shalom as well as a small synagogue in Lake Hoptacong, NJ. *Her story can be found in Chapter 23.*

Janelle McCammon was born to a Methodist minister and a mother who was a teacher. She and her husband, Raymond Rosenfeld, met at Emory University. They married in 1972 and have two children, Bryn Rachel and Seth Robert, whom they raised with a cherished Jewish identity. Janelle and her husband are actively engaged in Temple activities. Her husband serves as Temple Beth El's Board President. *Her story can be found in Chapter 16.*

Geralda Miller works as a reporter in Reno, Nevada. She continues her study of race and identity and graduated from the University of Reno in December 2009 with a master of arts in History. Geralda has found friends and a synagogue in Reno she calls home. *Her story can be found in Chapter 50.*

Mike Neulander was born in Miami, Florida, in 1957. He graduated from the University of Miami in 1980 with a B.A. in political science. He served in the Gulf War as a helicopter pilot in the 1st Cavalry Division, during which he received the Bronze Star Medal for aerial combat actions. He retired as a major. Married to the former Sharon Horton since 1980, he is father to Brandi and Ariel. *His story can be found in Chapter 24.*

Born in Haifa, Israel, **Ahuva Newman** graduated from the Hebrew University of Jerusalem with a B.A. in Hebrew literature, world literature, Hebrew grammar, and Jewish folklore. She holds a teaching certificate from HU as well. After moving to the United States, she obtained her M.A. in Guidance and Counseling from Wayne State University in Detroit, Michigan. Ahuva has been involved in Jewish education for over 30 years. *Her story can be found in Chapter 7.*

Arthur Ost retired from advertising and more recently taught French and Spanish at the college in San Mateo, California. Mr. Ost died in 2010. *His story can be found in Chapter 21.*

Rahel Pardo was born in New York state in 1949. She graduated from Syracuse University in 1971 and received her MSW from Yeshiva University in 1997. She married her beloved husband, Barak, in 1977 and then, under a *chuppah*, again in 1992.

They live with their two foster children (and various wildlife) on a farm and are informally involved in Jewish and Israeli causes. *Her story can be found in Chapter 36.*

B. Valerie Peckler lives in Boulder, Colorado, with her husband. They have two grown children: Jonathan and Rachel. Valerie, a science teacher, technical writer, poet and artist, is best known for her contribution to *Pirkei Imahot*: "Men create disciples; women create generations." *Her story can be found in Chapter 33.*

Naomi Pinchuk lives in Southfield, Michigan. She and Larry Horwitz, her husband of thirty-five years, have two daughters: Judith, a pediatrician, married with a two-year-old daughter, currently living in New York, and Beth, a social worker, living in Chicago. Naomi works as a geriatric social worker in West Bloomfield, Michigan. *Her story can be found in Chapter 29.*

David Charles Rosen has been Assistant Director at the University of Michigan Hillel since 2011. He and Jillian, his wife, live just a Frisbee throw away from the Big House (Michigan Football Stadium) in Ann Arbor. In 2008, Davey completed an MA in Informal & Communal Jewish Education from the Davidson School at the Jewish Theological Seminary where he also formed JamDaven, an interactive, pluralistic, music experience. *His story can be found in Chapter 46.*

Eve Roshevsky is staff executive in the Department on Religious Living of Women of Reform Judaism, The Federation of Temple Sisterhoods. After returning from Israel in 1969, she worked in book publishing, principally at Doubleday & Company, where she edited the memoirs of Isaac Bashevis Singer and managed the Anchor Bible commentary series. *Her story can be found in Chapter 45.*

Larry Schwartz grew up in the Pittsburgh neighborhood of Squirrel Hill. His strong Jewish identity was formed through home and synagogue life and active participation in USY and Camp Ramah. After graduating medical school, he lived for a year in Jerusalem, where he continued his passion for Jewish education by working with high school students coming to Israel.

Larry and his wife, Brandy, are active members of the Jewish community in Baltimore. Brandy teaches at a Jewish day school; Larry is completing a fellowship in pediatric anesthesiology and intensive care. *His story can be found in Chapter 44.*

Daniel Shapiro grew up in Montreal, where he attended Jewish day school. He currently lives in Los Angeles with his partner, Greg Roth, and their two children Lilly 9 and Noah 7, who both attend Jewish day school as well! *His story can be found in Chapter 37.*

New York native, **Robert Tennenbaum**, graduated from the High School of Music and Art, Pratt Institute School of Architecture, and Yale University Graduate Program in city planning. He was chief architect-planner for Columbia, Maryland, and participated in the redevelopment of downtown Baltimore and campus development for the University of Maryland. He has exhibited his work and has also licensed his images for holiday cards and other uses. *His story can be found in Chapter 8.*

Sofer, Master Teacher and Artist **Neil Yerman's** international reputation for working creatively with communities across the Jewish spectrum is well documented by over 60,000 Google posts. He is one of only two scribes in the United States approved by the Memorial Scrolls Trust in England to restore Holocaust Memorial scrolls. Yerman's original art has been featured in shows throughout the United States. Contact: http://NeilYerman.com or Facebook. *His story can be found in Chapter 19.*

Sara Zivian Zwickl is an attorney with a practice in the Detroit metropolitan area focused on probate and estate planning. She majored in vocal performance at the Interlochen Arts Academy and Indiana University. Singing is her passion, second only to husband, Tim, and three terrific children: Josh, Becky, and David. *Her story can be found in Chapter 30.*

About the Author

IN ADDITION TO *This Jewish Life: Stories of Discovery, Connection and Joy*, Debra Darvick is the author of 100+ essays that have appeared in national magazines and newspapers across the country, including *Newsweek*, *Good Housekeeping*, *Moment*, the *Forward* and others.

Her children's book, *I love Jewish faces*, celebrates Jewish diversity.

A provocative blogger with a loyal following, Debra keeps up with readers at debradarvick.com.

About Flora Rosefsky

NOTED FOR COLORFUL contemporary cutouts and mixed media drawings, as well as folk art illustrations based on the artist's life, community and heritage, Flora Rosefsky maintains a studio at D. Miles Gallery & Studios in Decatur, Georgia. She recently had one-woman shows at The Columbia Theological Seminary in Decatur and at The Fine Family Art Gallery in The Marcus Jewish Community Center of Atlanta, and has also been commissioned to create large community story quilts for institutions, including The Breman Museum, The William Breman Jewish Home of Atlanta, the Jewish Family and Career Services of Atlanta, and The Jewish Community Center of Binghamton, NY.

In addition to her fine artwork, Rosefsky's paper cutout illustrations have been published on the covers of *The Detroit Jewish News* and *The Atlanta Jewish Times* and have been used for various invitations, greeting cards and posters, including The American Jewish Committee-Atlanta chapter, The National

Council of Jewish Women-Atlanta section, National Hadassah, and Young Audiences of Atlanta.

Rosefsky is a teaching artist with Young Audiences of Atlanta, Fulton County School Arts Program, and leads workshops and classes at The High Museum of Art in Atlanta.

About Simchat Torah III

Flora Rosefsky says: "Inspired by memories and joyous themes from my Jewish heritage or remembering events in my life, I use scissors to create mixed media drawings with paper cutouts. The scissors become an extension of my hand, drawing lines in a fluid motion, just as a pen moves across a page. Paper cutouts and the freedom to draw with my scissors lets my subconscious sense of feeling right take over my more concrete, practical side, adding a spirit of spontaneity that is an integral part of each new work.

"*Simchat Torah*, a special holiday to joyfully celebrate the completion and beginning of reading the Torah, is noted for a special tradition of 'circling,' where synagogue congregants and friends hold various Torahs while walking around the sanctuary accompanied by singing and dancing. Simchat Torah III, which reflects this tradition, is part of the permanent art collection at The William Breman Jewish Home of Atlanta, Georgia."

m

The cover of this edition of the book is designed around "Simchat Torah III", an original painting by artist Flora Rosefsky, used under license.

Flora Rosefsky can be contacted at: or:· florageart@aol.com

Phone: 404-633-7896·

Fax: 404-633-6302

Colophon

READ THE SPIRIT Books produces its titles using innovative digital systems that serve the emerging wave of readers who want their books delivered in a wide range of formats—from traditional print to digital readers in many shapes and sizes. This book was produced using this entirely digital process that separates the core content of the book from details of final presentation, a process that increases the flexibility and accessibility of the book's text and images. At the same time, our system ensures a well-designed, easy-to-read experience on all reading platforms, built into the digital data file itself.

David Crumm Media has built a unique production workflow employing a number of XML (Extensible Markup Language) technologies. This workflow, allows us to create a single digital "book" data file that can be delivered quickly in all formats from traditionally bound print-on-paper to nearly any digital reader you care to choose, including Amazon Kindle®, Apple iBook®, Barnes and Noble Nook® and other devices that support the ePub and PDF digital book formats.

Supported by the efficient "print-on-demand" process we use for printed books, we invite you to visit us online to learn more about opportunities to order quantities of this book with the possibility of personalizing a "group read" for your organization or congregation by putting your organization's logo and name on the cover of the copies you order. You can even add your own introductory pages to this book for your church or organization.

During production, we use Adobe InDesign®, <Oxygen/>® XML Editor and Microsoft Word® along with custom tools built in-house.

The print edition is set in Minion Pro and Myriad Pro fonts.

Cover art and design by Rick Nease: www.RickNeaseArt.com.

This edition is republished based on an earlier edition published by Eakin Press.

Copy editing and XML styling by Stephanie Fenton and Celeste Dykas.

Digital encoding and print layout by John Hile.

formation can be obtained
CGtesting.com
he USA
924170414